STUDIES IN IMPERIALISM

general editor John M. MacKenzie

Established in the belief that imperialism as a cultural phenomenon had as significant an effect on the dominant as on the subordinate societies, Studies in Imperialism seeks to develop the new socio-cultural approach which has emerged through cross-disciplinary work on popular culture, media studies, art history, the study of education and religion, sports history and children's literature. The cultural emphasis embraces studies of migration and race, while the older political, and constitutional, economic and military concerns will never be far away. It will incorporate comparative work on European and American empire-building, with the chronological focus primarily, though not exclusively, on the nineteenth and twentieth centuries, when these cultural exchanges were most powerfully at work.

Britannia's children

Britannia's children looks at the roots of society's perception of racial difference through the establishment and diffusion of the image of imperial peoples in the period before and after the First World War. Focusing on materials produced for children, by textbook historians and the popular press, it provides an important study of both the socialisation of the young and the source of race perceptions in twentieth-century British society.

Britannia's children introduces the reader to the imperial images of the Indian, African and Chinese – created for the youth of Britain through their history textbooks and popular periodicals.

By close study of the characterisation of the 'other', shaped in this era, one can see how the young learned both the lessons of imperial allegiance and a perception of racial difference which would influence many generations to follow. This revealing book shows how society secures the rising generation in the beliefs of the parent society, and how the myths of race and nationality became an integral part of Britain's own process of self-identification.

Written for historians, educators and a wider audience with an interest in the issues of race and society, this book makes important reading for those who wish to understand both the popularisation of the imperial idea and the legacy of its workings in contemporary society.

Britannia's children

READING COLONIALISM THROUGH CHILDREN'S BOOKS AND MAGAZINES

Kathryn Castle

**MANCHESTER
UNIVERSITY PRESS**

Manchester and New York

Distributed exclusively in the USA and Canada
by ST. MARTIN'S PRESS

Copyright © Kathryn Castle 1996

Published by Manchester University Press
Oxford Road, Manchester M13 9NR, UK
and Room 400, 175 Fifth Avenue, New York, NY 10010, USA

Distributed exclusively in the USA and Canada
by St. Martin's Press, Inc., 175 Fifth Avenue, New York,
NY 10010, USA

British Library Cataloguing-in-Publication Data
A catalogue record for this book is available from the British Library

Library of Congress Cataloging-in-Publication Data
Castle, Kathryn, 1946–
    Britannia's children: reading colonialism through children's books and
magazines / Kathryn Castle.
        p.   cm.   – (Studies in imperialism)
    ISBN 0-7190-2853-1
    1. Great Britain – Colonies – Public opinion.   2. Imperialism – Public
opinion.   3. Public opinion – Great Britain.   I. Title.   II. Series: Studies in
imperialism (Manchester, England)
    JV1011.C33 1996
    325'.32'07041 – dc20   95-39215
                                                                                                                        CIP

ISBN   0 7190 2853 1   *hardback*

First published 1996

00 99 98 97 96   10 9 8 7 6 5 4 3 2 1

Printed in Great Britain
Biddles Limited, Guildford and King's Lynn

CONTENTS

ILLUSTRATIONS

GENERAL EDITOR'S INTRODUCTION

Most societies clearly reveal both their moral norms and their political ideologies through their efforts to acculturate the young. While this can be an area of contention as much as of agreement, there is a particularly powerful urge to consensus in the training of youth, since their exposure to too much disagreement can seem to have socially disruptive or politically subversive results. It is indeed one of the notable characteristics of the late nineteenth and early twentieth centuries that many European countries, their imperial territories, and rapidly Europeanising imitators like Japan, established a powerful zone of intellectual, ideological and moral convergence in the projection of state power and collective objectives to children.

A variety of media were bent to these ends: school textbooks, juvenile journals, a host of adventure stories and hagiographical biographies, religious and youth organisations, some aspects of the theatre and later the cinema, as well as advertising and visual aspects of collectable ephemera. In some countries, many of these materials were subjected to direct state control (this was true of Japan for example), but in those where central governmental direction was relatively light (as in Britain), the consensus seems to have been achieved by voluntarist means.

In the past quarter-century or so there has been a growing awareness of the value of school texts in exposing the dominant ideology and objectives of those concerned with youth training, and thus of the elites most concerned with creating a degree of social conformity. There have also been studies of much juvenile literature as revealing the fantasies and attitudes of their adult creators. Kathryn Castle succeeds in bringing both of these together. Her focus is specifically upon representations of other societies in British texts, both those designed for instruction in schools and for entertainment in the home. Her 'others' are mainly those who were rendered strangely and deceptively familiar through imperial rule or commercial connection. By expanding her horizons to Africa, India and China – with many allusions to other non-European peoples – she makes a notably wide-ranging contribution to the discussion of representations of others that has been such a significant aspect of much recent scholarship.

John M. MacKenzie

ACKNOWLEDGEMENTS

This book originated in the research which I undertook for a PhD dissertation, and has covered more years than my family, friends and colleagues could have envisaged. For the space and time to undertake the project I am indebted to the Faculty Research Committee of the University of North London for sabbatical leave at critical periods of writing and editing. I should like to thank in particular Professor Denis Judd of the University and Dr Richard Aldrich of the Institute of Education for their help in the early years. As the project came near to completion John MacKenzie gave valuable criticism. The shortcomings of the book remain my own.

Friends and colleagues have given invaluable support. Merle Collins, the late Howell Daniels, Gillian Darcy, Richard Dunn, Sheila McElligott, Margaret Rustin, and Andrew Wright have each in their own way made this an easier task. My family have not only put up with what seemed like an endless project, but were instrumental in making it happen. My daughter, Tanya Kreisky, proofread endless versions of the text, and generously gave of her time and computer to prepare the manuscript. My partner, Paul Sutton, lived with the book in good humour and helped me to retain mine. To him, to Tanya, and my parents, this book is dedicated

KAC

INTRODUCTION

PRICE ONE PENNY.] **MANY SPLENDID PRIZES OFFERED WITHIN.**

No. 560.—Vol. XI.]　　　JUNE 3, 1903.　　　[ALL RIGHTS RESERV

When a nation extends itself ... it meets with other nationalities which it cannot destroy or completely drive out, even if it succeeds in conquering them ... this presents a great and permanent difficulty to contend with.
Sir J. R. Seeley, *Our Colonial Expansion*, 1887

As this book nears completion there seems little cause for complacency over the future of Britain's multiracial society nor for the decrease of racial enmity in the wider world. Racism and its corollary, prejudice, still haunt the streets of Great Britain, erupting with ever greater frequency into a violence and intimidation which scar the social fabric. The incorporation of stereotypical attitudes toward former 'subjects of Empire' continues to produce a popular imagery found in both the print and visual media. For example, the subtext of reassurances that the reversion of Hong Kong to the Chinese will not produce a 'flood' of emigrants to Britain is not far removed from the long-standing fears of an invasion of the 'Yellow Peril'. The impact of the popular diffusion of the imperial ethos, and its legacy of images and anxieties, particularly in attitudes toward race and nationality, sustains a contemporary as well as an historical imperative in seeking a greater understanding of its significance in the social history of the twentieth century.[1]

The 'great and permanent difficulty' of the imperial past surfaces repeatedly in the debate over education suitable for a rising generation. In the 1960s significant advances were made in removing excessive nationalism from school history. The past ten years, however, have seen a desire on the part of government and 'traditionalists' in the historical profession to 'recapture' the ground for British study, and a reactivating of the debate on the uses of history. Talk of education for citizenship, particularly in the wake of the jingoism of the Falkland conflict, runs close to the risk of falling into the same self-serving delusions held by authors of textbooks in the earlier years of this century. The contemporary debate over the history syllabus illustrates again how the past may be activated to ends which 'abuse' the discipline, and that the dangers of the nationalist bias examined in this study remain to be challenged.[2]

That the education of Britain may not serve the needs of all communities within its borders can be observed in the moves for separate schooling by ethnic groups. The failure of the majority culture to incorporate all its citizens or to deal with their histories and cultures within the existing materials and programmes for schools has resulted in a dimension of withdrawal and self-directed study for children of the Afro-Caribbean and Asian community. This in itself passes comment on the degree of adjustment and recognition made by the

British educational establishment to the post-imperial realities of the nation.[3]

This study seeks to expand upon useful scholarly work in the field of popular imperialism, and particularly that which has centred its attention on the exposure of the young to the world of Empire. Valerie Chancellor was the first to examine critically the texts of nineteenth-century England for service to ideals which served the interests of the state and controlling elites. E. H. Dance's *History the Betrayer* carried forward the analysis of a discipline whose search for the 'truth' has been distorted in its excessive nationalism. J. A. Mangan's collection of essays on the imperial curriculum has provided wide-ranging examples of the permeation of racist ideology in the schooling of pupils at home and abroad. This study owes much to the pointers of Frank Glendenning's unpublished PhD thesis on images of race in the French and British textbooks of the imperial era.[4]

More attention has been paid to the popular press in a period when juvenile periodicals were proliferating and serving as successful transmitters of imperial propaganda. Jeffrey Richards' collection of writings on *Imperialism and Juvenile Literature* casts a wide critical eye over the contents of journals and novels in the period of romantic adventure fiction, and draws interesting conclusions on the factors which promoted the imperial formula and shaped its expression. Martin Green's excellent study of adventure fiction, *Dreams of Adventure, Deeds of Empire,* is an essential starting point for anyone interested in heroic myth-making and the relationship between historical figures and adventure heroes. Patrick Dunae and Louis James have concerned themselves with the impact of such ideas on the young reader, as have studies emerging from historians operating in the fields of education and social history. The position of women in the Empire and notions of masculinity in the imperial fiction have increasingly engaged the attention of scholars, whose analyses have confirmed the important part played by juvenile publications in the formation of attitudes in the young.[5]

Bringing together sources from both the formal education of the classroom and the literature of the streets and home was prompted by the approach of such works as John MacKenzie's *Propaganda and Empire,* which has emphasised the interactive and cooperative relationship between formal and informal agencies of social control in the dissemination of imperial ideas. H. E. Cooper's work has also illustrated the interdependence of the world of leisure and formal learning, a thesis developed in John Springhall's book on youth movements in the period. Whether one accepts the concept of hegemony in the permeation of ideas of the age, it is impossible now to refute the wide acceptance of a discourse which internalised an ethos derived from the imperial experience.[6]

While 'influence' is difficult to evaluate with certainty, enough evidence has been gathered to point to the establishment of the ideas within society at large. Circulation figures for publications such as the *Boy's Own Annual* and the Harmsworth weeklies topped one million per issue. Anecdotal evidence from biographical works has now been supplemented by more thorough oral histories, such as Stephen Humphries' *Hooligans or Rebels*, which examine the impact of the deluge of imperial rhetoric in schools and printed materials. While Harmsworth's claim to be the major recruiting organ for the British armed forces cannot be accepted unreservedly, there is little doubt that the sheer volume and invasive nature of imperial propaganda directed at the rising generation did help to shape images of self, and certainly of the 'others'.[7]

Contemporary studies of racism in children's books, both in Britain and abroad, suggest that the inclusion of stereotypical images does affect the idea formation of children at a vulnerable stage in their development. Academic studies are buttressed by the judgements of affected groups, who, faced with the continuation of racist imagery in texts, popular books, and classroom practice, have shown their dissatisfaction by producing alternative materials and forming pressure groups to monitor the dangers of false representation. Studies of the misunderstandings which can be produced by 'false history' and distorted characterisation have emerged from societies, like Northern Ireland and post-war Germany, where violence and repression have been linked to adulterated views of the past.[8]

In the late nineteenth century, a particularly strong relationship developed between education, the juvenile press and the imperial propagandists. Arguably the most fertile ground for their shared agenda was the 'story of Empire'. The high tide of British imperialism corresponded with the expansion of history in the school curriculum, the growth of respectable periodicals, and the perception of a need to reinvigorate public morale and national pride. At the same time the expansion of literacy and fears of degeneracy prompted a concern that conveying the imperial discourse to a wider audience was essential.

In former years the burdens of Empire or of the State fell on the shoulders of a few, now the humblest child found on the benches of a primary school will in a few years' time be called upon to influence the destinies of not only fifty four millions of white, but also three hundred and fifty millions of coloured men and women, his fellow subjects scattered throughout five continents of the world. Such overwhelming responsibilities have never before in the history of the world fallen upon any people.[9]

Few doubted that history would take a central role in the process of producing imperial citizens. Moral instruction and civic initiation of the young were central concerns of the Board of Education directives, educational journals, the newly formed Historical Association and the publishers of texts for the expanding market. Character formation became a primary objective of history lessons, and the successful text was one which emphasised the conflict, romance and heroism of the British past. Both potential leaders and followers, it was felt, could be secured in a shared community of values and 'Britishness' through the experience of an imperial identity, hopefully subsuming social and class antagonisms in the process.[10]

The textbook market grew in response to rising student numbers and the expansion of history in the curriculum, while university historians and public school masters came forward to provide approved books for the junior and senior audience. Historians such as Peter Fryer and Marc Ferro have studied the influences on these new textbook authors and argued that it was the nineteenth-century defenders of Anglo-Saxon values whose imprint was felt most strongly in the narrative. The importance of the Oxford and Cambridge schools of history was evident, in the debt to Froude, Seeley and Egerton, as well as the guidelines for history teaching produced by two influential Oxford historians, C. H. K. Marten and M. W. Keatinge. Marten and Keatinge also produced two widely used texts for senior classes. Historians, therefore, most closely involved in the production of materials for classroom use and teacher guidance were closely linked with imperial advocates and generally shared their view of the subject's usefulness in propagating imperial aims.[11]

Joining the camp was the editor of *Boys of the Empire*, who set a course to 'nurture and strengthen a spirit of patriotism and loyalty'. This was a sentiment little different from the Board of Education's suggestion that students 'should feel the splendour of heroism, the worth of unselfishness and loyalty to an ideal, and the meaning of cruelty and cowardice'. The opportunity for out-of-school hours to be filled with popular magazines was seized upon by publishing houses, and the years from 1880 to 1918 witnessed an extraordinary proliferation of periodicals aimed at the expanding market. That profit might be linked with social improvement was made explicit. Editors declared their determination to exterminate the 'gutter literature' which they claimed had contributed to national decline, and set out 'to carry the war into the enemy's camp, and flood the market with good, wholesome literature'. *Pluck* advertised itself as 'exciting enough to meet popular taste ... but devoid of any unhealthy tone'. Over 149 magazines were launched in these years, catering to all sections of the youthful population. The rise of the Amalgamated Press, Harmsworth's highly successful and diverse range of juvenile papers, is one of the success stories of the era. Within this intensely competitive and lucrative market the world of Empire and its cast of subject peoples became a dominant feature.[12]

The 'crossover' between these two worlds, of school texts and leisure pursuits, was a common occurrence and helped to blur and merge the function of 'instruction' and 'entertainment'. In a sense both worked together to fashion an Empire for the young. For the youngest pupils there was little difference between the stories in their readers and the papers or annuals they might read for pleasure. Stories by popular adventure writers appeared in both, and it was not uncommon for fiction writers to turn their hand, like Kipling and Henty, to the history textbook. Senior pupils could break from preparation for examinations which stressed the military successes of Empire and find famous military men recounting their experiences in periodical features such as 'Great Sieges in History' or 'Pictures from the Book of Empire'. Activities such as the Boy Scouts and Girl Guides, the Duty and Discipline Movement, Empire Days and the other agencies of socialisation stressed values which were echoed or advertised in both school and leisure materials, and again served as bridges between the more and less formal agencies of children's instruction.[13]

If one accepts that there was the intention, the opportunity and the agencies to transmit the imperial message into a child's world, this study turns to an aspect of the discourse which has been somewhat neglected. While a good deal of scholarly attention has been paid to the propagating of Anglo-Saxon values and ideals of British 'character' through the literature produced for youth, and to a lesser extent the textbooks, much less attention has focused on the creation of the cast of 'imperial subjects'. While heroics and historical myth-making helped to activate and inculcate a belief in manliness, service, athletic prowess, honour, courage, and fair play, with a firm underpinning of Christian sensibilities, they also injected the 'mirror image' of the 'other', alien beings.[14] These were the 'supporting cast' in the story of Empire, without whom the testing of self in conflict or the assumptions of superiority became meaningless. While contingent upon the British view of the past, and the racial assumptions of the age, these 'subject peoples' nonetheless assumed an identity which became self-sustaining and real to the reader. They too, within the imperial ethos, were given a 'history' and an identity which merit examination.

This is a study of the images of the Indian, the African and the Chinese peoples as they appeared in the textbooks and periodicals of the imperial era, and as they remained in such materials and the social discourse for generations after the 'reality' of Empire had gone. From the pages of the history textbooks they first emerge in the 'official' world of received wisdom, on the sidelines of great events or occasionally, briefly, central to a conflict or atrocity which furthers the interests of imperial expansion. The popular press built upon these images, filled in the contours of the characterisation, and expanded the cast of characters. Tracing this process across both school and leisure hours helps to evaluate the extent to which the imperial discourse dominated the world of the 'learning' child, and the degree of mutual reinforcement which occurred when projecting the imagery of imperial assumptions. Looking at three different 'subjects' suggests how a specific image grew out of the imperial and national needs of the pre-war Empire, and the particular historical, economic or social conditions which affected the perception of each group. Did, for example, India's primary position as 'jewel of the Empire' promote a more positive or defensive view of its peoples? Did the history of slavery affect Britain's view of the African peoples? How does opium figure in a conception of the Chinese character? Looking in greater detail at the cluster of characteristics which built the stereotypical views of each group also reveals the process of racial mythologising which was central to the maintenance of Empire strength. An important part of the Empire was built not just in the railways of Africa or the civil service of India, but in the characterisation of its peoples. Here, in the creation of the imperial subject, are betrayed the deepest hopes and fears of the imperialist nation, where the illusion of superiority creates a security of control and acceptance of power in reality unobtainable.

For this study a wide range of materials has been examined. The selection of textbooks rested upon a desire to cover those produced for both junior and senior readers, and to include those which were recommended by the inspectorate and enjoyed successive reprinting. The periodicals from which examples are drawn represent the relatively more expensive, penny journals produced for a middle-class and public-school market, like the *Boy's* and *Girl's Own Paper* and the *Captain*, and the newer publications for working-class readers, weekly halfpenny papers like *Marvel*, *Pluck* and the *Magnet*. The question of whether there were class- or gender-specific images will be considered, and it is apparent that in the cheaper weekly papers adventure stories replaced the instructive elements of middle-class annuals. Girls' papers did place the British character in a different relation to the 'native', and this is suggested in the discussion of the romantic and picturesque. However, it is also clear that papers crossed class and gender boundaries, that working-class youth read the 'improving' annuals when possible, and that girls picked up their brothers' magazines and enjoyed them. While most studies have considered the imperial message a province of male socialisation, it is clear that within the constraints of the role deemed appropriate for imperial girls, there was ample scope for service to Empire, and correspondingly a need for nurses, teachers and missionaries to understand the peoples they might serve. The final chapter suggests that the imagery not only transcended class and gender lines, but also extended in time through the twentieth century. Between the wars, despite alterations in the imperial 'realities', the images of Indian, African and Chinese peoples showed that this Empire retained its life in both textbooks and annuals.[15]

Both the history textbooks and the children's periodicals offered to the young a version of how to relate to the imperial world and to the peoples who lived within it. While dominance over 'imperial races' was a primary message, it is also true that exposure to models of acceptable and non-acceptable behaviour might assist in the process of individuation and self-definition in a child's formative years. And if character was defined through conflict, then the 'alien' played a key role in questions of identity and status, as the young Briton differentiated him- or herself from the wider world. Securing youth into the imperial ethos involved both positive identification with Britishness and a distancing from the undesirable 'other'. Images of race created to satisfy imperial prerogatives therefore answered deeply felt needs in the population as a whole, and were a testing ground for their own strengths and weaknesses. The complementary nature of the projection of national identity and the process of self-definition strengthened the impact of racial imagery in this era, and goes some way to explaining the tenacity of its hold on public consciousness in the post-imperial period.[16]

In the fullest sense, this is a study of the role that racial imagery can play in any society, past or present, and more particularly in securing the allegiance of the young to values and institutions threatened by the forces of change. By examining the image of the 'other' in materials ostensibly dissimilar in function, and noting the essential similarities and reinforcing relationships between school and popular materials, one discovers how pervasive and controlling was the logic of racial and national superiority. By exploring the picture of the 'imperial' Indian, African and Chinese, the source of long-lived distortions and misconceptions becomes clearer. The ghosts of these images continue to haunt our daily lives, and by looking closely at the process which gave them life in the minds of earlier generations, both an essential construct of the imperial world and the 'invisible Empire' of our own can be recognised, demythologised and perhaps laid to rest.

Notes

1 The Home Office estimates 120,000 racially motivated attacks a year. Congress for Racial Equality advertisement, *The Independent*, 1 July 1994.

2 UNESCO, *Looking at the World Through Textbooks*, Paris, 1946; R. Preiswerk, ed., *The Slant of the Pen*, Geneva, 1980; R. Dixon, *Catching them Young*, London, 1977; G. Klein, *Reading into Racism*, London, 1985, chapter 5; G. McDiarmod and D. Pratt, *Teaching Prejudice*, Toronto, 1971; 'History men battle over Britain's future', *The Times*, 9 May 1994; Christopher Hill, 'Lies about crimes', *The Guardian*, 29 May 1989; P. Marshall in J. Gardiner, ed., *The History Debate*, London, 1990.

3 P. Fryer, 'Black perspectives on British education', in J. Gundara, C. Jones, K. Kimberly, eds, *Racism, Diversity and Education*, London, 1986.

4 V. Chancellor, *History for their Masters*, Bath, 1970; E. H. Dance, *History the Betrayer*, London, 1960; J. A. Mangan, ed., *The Imperial Curriculum*, London, 1993; F. Glendenning, *The Evolution of History Teaching in British and French Schools in the 19th and 20th Century with Special Reference to Attitudes to Race and Colonialism in History Textbooks*, unpublished PhD, Keele, 1975.

5 J. Richards, ed., *Imperialism and Juvenile Literature*, Manchester, 1989; M. Green, *Dreams of Adventure, Deeds of Empire*, London, 1980; P. Dunae, 'Boys' literature and the idea of Empire', *Victorian Studies*, vol. 24, autumn, 1980, pp. 105–22; L. James, 'Tom Brown's imperialist sons', *Victorian Studies*, vol. 18, autumn, 1973, pp. 89–99; G. Avery, *Childhood's Pattern*, London, 1975; K. Drotner, *English Children and their Magazines*, New Haven, 1988; K. Boyd, 'Knowing their place', in J. Tosh and M. Roper, eds, *Manful Assertions*, London, 1991; V. Ware, *Beyond the Pale*, London, 1992; J. A. Mangan and J. Walvin, eds, *Manliness and Morality*, Manchester, 1987.

6 J. Mackenzie, *Propaganda and Empire*, Manchester, 1984; H. E. Cooper, *British Education, Public and Private, and the British Empire, 1850–1930*, unpublished PhD, University of Edinburgh, 1979; J. Springhall, *Youth, Empire and Society*, London, 1977; J. Gillis, *Youth and History*, London, 1981.

7 S. Humphries, *Hooligans or Rebels*, Oxford, 1981; E. S. Turner, *Boys will be Boys*, London, 1948, pp. 115–16; R. Roberts, *The Classic Slum*, Manchester, 1971, pp. 160–2; J. Springhall, *Coming of Age: Adolescence in Britain, 1860–1960*, London, 1986, pp. 130–3.

8 D. Milner, *Children and Race; Ten Years On*, London, 1983; McDiarmod and Pratt, *Teaching Prejudice*, chapter 1; Klein, *Reading into Racism*, chapter 1; Afro-Caribbean Educational Resources Project, *Racism and the Black Child*, London, 1982; Centre for Contemporary Cultural Studies, *The Empire Strikes Back*, London, 1982; Fryer, 'Black perspectives on British education'; J. Del Fattore, *What Johnny Shouldn't Read*, London, 1992.

9 Lord Meath, *Essays on Duty and Discipline*, London, 1911, no. 6, p. 59.

10 B. J. Elliott, *The Development of History Teaching in England, 1918–39*, unpublished PhD, University of Sheffield, 1976, chapter VI; Board of Education, *Suggestions for the Consideration of Teachers and Others Concerned in the Work of Public Elementary Schools*, London, 1905, 1914; F. Adkins, 'Significant history for the upper standards', *History*, vol. 1, no. 1, 1912, pp. 20–33; W. H. Webb, 'History, patriotism and the child', *History*, vol. 2, no. 2, 1913, pp. 53–4; P. Horn, 'English elementary education and the growth of the imperial ideal', in J. A. Mangan, ed., *Benefits Bestowed*, Manchester, 1988, pp. 39–55.

11 P. Fryer, *Black People in the British Empire*, London, 1989, pp. 73–9; M. Ferro, *The Uses and Abuses of History*, London, 1984; J. Kenyon, *The History Men*, London, 1983; H. C. Duckworth, *The Evolution of the History Syllabus in English Schools, with Special Reference to the Influence of the Public Schools 1900–25*, unpublished MPhil, University of London, 1972; Elliott, *The Development of History Teaching in England for Pupils Aged 11–18*, p. 138; Cooper, *British Education, Public and Private, and the British Empire, 1850–1930*, p. 229; P. M. Kennedy, 'The decline of nationalist history in the West', in W. Z. Laquer and G. L. Mosse, eds, *Historians in Politics*, London, 1974, pp. 329–52; M. W. Keatinge, *Studies in the Teaching of History*, London, 1910; C. H. K. Marten, 'Some general reflections on the teaching of history', *History*, vol. 2, no. 2, 1913, pp. 86–98; R. Aldrich, 'Imperialism in the study and teaching of history', in J. Mangan, ed., *Benefits Bestowed*, Manchester, 1988, pp. 23–38.

12 *Boys of the Empire*, vol. 1, no. 1, 1900; Board of Education, *Suggestions for the Consideration of Teachers*, p. 11; B. G. Johns, 'The literature of the streets', *Edinburgh Review*, January, 1887, p. 63; *Pluck*, vol. 1, no. 6, 1895; J. Springhall, 'Healthy papers for manly boys', in J. Richards, ed., *Imperialism and Juvenile Literature*, Manchester, 1989, pp. 107–25; P. Dunae, 'New Grub Street for boys', in J. Richards, ed., *Imperialism and Juvenile Literature*, Manchester, 1989, p. 23; Turner, *Boys will be Boys*, pp. 110–15; J. Field, *Toward a Programme of Imperial Life*, Westport, 1982, pp. 112–13.

13 M. Starr, *Lies and Hate in Education*, London, 1929, p. 44; C. R. L. Fletcher and R. Kipling, *A School History of England*, Oxford, 1911; G. A. Henty, *The Sovereign Reader*, London, 1887; Longman's Empire Readers in 1905 contained stories by Jules Verne, Captain Marryat, and Ryder Haggard; A. Jenkinson, *What Boys and Girls Read*, London, 1940, found half of secondary school teachers used magazines like *Gem* and *Magnet* in senior elementary schools.

14 J. A. Mangan, 'Noble specimens of manhood: schoolboy literature and the creation of a colonial chivalric code', in J. Richards, ed., *Imperialism and Juvenile Literature*, Manchester, 1989, pp. 173–94; J. Bristow, *Empire Boys*, London, 1991, p. 59.

15 Avery, *Childhood's Pattern*, p. 206; Drotner, *English Children and their Magazines*, p. 179; W. Forrester, *Great Grandma's Weekly*, London, 1980, p. 14; K. Reynolds, *Girls Only*, London, 1990, p. 26; *The Girls' Empire Annual* of 1902 claimed 'for the readers of the *Girls' Empire* patriotism is not merely a flimsy emotional catchword, but something of vital actual import'.

16 Milner, *Children and Race*, p. 78; J. Walvin, *A Child's World*, London, 1982, p. 122; J. S. Bratton, *The Impact of Victorian Children's Fiction*, London, 1981, pp. 27–30; Field, *Toward a Programme of Imperial Life*, chapter 7.

CHAPTER ONE

The untold millions:
India in history textbooks

In S. R. Gardiner's *A Student's History of England*, first published in 1892, he wrote that it was his intention to explore 'the peace and civilisation which it was the glory of British statesmen to introduce into India'.[1] This statement, from one of the most influential historians of his age, cites the history of British India as the supreme example of the imperial ethos at work. Both junior and senior texts of his contemporaries felt obliged to describe with varying degrees of wonder, pride, and responsible scholarship how a small island nation had managed to gain control of vast territories and peoples, and export, with significant success, British values and institutions. This was the story which textbook authors agreed was an essential part of the education of a rising generation of imperial citizens.

Historians lived and worked within a society where popular lore and emotive memories had imbued events like the Indian Mutiny with associations they would have found difficult to deny. Added to this popular consensus was a concern that Britain's future should rest upon an appreciation of its 'glorious past', making of Empire historians patriots as well as scholars. Against a backdrop of promoting the 'wonderful development of the Anglo-Saxon race' and 'preserving that fabric from harm', textbook historians approached British India as the primary example of imperial achievement. It was within these controlling imperatives that India entered the texts of school history.[2]

The image of India and its peoples emerged from what was included in the text and also through what was omitted, from general observations on the 'condition' of India and the assessment of individual figures, and finally through the comparisons which were inevitably drawn between English actions and character and those of the 'other'. One of the most important considerations in the history textbooks' treatment of British India was the selection of events chosen to illustrate the historical relationship between the two nations. Most writers conformed to a similar pattern of historical development, beginning with the establishment of the East India Company, moving to the struggle for supremacy with the French in the eighteenth century, emphasising the years of Mutiny, and finishing with the relative tranquillity of the post-Mutiny consolidation.[3] Within this chronology, the student was encouraged to view India's 'history' as commencing with its recognition by the Western world, a clear sign that inclusion was contingent upon the imperial connection. For example, discussion of the 'state' of India in the eighteenth century represented a context only for understanding the opportunities afforded for penetration by European powers. In 1899 George Carter's description of the 'Moghul Empire' showed a characteristic attitude toward the relevance of indigenous Indian history:

It was a disordered state ... with an entire absence of anything like patriotism and unity, an easy prey to a foreign invader.[4]

India appeared in a state of anarchy and confusion, with a population ravaged by the constant warfare of constituent states, indeed hardly a nation at all by European standards. In the textbooks it was this disorder which both invited and justified the imposition of foreign control. Apart from offering the student the kind of background information which paved the way for the European presence, there were also some descriptive passages on the 'races' which inhabited the subcontinent, but here again the detail was directly linked to the evolution of British rule. Osmond Airy asserted that 'our Empire in India had been possible because the inhabitants were not one race, but many races'. From the Anglo-Saxon perspective diversity was presented not as a rich cultural asset, but as a riot of competing linguistic and religious groupings without a unifying and stabilising core. Students must have felt their distance from 'the Hindoos of 3,000 castes, with the worship of innumerable gods and endless diversity of ritual'.[5]

A concern with racial differentiation and hierarchies reflected the penetration of social Darwinism, as did the measuring of other races against the superior position of Anglo-Saxon characteristics. An historian might divide the Indian peoples into the non-Aryan, the Aryan invaders and the Hindu, describing them respectively as 'flat nosed savages', 'a primitive civilisation', and an uneasy 'mixture' of the other two.[6] In 1912 Warner and Marten, borrowing an observation from Lord Curzon, offered a view on the diversity which was India.

> The inhabitants of a vast continent speak 50 languages and vary in colour from the light brown of northern Pathan to the black of southern Tamil; and they are divided into races which, in the words of a recent viceroy, differ from one another 'as much as an Esquimaux from a Spaniard or Irishman from Turk'.[7]

From this 'vast mass of different elements', they argued, a stationary civilisation had emerged, where no 'cohesion or unity was possible'. Remarks such as these did little to encourage either tolerance or understanding of India and its peoples. Rather the country emerged as a strange and disordered community, clearly inferior to the progressive and dynamic integrity of the European model. Only occasionally in the junior readers can one find the older image of a 'romantic' India which had been held in the eighteenth and earlier nineteenth century. In 'stories' of Empire, rather than texts for the senior student, the 'great and mysterious empire of India which has always exercised a fascination over men's minds' might still find expression.[8] For the older pupil, reflecting the appropriate lessons for a potential servant of Empire, the 'land of mystery' gave way to the more pragmatic and immediate concerns of order, efficiency, and control. Difference now prompted stern ethnocentric judgements, and students encountered a derisory attitude toward practices of worship of 'animals such as the cow, and the monkey, or anything unusual such as peculiarly shaped stones and trees'.[9]

India's unstable society and the disorderly conduct of its population were underscored in the texts by the characterisation of those who resisted the European advance into their territory. While J. F. Bright offered a rather vague picture of the Mahrattas 'dreaming of restoration of their national greatness', the majority of historians agreed with S. R. Gardiner that they were no more than 'freebooters on a large scale' and an 'imminent danger' to British interests. J. M. D. and J. M. C. Meiklejohn in 1901 claimed that 'they were disturbers of the peace of India, and had therefore to be put down'. Opponents of law and order, brought by the advance of British power, were generally treated with a summary justice in the histories. The Omans' choice of words reflects this judgement on a people 'finally crushed in 1817–18'. The 'warlike clans' of pre-imperial India became symbolic of the unregulated strife which had brought India into chaos, and were seen to bear a major responsibility for the intervention of external powers.[10]

Some respect was accorded to those pre-Mutiny rulers, however hostile, who represented a recognisable code of military or civil conduct. Haider Ali, Muslim ruler of Mysore in the eighteenth century, was one such figure. York-Powell and Tout provided an explanation for the textbook admiration of the 'Master of Mysore'.

> A tall, robust, strong, active man of fair and florid complexion, a bold horseman, a skilful swordsman and an unrivalled shot ... a Mohammedan, but tolerant and kindly to his Hindu neighbours ... the old soldier held his own until his death in 1782.[11]

Much like the Sikh leader, Ranjit Singh, 'Lion of the Punjab', Haider was respected as a formidable opponent, and presented as the exception in leaders of his era, one who recognised the need for religious conciliation rather than conflict. Also, crucially, the textbooks admired the fact that he appreciated the potential of British power, while his death removed the possibility of effective resistance. The description of this 'enlightened despot' was revealing for the standards which texts applied in judging the 'good leader'. He was light-skinned, athletic, brave in battle, fair and tolerant, in fact, remarkably English.

The Sikhs, despite opposing the British in two bitter wars of the nineteenth century, also earned admiration for their behaviour. The characterisation of their practices stands in contrast with dismissive attitudes toward other Indian peoples.

> They were a religious sect who maintained the abolition of caste, the unity of the godhead, and purity of life, and were distinguished for the steadiness of their religious fervor.[12]

Warner and Marten, writing in 1912, found that the 'steadiness and zeal' of the Sikh could be compared to 'Cromwell's famous Ironsides'. This was one of the very rare instances in which any foreigners were accorded the status of shared characteristics with the British, and showed the unique position occupied by the Sikh in the history of British India. Part of this approval rested upon a 'steadfast loyalty' in the betrayals of 1857, the events which strongly influenced the negative image of Indian subjects. But part was also the clear line which had been drawn, as in the case of Haider Ali, between qualities accorded respect in the West, and those which represented a regressive and obstructive Indian leadership.[13]

For the student, however, despite the mention of worthy opponents in battle or the loyal Sikh, exceptions did not nullify the conclusion that a country in chaos needed the order and peace brought by British rule. S. R. Gardiner summed up what many of the textbooks suggested in surveying the 'state of India' on the eve of British expansion.

> England cannot but perceive that many things are done by the natives of India which are in their nature hurtful, unjust, or even cruel, and they are naturally impatient to remove evils that are evident to them....[14]

That the Indian peoples were, according to the characterisation, exploited and static masses crushed by the greed and military ambitions of their leaders exemplified one such 'evil', and was commonly mentioned in the texts. This image was a strong underpinning of the students' understanding of the case for British intervention, and stressed the need to move India closer to the European model of government. Local power structures were portrayed as not only incompetent, but of doubtful legitimacy by Western standards.

> The nawabs and viziers ... held sway merely because they themselves or their grandfathers, had been successful soldiers who had overthrown competitors: they had no dynastic rights like the monarchs of Europe.[15]

From this highly selective representation of Indian society during the early years of British interest emerged, in the words of one text, the simple choice between 'outrage and misery' or 'peace and settled government'. A few examples of the flawed society and character of the prospective imperial domain sufficed to justify, if not explain, the growth of British power. For most students, it was expected that an emotional, perhaps moral sensibility would secure an understanding of the dynamic of intervention, and in this process reaction to the characterisation of India, rather than its history, was paramount.[16]

In this process the textbook treatment of the 'heroes' of the British story is illuminating. Guidelines of the Board of Education in 1914 show how central to the learning experience was the incorporation of lessons of character.

> The teacher should place in relief those actions of heroes and heroines which exhibit their highest qualities but should take care not to raise them too far by the omission of their faults and shortcomings.[17]

The exploits of Clive and Hastings were familiar to the young from texts and popular reading. Their presentation in history readers and textbooks not only sheds light on the 'heroic' symbols of Empire, but also crucially contrasts with the 'subject' people. In the junior readers and simpler texts the need for clarity and compression tended to work to enhance the *'Boys' Own'* qualities of the two men. Arguably this uncomplicated version of history was deemed most appropriate for a readership of potential followers, rather than active participants in colonial events. If only a few sentences were to be included it sufficed to describe Clive as 'England's Champion', 'deliverer', or 'avenger' of the Black Hole. While Hastings was less directly associated with stirring deeds and therefore appeared less often in the readers, the texts for lower forms did encapsulate his career in descriptions of 'glorious service' or through a simple image. J. R. Green's junior text asserted that 'after a century of great events Indian mothers still hush their infants with the name of Warren Hastings'. These brief and uncritical references to the two Englishmen suggested a rather effortless 'mastery' over the Indian environment. To Clive was attributed both success over troops who 'fled in terror' at his advance and a 'touching devotion' from his own sepoys. Hastings appeared a strong and just statesman, towering over the intrigues of corrupt local leaders. They became heroes not only to the reader, but also to the exploited masses of the areas they brought under British influence. The Indian image was clearly co-opted and directed to supporting the 'heroic' imperatives of a one-dimensional view of British leadership, an important validation of Empire for the younger reader. The 'Empire stories', directed toward those who were both impressionable and perhaps leaving school with little more to their history lessons, represent a stark example of the patriotic message for the working-class pupil.[18]

The role played by India was rather more complex, however, in those senior texts which dealt with the controversial aspects of Clive's and Hastings' careers. Throughout the period history textbooks did introduce the student to the accusations levelled against both men in their lifetimes. What is notable in the years leading to the First World War is the manner in which the authors of the texts, whatever reservations they might have had of the methods employed by the men, attribute culpability for their actions. Few offered a very positive view of the East India Company, acknowledging the uneasy mix of profit and good government, and most credited the two men with a positive move away from Company rule. However, when dealing with the charges of corruption and irresponsibility which emerged from the careers of both men, it became increasingly clear through the early years of the twentieth century that it was India itself which shouldered a large portion of blame for such irregularities. Both Clive and Hastings, in this version of events, paid a heavy price for their long periods of service abroad, emerging infected with the corruption and venality endemic in the 'nature' of India. Clive was doomed by 'the oriental falsehood and treachery to which he stooped', and by the 'laxity and unscrupulousness of Indian politics'. Carter observed that 'the shock was so great that he went mad, and died shortly afterward'.[19]

Hastings was accused by Gardiner of 'soiling the English name' by 'lending troops to an Eastern potentate ... certain to abuse a victory won by their arms'. Listening to the advice of 'native princes' became a major failing in Hastings' errors of judgement. Innes summed up the most important aspects of his career:

He unfortunately allowed methods to be employed which were a matter of course in oriental warfare and oriental courts, but were thoroughly repugnant to European ideas. The lesson had not yet been learned that in dealing with peoples whose moral standards are different from those of Europe, the white man must hold to the white standard that is not only the right course, but the course that pays best in the long run.[20]

It becomes clear that even in the senior texts there was a growing reluctance to tarnish the reputation of Clive or Hastings by holding them or defects in the 'British character' responsible for their actions. While the riches and intrigues of the oriental life might appear seductive, in the end and with the hindsight tempered by the Mutiny, what was threatened was not only their own natural virtues but the investment of their country. They had not yet learned the 'lesson' of Empire, that moral standards cannot be seen to be compromised, and the consequences of laxity can be dire. As is so often the case, however, it was the 'temptress' who bore responsibility and the Indian who was cast as immoral, dangerous, untrustworthy and invasive. Good reputations were soiled, and good men ended their days in suicide or alienation. This was a heavy burden for India to bear, and certainly helped to diminish the young reader's sympathies for a local population exploited by both princely and British profiteers. Clive's and Hastings' 'crimes' were reduced to misdemeanours, and historical judgement acquitted them in a context of provocation beyond reasonable limits. Any blemish upon their reputations was seen to be the mark of India and its peoples. Theirs were cautionary tales, and the best defence was to maintain a safe distance from the Indian. 'Holding to the white standard' was not only safe and virtuous, but a safeguard of something more valuable than quick riches. The threat to Empire of overly close contact with the ruled was a basic tenet of British India in the late nineteenth and early twentieth century, and history textbooks suggested that the past showed ample justification.[21]

In 1914, a Board of Education circular recommended that students also learn 'the meaning of cruelty and cowardice'. In contrast to the generous judgements of their own servants of Empire, historians found few Indian leaders who merited forgiveness for their errors. The textbooks exhibited a belief that there were a number of significant 'villains' in the history of British India. These images were instrumental in shaping the imperial Indian. The characterisation of Siraj ud Daula and Nana Sahib centred upon their association with 'outrages' perpetrated against the British, respectively the 'Black Hole' of Calcutta' and the siege of Cawnpore. These individuals became the personification of the 'oriental methods and morals' which would be set against British character and conduct.[22]

In the late nineteenth century the story of the 'Black Hole' remained alive within the popular imagination, fuelled by the memoirs of J. Z. Holwell, commander of the garrison of 170 soldiers left at Fort William in June of 1756. Historians of the late twentieth century acknowledge the significance of the event's impact upon public perceptions, citing Holwell's account as one 'which would ignite generations of British schoolboys with passionate indignation and outrage against the "uncivilised natives" of India'. M. E. Chamberlain, in 1974, explained how the episode 'lived on in English folk memory, the first in a long series of incidents which were to have totally different meanings for the two sides'. Within the modern perspective, both British and Indian historians have re-evaluated the role of Siraj ud Daula, suggesting that 'he himself had neither ordered such torture nor been informed of it'. A more balanced view makes him 'neither the monster of English legend nor the hero of some later Indian nationalist propaganda'.[23]

In history textbooks written nearly 150 years after the event, one can observe little desire on the part of the authors to reassess the image of the Indian held responsible for a 'deliberate' and 'conscious' atrocity against the British. As little information was given on the context of his rise to power in Bengal, or the civil and military considerations which informed his actions, Siraj's behaviour in relation to the British was presented as having no rational motive whatsoever. His actions in directing forces to Fort William were portrayed as those of a 'cruel young man who hated the English', or as a 'youth with monstrously inflated ideas of his own power and importance' who 'decided to pick a quarrel with the British'. While some texts used more restrained language in their treatment of the young nawab, the basis of his sudden 'decision to seize British property at Calcutta' was not clarified.[24]

The adjectives used by textbook historians to describe Siraj ud Daula echoed the general criticisms of Indian leadership. He was seen as 'weak', 'cruel', 'debauched', 'effeminate', 'despotic', 'stormy', 'treacherous', 'vicious' and 'monstrous'. As his place in the texts put him in close proximity to Clive, the 'avenger', the student must have noticed the comparison, if only to forgive Clive his difficulties in dealing with such apparently corrupt and immoral beings. Even those texts which restrained from calling Siraj 'bloodstained' treated the young ruler as unmanly and subject to the tempestuous and petulant behaviour of the 'pampered prince'. Historical readers described his laughter at the death throes of 'innocent British victims'.[25]

Another prototype of the 'villain' in British India was Nana Sahib, who entered the texts in the discussion of the Mutiny of 1857. Little is learned of him beyond his role in the 'massacre' at Cawnpore, where 400 British subjects had surrendered, been guaranteed safe passage, and subsequently perished.

As had been the case with the 'Black Hole' before, the deaths of British men, women and children sparked off a wave of revenge and reprisals, which exacerbated the racial animosity between European and Indian. In dealing with the actions of Nana Sahib, the texts did not place his opposition to the British within a context of conflicting attitudes toward British policy. Sahib's loss of status through the doctrine of 'lapse' did not enter the narrative. Only Gardiner mentioned a 'hatred of the British on account of the wrongs which he conceived himself to have suffered'. Airy diminished his motivation to the 'refusal of a pension'. Many texts referred to no more than 'dire treachery'. If anything, he emerged as more 'evil' than Siraj ud Daula in his 'cold blooded betrayal'. This was favoured ground for the historical readers, who provided images of the 'horrors' – scenes of 'Englishmen and women slaughtered like sheep ... hacked and mutilated'. In summoning appropriate fear and revulsion from the younger reader, authors designated Sahib a 'monster', the 'fiend in human shape'.[26]

The 'energising myths' of imperial literature, identified by Martin Green, have their counterparts in the writings of the textbook historians. The cluster of images which form around Cawnpore and the 'Black Hole' are important components. Against the outrage of Calcutta stands the figure of Clive and his 'revenge' at Plassey, a critical part of the heroic construct of British imperialists. Just as Warren Hastings entered the dreams of Indian children, so the heroes and anti-heroes would enter the English child's consciousness. Siraj ud Daula and Nana Sahib were described as nightmarish figures, perpetrating dreadful deeds not only against the forces of Empire, but also against unprotected dependants. In response, the child seeks safety and reassurance – Clive and the force of the British Empire. The sense of danger which was inherent in contact with the oriental world was forcefully brought home in the characterisation of the Indian leaders. Just as subsequent administrators in India would justify harsh controls, social segregation, and protection of their women after the event, so the schoolchild would absorb with the highly derogatory images of the Indian a desire for safe containment and a support for the continuation of British rule. The textbooks encouraged this response by eliminating any suggestion that the British posed a threat to either the individual or collective identity of India. Violence was not viewed so much as a failure of policy or diplomacy but rather as an opportunity for a crude propaganda exercise. Consequently, the 'villains' of British India operated in the textbooks much like their counterparts in the adventure story. Projected on to them were all the uncomfortable aspects of the struggle for power on the subcontinent, when heroics gave way to violence and coercion. Once characterised as the source of such evil deeds, the two leaders offered compelling evidence of the need for expanded British controls.[27]

In the post-Mutiny era, the image of an Indian ruling elite underwent significant transformation. The 'pacified' princes were a key image in the textbook descriptions of the 'Pax Britannica', again underpinning the course of government on the subcontinent. With the demise of the East India Company and the unity of Empire focused on the Empress-Queen Victoria, alliances between the official presence in India and 'independent' feudal princes furthered the 'quiet, steady work' which was seen as the hallmark of the era. Textbooks clearly tied in the peaceful, progressive Empire in India with this sign of mutual cooperation, in which the conservative upper orders linked with the officials of Empire in their loyalty to the British monarch. The manipulation of the image of India's own leaders in supporting the idea of imperial rule had taken a new turn. Before the Mutiny, the authors had been careful to cast native leadership as regressive and obstructive, scheming, quarrelling and exploiting their peoples. This had fitted a narrative which celebrated the intervention of Europeans and the gradual expansion of British power. After the Mutiny, the most important image to project was of peace and security. Pro-Western princes, 'working well for their people' and protected by the British, provided a sense of unity around shared class and material values. The *Oxford Survey of the British Empire* noted in 1914 that princes who had benefited from British education were 'practically English gentlemen'. Hawke in 1911 stressed that the princes 'trust the British government as an impartial protector of their interests'. Those who a century before had been designated 'oriental tyrants' now became the natural leaders of their people. Little detail was provided on these allies, perhaps because it might lead to difficult questions. If the imperialist claimed to offer India a way forward out of its static and conservative past, it might seem rather confusing or contradictory for the Empire to ally itself with feudal land owners, who certainly did not represent the forces of progress or change for the masses. It was enough, apparently, to inform the reader that these were 'loyal' and 'deferential' friends. These 'puppet rulers' were supported in the texts as buttressing the stability of the imperial edifice, and recognising the value of the imperial connection. History had come to accept the 'benevolent' despot in India in exchange for the security of British rule.[28]

While few texts wished to disturb this view of post-Mutiny India, there was some mention of new voices emerging from the vernacular press and the nationalist movements. Here, arguably, was the modernising force in India and the attitude taken toward these persons and organisations in the history texts reveals more of the acceptable 'imperial Indian'. Careful not to designate them as 'leaders', instead they joined the ranks of 'troublemakers', intent on leading their people astray with 'silly and seditious journalism'. Texts in this instance passed on to readers the prevailing attitudes toward the educated Indian. Oman expressed a typical view in his anxiety about a 'half educated literary proletariat'. As partners in Empire, the wholly educated, one concludes, are those who, like the 'tame' princes, had imbibed the ethos of gentlemen rather than the unsettling study of Western political thought. Education for Empire, as was the guiding principle in the history texts for English schoolchildren, was to produce support for, not difficult questions about, the British influence in India. Textbook allegiances followed the lines of British policy in the late Empire, expressing positive views of the loyal elite, and discrediting as sedition the emerging nationalists.[29]

No single incident in the history of British India so hardened the hearts and minds of the English toward their Indian subjects as did the Mutiny of 1857. If the 'Black Hole' and Cawnpore illustrated the duplicity of Indian leaders, it was the Mutiny which shook the Empire to its core, and presented the spectre of collective betrayal. First-hand accounts of the Mutiny had become available to the British public soon after the event, conditioning public anger and outrage. Reinforcing and reflecting these established attitudes, the history texts stretched their narrative to its emotive limits. Indeed, authors were reduced to the admission that words were inadequate to convey fully such awful events. Livesey was just one of those who confessed his failure to encompass the 'innumerable outrages'.[30]

Although there was a common sense of the horrors of the rebellion and a patriotic pride in the success of British arms, the textbooks did nonetheless exhibit significant differences in their treatment of the mutineers. This offers an interesting insight into influences on the history written for schools, and the imagery of the Indian peoples within it. From 1890 to the turn of the century, historians on the whole adopted a more balanced approach to the causes of the Mutiny and a more objective assessment of the conduct of the war and its immediate aftermath. J. F. Bright's multi-volume *History of England* used in the 1890s reflected both the author's liberal sentiments and a more judicious stand on the plight of the native soldier.

> The sepoy was not only a soldier but a member of a nation ... liable to be influenced by the social and political feelings of those around him ... brave men fighting after the nature of their kind for a national liberty which they loved or for a religion in which they devoutly believed.[31]

This historian was also critical of British reprisals. When describing the post-Mutiny executions of the rebels he presented an act 'apparently indiscriminate ... a batch of 12 executed merely because their faces turned the wrong way'. He went so far as to charge his own countrymen with showing 'in a cruel fashion ... their incapacity for understanding the rights or feelings of those opposed to them'.[32]

Even the junior readers of the early years admitted errors of judgement. Macmillan's popular series, published between 1891 and 1895, questioned the 'deliberate attempt by the English to force some to sacrilege'. Charlotte Yonge's junior history pointed to the consequences of an English arrogance which alienated influential sectors of the Indian community.

> The British did not take pains, as a rule, to show friendly courtesy to the grave and dignified Hindoos, often of high rank ... and though the native might cringe and obey, he laid up hatred in his heart.[33]

Gardiner observed in his senior text of 1892, when considering the motivation of the mutineers, that 'the British government had not shown itself sufficiently careful of their feelings and prejudices'. Airy showed some sympathy for the sepoy's anxieties in 1893 when he recorded that the loss of caste presented a 'most dreaded calamity'. Most texts of the 1890s noted in the same vein that the Indian people were concerned at the loss of their native leaders, and that the doctrine of lapse 'had given great offence'.[34]

By 1900, however, the tone was becoming harsher and the judgements more uncompromising. York-Powell and Tout in that year described a Bengal army 'pampered and spoiled by foolish indulgences'. Grievances previously viewed as legitimate were now often explained by the operation of character defects and misunderstandings. Many noted the 'fears of a suspicious race'. Derogatory adjectives punctuated and altered the narrative: the 'punctilious Brahmin and the bigoted Musselman came to believe that new ammunition was greased'. Some recognition of nationalist stirrings was now relegated to the 'rumours' and 'mischief' of the unscrupulous, while weak-minded soldiers succumbed to sedition in their midst. Oman and Oman captured this view in 1904 when describing 'a foolish rumour which set the army in a flame'. Insensitive policy decisions by the British now read as the sepoy's 'misunderstanding' of basically good intentions. While earlier histories had accepted the shortcomings of Dalhousie's policies, particularly the projected annexation of Oudh, Innes in 1907 presented a rather different version of events.

> Its kings had been warned over and over again, that if they did not mend their ways their dynasty would be deposed.[35]

By 1912 Warner and Marten had placed the explanation for the rebellion firmly in the Indian camp, concluding that 'Western reforms mystified and unsettled the Indian mind, and natives thought the world was being turned upside down'.[36]

As the shortcomings of the Indian peoples came to bear the blame for the Mutiny, so the suggestion of punitive action by the Europeans began to disappear from the history texts. Whereas it was quite common before 1900 for authors to accept that circumstances had created the possibilities of over-reaction by British soldiers – 'a ferocious if natural desire for revenge' – later works played down the reprisals. Details of mutineers blown from cannons were replaced by such terse assertions as 'the treachery and cruelty of the sepoys was punished with ruthless severity'. Keatinge and Frazer in 1911 observed only that 'the tragedies of the Mutiny made it impossible for the British to be altogether merciful'. There was to be no suggestion that the British had ever been 'out of control', or had deviated from an honourable military tradition.[37]

The textbook historians' treatment of the Indian Mutiny did change over time and included significant alterations in the image of the Indian mutineer. A consideration of the possible reasons for the hardening of attitudes toward the Indian and the increasingly uncritical assessment of British actions suggests that the histories of the period were clearly responsive to the needs of Empire. By the early 1900s it became increasingly important to reassure the student that Empire was 'still the most important fact in modern history'. Writing in a period which included the Boer War, fears of national degeneracy, and challenges to national interests from European competitors, historians constructed a past which emphasised the stability and strength of the imperial ethos. With these considerations to the fore, there was increasingly little room to consider the Indian as aggrieved, discontented, angry or exploited. The same texts which dismissed the Mutiny as a 'protest' movement also discounted the rise of Indian nationalism in the late nineteenth century and denigrated the rise of a political press. The over-riding concern was with the safety of Britain's position in India. It became less important to learn from the errors of the past than to eradicate them. In the process, the image of the Indian lost a fragile claim to a rational and independent voice, while British actions moved increasingly beyond reproach. Opposition to the British, whether in 1857 or later, rested now in 'misunderstandings', irrational fears, and the rumour of sedition. As British 'heroism' and good intentions became the most significant 'facts' in school histories of the Mutiny years, subjects who failed to recognise their own best interests assumed responsibility for the resort to armed conflict. As *The Oxford Survey of the British Empire* advised in 1914, a concentration on the 'heroism of the British' ensured that a study of the Mutiny 'added to rather than diminished British prestige'.[38]

While this may have been the case, and undoubtedly was the purpose, Empire's gain was history's and the Indian peoples' loss. The co-opting of the image of India and its peoples to support British intervention and control had become extraordinarily self-serving by 1914. This trend can be seen particularly in the case of the Indian Mutiny, the most emotive and significant event in the relations between subject and imperial power. In the texts, a conflict of interests or a question of policy became transformed into a struggle between the character and values of two peoples, with the behaviour of the Indian attesting to a need for guidance and control. Authors could not allow an interpretation which acknowledged nationalist aspirations, for to accord such a discourse to resistance challenged the long-standing image of an India of inchoate political awareness. Were Indian aspirations to be legitimised, the image of disorder and chaos upon which British intervention was predicated would be challenged as a permanent characteristic of Indian society. If textbooks credited the local press or the Indian National Congress with a growth of national identity, the future of Empire could not be secure. Texts reflected the official view that at this stage of development India's best interests were secured by its imperial connections, while internal dissension was relegated to the turmoil which must be kept at bay. Historians writing for the young stressed the benevolent power of a paternal force – echoing Curzon's view at the turn of the century.

> We cannot take the natives up into the administration. They are crooked and corrupt. We have got therefore to go on ruling them and we can only do it with success by being both kindly and virtuous. I dare say I am talking rather like a schoolmaster; but after all, the millions I have to manage are less than schoolchildren.[39]

Curzon's words are particularly illuminating in the context of this study. They articulate the unspoken text of the histories, that English schoolchildren should be prepared to take up the mastery of their fathers. And also that it was imperative, given the character of India, that they do so.

Where did that leave the 'imperial Indian'? It is arguable that the authors of the history texts knew no more of the Indian than they represented, and that their own knowledge of the Empire rested upon the ethnocentric history they had themselves studied and credited in their works. In their assessment of Indian character they were clearly echoing the prevalent ideas of the era, the delivered dogma of scientific racism, the racial hierarchies of the evolutionists and the Spencerians, and 'progressive' history. However, they had both a captive audience and the 'legitimacy' of scholarship. By preparing the young to accept rather than challenge popular knowledge the critical edge of 'history' in British India was abandoned.[40]

The messages would be mixed but mutually reinforcing. At one end of the spectrum were the 'exceptional Indians', few in number and distinguished by the adoption of European values and manners. As might be expected, they represented an 'elite' which had risen above the 'teeming masses'. Without exception, entry into this exclusive club was based on 'passing' with as many characteristics of the Anglo-Saxon as possible. Class distinctions played a major part in this dispensation. The princes of the Raj were seen as indispensable allies, and while the texts stressed the protective role of the British in their regard, this alliance clearly maintained wealth and status for both parties. This convergence of conservative interests relieved the elite from the generally harsh stereotyping of their predecessors, and moved them from the ranks of 'oriental' to 'benevolent' despots.

The 'other face of India', those who had contested progress and thereby invited suppression, proved, in Sir Charles Oman's words, that 'the British bayonet was still needed'. The picture drawn of 'cruel despots' who exploited their own peoples, pursued violence with a 'ruthless disregard for human life', and lived by the principle of power without responsibility, operated in the texts to help secure youth's belief in the 'adventure' of history as an armed struggle. This was the 'real' India, of strange and 'alien' practices, whose existence caused such problems for the successive servants of Empire. This aspect of 'imperial India' worked to discredit the unacceptable difference of Indian culture and by so doing redeemed the lapses of Clive and Hastings, justified excesses of revenge after the Mutiny, and labelled as troublemakers the nationalist camp. This was the province of 'old India', unenlightened, and unable to offer its millions either protection or progress. These were the forces which would be replaced by the alliance of pro-Western prince and Raj official, allowing India to advance from 'infancy to political manhood'.[41]

The history texts were, of course, really only interested in the clashes of the 'great figures' on the historical stage, British and Indian. However, the claims of progress and benevolence which attached to the authors' descriptions of British intentions abroad could be illustrated in the treatment of India's 'teeming masses', caught between the acceptable princes and the unscrupulous or seditious nationalists. In most texts the inhabitants of India were described as prisoners of conditions once known in medieval Europe. Poverty and ignorance, assisted by the caste system, made for an essentially static and conservative peasantry. It was common in the rhetoric of the era to compare these uncivilised 'rungs' on the evolutionary ladder with the progress to adulthood, and so childlike emotions and superstitions became part of the picture. Having established this image in the mind of British schoolchildren, the Empire assumed a natural parental role. India received education, hospitals, roads, railroads, irrigation and sanitation as part of the 'quiet and steady' benefits of guardianship. These children of India were the 'vast responsibility' which textbooks emphasised as a major feature of the imperial relationship, and texts presented the 'masses' as giving mute assent to an open-ended extension of British control.

> It is true that India was won by the sword, but England has given peace and prosperity to 300 million of that vast dependency ... freedom and justice to the struggling masses of people of all races and religions, who if left to themselves, would perish by war and brigandage.[42]

Considerations of profit and loss did not sit comfortably with such sentiments. Historians did not concern themselves with Britain's 'dependency' on the wealth generated by the control of India. Having explained the transition from company rule to 'disinterested' administration as a diminution of the 'venal motive' in conquering the subcontinent, history confined itself to demonstrating the administrative and social reforms associated with direct rule. The economics of Empire were relegated to the geography texts, leaving to history the 'higher ground' of law and politics. The historians of the late nineteenth century de-emphasised the merchant's role in British expansion, and this was particularly evident in India, where trade had once brought the unacceptable temptations of corruption, and was now dissociated from imperial ambitions.[43]

Textbook historians generally shared three priorities in writing of British India – instil a sense of pride in Empire through its past, secure the commitment of the rising generation to holding on to it, and make the connections between these successes and racial/national identity. When one looks at the images of the Indian operating in these narratives, it is apparent how the configuration of individuals and the choice of events lend themselves to the imperial ethos, indeed are crucial in convincing the young of the justice of the imperial case. The realities of power could not allow a very positive view of one's subjects – too much sympathy on the part of the young might unravel the case for control. The uncertainties and anxieties felt about the state of Britain and its world position after 1900 helped to harden the images further, signifying the direct relationship between national interests and the shape of the 'other'. The revision of Mutiny history illustrates clearly just how responsive the history narrative had become to external considerations. Historians of British India offered the schoolchild images tailored to meet imperial priorities – one-dimensional, non-negotiable, and ultimately self-serving. Not only these pupils in their adult lives, but succeeding generations who read these long-lived texts, would continue to believe in an India which was created, rather than revealed, by the historians of Empire.

Notes

1   S. R. Gardiner, *A Student's History of England*, London, 1892, p. 859.
2   T. Livesey and B. Besonthorp, *Macmillan's History Readers*, London, 1891–95, p. 224; R. Walker and G. Carter, *Local Examination History of England*, London, 1905, p. 103; A. Innes, *History of England*, Cambridge, 1907, p. vi.
3   F. Glendenning, 'School history textbooks and racial attitudes, 1804–1911', *Journal of Educational Administration and History*, vol. 5, 1973, pp. 40–1.
4   G. Carter, *History of England*, London, 1899, p. 84; also G. Warner and C. H. K. Marten, *Groundwork of British History*, London, 1912, p. 466; Gardiner, *A Student's History of England*, p. 859; F. York-Powell and T. Tout, *History of England*, London, 1900, p. 898.
5   J. R. Green, *A Short History of the English People*, London, 1894, p. 1659; M. Keatinge and N. Frazer, *A History of England for Schools*, London, 1911, p. 506; York-Powell and Tout, *History of England*, p. 785; *Avon Historical Readers*, London, 1895, p. 85; O. Airy, *Textbook of English History*, London, 1893, p. 496; Warner and Marten, *Groundwork of British History*, p. 467.
6   York-Powell and Tout, *History of England*, p. 995.
7   Warner and Marten, *Groundwork of British History*, p. 466.
8   Warner and Marten, *Groundwork of British History*, p. 466; C. L. R. Fletcher, *Introductory History of England*, London, 1909, pp. 110–12; R. S. Rait, *School History of England*, Oxford, 1911, p. 92; Livesey and Besonthorp, *Macmillan's History Readers*, p. 31; *Avon Historical Readers*, p. 85.
9   York-Powell and Tout, *History of England*, pp. 785, 995; Carter, *History of England*, p. 84; see also M. E. Chamberlain, *Britain and India*, Newton Abbot, 1974; P. Mason, *Patterns of Dominance*, London, 1970.
10 J. F. Bright, *A History of England for Public Schools*, London, 1887–1901, p. 799; Gardiner, *A Student's History of England*, p. 859; J. M. D. Meiklejohn and J. M. C. Meiklejohn, *A School History of England*, London, 1901, p. 451; Sir C. Oman and M. Oman, *A Junior History of England*, London, 1904, p. 239.
11 York-Powell and Tout, *History of England*, p. 1001; see also Green, *A Short History of the English People*, p. 1712; Gardiner, *A Student's History of England*, p. 758; Carter, *History of England*, p. 118; M. O. Davis, *The Story of England*, Oxford, 1912, p. 283.
12 *Avon Historical Readers*, p. 494.
13 Warner & Marten, *Groundwork of British History*, p. 688; V. G. Kiernan, *The Lords of Human Kind*, London, 1969, p. 55; Bright, *A History of England for Public Schools*, p. 293; Carter, *History of England*, p. 217; A. Hassall, *A Class Book of*

English History, London, 1901, p. 548; Innes, *History of England*, p. 542, Keatinge and Frazer, *A History of England for Schools*, p. 514.

14 Gardiner, *A Student's History of England*, p. 954.

15 Innes, *History of England*, p. 373.

16 Gardiner, *A Student's History of England*, p. 804; V. Chancellor, *History for their Masters*, Bath, 1970, pp. 38–66.

17 Board of Education, *Suggestions for the Consideration of Teachers and Others Concerned in the Work of Public Elementary Schools*, London, 1914, p. 9.

18 A. Hassall, *The Making of the British Empire*, London, 1896, p. 52; J. C. Curtis, *Outlines of English History*, London, 1901, p. 58; G. Bosworth, *A History of the British Empire*, London, 1905, p. 228; Rait, *School History of England*, p. 95; Green, *A Short History of the English People*, p. 1710; Carter, *History of England*, p. 64; Meiklejohn and Meiklejohn, *A School History of England*, p. 379.

19 Meiklejohn and Meiklejohn, *A School History of England*, p. 379; Warner and Marten, *Groundwork of British History*, p. 469; Green, *A Short History of the English People*, p. 1648; York-Powell and Tout, *History of England*, p. 998; Gardiner, *A Student's History of England*, p. 802; Carter, *History of England*, p. 88.

20 Gardiner, *A Student's History of England*, p. 802; see also Innes, *History of England*, p. 400.

21 P. Mudford, *Birds of a Different Plumage*, London, 1974, p. 153; Mason, *Patterns of Dominance*, p. 95; Chamberlain, *Britain and India*, p. 101.

22 Board of Education, *Suggestions for the Consideration of Teachers and Others*, p. 9; Glendenning, 'School history textbooks and racial attitudes', pp. 41–2.

23 Letter of J. Z. Holwell, reprinted in T. Charles Edwardes and B. Richardson, *They Saw it Happen*, Oxford, 1974, pp. 278–85; S. Wolpert, *A New History of India*, Oxford, 1989, pp. 179–80; Chamberlain, *Britain and India*, p. 45.

24 *Avon Historical Readers*, p. 77; Rait, *School History of England*, p. 95; Warner and Marten, *Groundwork of British History*, p. 471; Davis, *The Story of England*, p. 283.

25 Livesey and Besonthorp, *Macmillan's History Readers*, p. 54; Carter, *History of England*, p. 86; Meiklejohn and Meiklejohn, *A School History of England*, p. 358; Bright, *A History of England for Public Schools*, p. 1118; Oman and Oman, *A Junior History of England*, p. 253; *Avon Historical Readers*, pp. 78–9.

26 Chamberlain, *Britain and India*, p. 94; Gardiner, *A Student's History of England*, p. 953; Airy, *Textbook of English History*, p. 498; Keatinge and Frazer, *A History of England for Schools*, p. 514; Rait, *School History of England*, p. 171; Livesey and Besonthorp, *Macmillan's History Readers*, p. 35; *Avon Historical Readers*, p. 96; T. Livesey and B. Besonthorp, *History of England*, London, 1908, p. 93; A. Buckley, *History of England for Beginners*, London, 1904, p. 351; A. W. Dakers, *Jack Historical Readers*, London, 1905, p. 141.

27 Warner and Marten, *Groundwork of British History*, p. 692; M. Green, *Dreams of Adventure, Deeds of Empire*, London, 1980, p. 31 for Clive as 'Boy's Own' hero.

28 Meiklejohn and Meiklejohn, *A School History of England*, p. 449; Bright, *A History of England for Public Schools*, p. 233; J. A. Herbertson and O. J. Howarth, *Oxford Survey of the British Empire*, Oxford, 1914, p. 305; E. Hawke, *The British Empire and its History*, London, 1911, p. 315; Hassall, *The Making of the British Empire*, p. 593; Rait, *School History of England*, p. 171.

29 C. Bolt, *Victorian Attitudes To Race*, London, 1971, p. 192; Bright, *A History of England for Public Schools*, p. 233; York-Powell and Tout, *History of England*, p. 1019; Oman and Oman, *A Junior History of England*, p. 734; Warner and Marten, *Groundwork of British History*, p. 698.

30 Bolt, *Victorian Attitudes To Race*, pp. 157–8; 'The Indian Mutiny in fiction', *Blackwoods Magazine*, vol. CLXI, 1897, pp. 218–31; T. Livesey (with B. Besonthorp), *Granville History Readers*, 1902, p. 192; see Bright, *A History of England for Public Schools*, p. 292; R. Pringle, *Local Examination History*, London, 1899, p. 138; Warner and Marten, p. 692.

31 Bright, *A History of England for Public Schools*, pp. 292–8.

32 Bright, *A History of England for Public Schools*, pp. 305, 318, 328.
33 Livesey and Besonthorp, *Macmillan's History Readers*, London, p. 182; C. Yonge, *Westminster Reading Books*, London, 1890–92, p. 98.
34 Gardiner, *A Student's History of England*, p. 952; Airy, *Textbook of English History*, p. 498; Bright, *A History of England for Public Schools*, p. 295; Carter, *History of England*, p. 215.
35 York-Powell and Tout, *History of England*, p. 1015; Carter, *History of England*, p. 216; Hassall, *The Making of the British Empire*, p. 558; Meiklejohn and Meiklejohn, *A School History of England*, p. 428; Oman and Oman, *A Junior History of England*, p. 242; Innes, *History of England*, p. 483.
36 Warner and Marten, *Groundwork of British History*, p. 690; Bosworth, *A History of the British Empire*, p. 281; Hassall, *The Making of the British Empire*, p. 558.
37 Airy, *Textbook of English History*, p. 498; Gardiner, *A Student's History of England*, p. 952; Oman and Oman, *A Junior History of England*, p. 244., Keatinge and Frazer, *A History of England for Schools*, p. 513.
38 Hawke, *The British Empire and its History*, p. 3; Herbertson and Howarth, *Oxford Survey of the British Empire*, p. 173.
39 Mudford, *Birds of a Different Plumage*, p. 208.
40 Rait, *School History of England*, p. 171; D. Gordon, *The Moment of Power*, Englewood Cliffs, 1970, pp. 116–17; V. Chancellor, *History for their Masters*, Bath, 1970, pp. 141–2; D. Kuya, 'Racism in children's books in Britain', in R. Preiswerk, ed., *The Slant of the Pen*, Geneva, 1980, pp. 26–45.
41 Sir C. Oman, *A History of England*, London, 1895, p. 734.
42 Meiklejohn and Meiklejohn, *A School History of England*, p. 450; see also A. J. Greenberger, *The British Image of India*, Oxford, 1969, pp. 42–3.
43 For geography texts see J. MacKenzie, *Propaganda and Empire*, Manchester, 1985, p. 186; P. Murrell, *The Imperial Idea in Children's Literature, 1840–1902*, unpublished PhD thesis, University of Swansea, 1975; Green, *Dreams of Adventure, Deeds of Empire*, pp. 25, 31.

CHAPTER TWO

Princes and paupers:
India in children's periodicals

India's primary position in imperial history was also reflected in the popular children's press before the Great War. The more 'respectable', like the *Boy's Own Paper*, featured both fictional and non-fictional pieces, while the 'less serious' of the papers – *Magnet* and *Gem* – contained stories, 'did you know' facts and comic inserts. One can easily imagine a child putting aside a textbook and turning to a penny paper, there encountering figures familiar from his/her school history. A wide range of images of the Indian peoples emerged from the juvenile periodicals, forming a rich source of 'information', and augmenting material learned in the classroom.

The non-fiction in the periodicals occupied a middle ground between the world of the textbooks and the adventure stories. Those papers which set out to instruct as well as to entertain the reader contained 'true life' features from British India, both past and present. The royals, as they continue to be, were figures of great interest.[1] Both Queen Victoria and George V as Empress and Emperor of India were portrayed in actual and symbolic relations with their subjects. Their actions were viewed as instrumental in securing the continuing loyalty of the dominions, and both were cast to embody the care and concern of the monarchy toward subjects abroad. A picture of the Queen photographed while diligently attending her Hindustani lessons had a caption which captures the spirit of this imperial harmony.

> The princes and paupers of that country recognise in this imperial self-devotion a mark of tender care and parental attention toward her subjects in the East.[2]

Mingling with this image of the Queen as dedicated Empress were conventions of Empire and of gender. She was pictured in her study, no closer to the actual Indian population than the pages of a book, although presumably learning the language so that she can converse with her subjects. It would be an ungrateful 'child' of the East who failed to respond to the tender solicitations of the mother Empress.

Royal visits abroad more often featured the male royals. The visit of George V to 'Imperial Delhi' in 1911 showed the British sovereign in action. Again, photographs provide a message on the nature of the imperial connection. The King-Emperor is pictured in the act of dispensing gifts from the throne – education, privileges for the native army, and 'kindly remissions for poverty stricken debtors'. The local 'nawabs' make 'obeisance' to their ruler. One, the Begum of Bhopal, is quoted in the article as observing 'that British monarchs, as none before, ruled in the hearts of the people'. This constituted another model of imperial harmony – enlightened monarch, loyal Indian elites, and charity for the masses. Not even the local press, portrayed in the textbooks as potential troublemakers, were allowed to disturb the order of the day. Indeed, a 'paper of somewhat advanced views' was moved to credit a King who 'knew more of us than we knew ourselves'. The Indian peoples behaved in the royal presence like model subjects, deferential, submissive, and grateful for his royal benevolence.[3]

Evidence of loyalty seemed necessary in the years between the Boer War and the First World War. The annuals obliged by providing examples from the arena of military service. The *Boy's Own Paper* in 1906–7 carried a series of memoirs which included the figures of exemplary Indian soldiers. In 'A brave man', Col. James Fitzgerald praised the gallantry of a jemadar who risked his life for the British during the 1857 Mutiny. It was his 'pluck and endurance' in volunteering to ride the lead elephant across a swollen river which allowed essential resupply of British forces. The same issue celebrated the career of the Sikh Jawahir Singh, who distinguished himself during the Boxer Rebellion, becoming a 'native officer' on his deathbed. In 1913 and 1914 both *Young England* and the *Boy's Own Annual* carried features and pictures of the Indian Army regiments and the Indian Camel Corps, who had provided 'invaluable service' in China and Egypt. In addition, anxiety about the vulnerability of imperial ties during the First World War was allayed by stories of the 'steadfastness' of Indian soldiers serving in France and Belgium. Building upon the images of deference to the British sovereign in peacetime, recruits from India to the British cause in war reassured the reader that these were subjects prepared to make the ultimate sacrifice for a cause they held as their own.[4]

Service was not confined to the military arena, and the field of play could prove as telling as the field of war. Unlike other imperial subjects, such as the African or the Chinese, the Indian was accepted into the ranks of the sportsman, in particular the cricketing fraternity. Exceptional athletes such as the cricketer Ranjit Singh earned many tributes in annuals such as the *Captain* and the *Public School Magazine*, directed at the 'better sort' of reader. Ranjit was very popular and very English, seen posing in his whites and leaning upon a smart motorcar. J. A. Mangan has called sport the 'umbilical cord' of Empire, and the juvenile press helped to strengthen the link. While the reality of Ranjit's status as an outstanding cricketer might have involved a complex interplay of assimilation, adaptation and resistance to the forces of Britishness, the annuals stressed the role of sport in eradicating 'native' characteristics. Cricket in particular functioned as a sign of class allegiances and signalled the community of interest between high caste in India and the English public school. The Indian cricketer, like the soldiers in France or Belgium, was helping the side to win. Inclusion in sporting teams as well as in the military fitted well with the textbook descriptions of the Indian elite as nearly 'English gentlemen'.[5]

Another meeting point for upper-class Indian and British officials was the hunt, in pursuit of elephant, tiger or pig. Incorporating the physical exertion of sport and the dangers of war, the hunt added to the adventure of exotic locations. This was a favoured aspect of the Indian experience, as the vast majority of articles rested upon the memories of those who had recently returned from colonial service or were recalling Indian boyhoods. These extracts fill in details on the lives of the Indian rajahs 'at home', when they are not playing cricket or providing support for the British monarchy. *Young England* in 1913–14 provides a number of good examples of hunting memoirs. In 'An elephant hunt worth watching', the Viceroy and Maharajah motor through Mysore to watch an elephant round up. The viceregal party was presented as a social and official meeting point, as they discussed important matters 'over a quiet tea and then motored on'. In 'Out for the jungle pig' in the same issue, a much more active pursuit of game is described, and the reader is reminded that this is not 'child's play'. The value of India as a stimulating and adventurous environment is reflected in the assertion that 'sportsmen in the wilds of India find plenty to keep them alert'. The Maharajah is characterised as an amiable host, who 'in curiously good English told amusing stories'. These true-life adventures in the contemporary Empire, when added to the images from sport, war and official celebrations, were central to the projection of very positive relations between the princes and the agents of Empire. The Maharajah was appreciated for providing an experience both thrilling and familiar, creating a setting where the hunters' satisfaction felt 'like lads returning from a well fought game in the twilight of an English spring'.[6]

The periodicals did not neglect, however, the fact that the relationship with India and its peoples worked on other levels as well, and incorporated into their picture of Empire the practical and less heroic relations of the imperial world. It was perhaps in these more prosaic encounters that the young middle-class reader might come closer to an imagined future as civil servant, investor, missionary or nurse. These 'every day' relations gave detail and depth to the 'quiet, steady work' of the Empire. It was the management of an Indian workforce on which the Agent General of Natal offered his advice in *Young England* in 1899. These were Indian 'coolies', imported to replace the unreliable local workers. For the potential emigrant to outposts of Empire this could be useful information. The picture was a mixed one. While the workers were described as 'useful and almost indispensable', the Agent also admitted that there were problems of control and respect for local law. Because 'this section of the population is responsible for more crimes than all the whites' a strict watch was needed over the sale of intoxicating liquors. Although the harsh Indian environment had created in its peoples an awareness of the 'need for daily toil', strict discipline would be needed to keep them in line with social and civic expectations. The potential manager would recognise these flaws in the Indian character in order to marshall their resources as a workforce, essential to deploy in parts of the Empire where 'the native Kaffir are too lazy or too independent' to be relied upon. In a series designed for 'go ahead young men with modest capital', useful information involved both understanding the value of a mobile imperial labour force and the ability to direct these energies toward useful ends.[7]

The images of India revealed so far all share the common characteristic of having been incorporated into the 'service' of Empire, voluntarily and in a spirit of mutual benefit. All in one way or another were pictured as willing participants in the maintenance of British power, in India, on foreign battlefields, or South Africa's railways. For the elites or the military, dominance was subsumed in the context of class or command structures. Weaknesses in the 'ordinary' workers' behaviour became the target of harsh but essential discipline. All were expected to play the game by the English rule book, and presenting the Indian as willing to recognise the boundaries helped to preserve the image of an Empire whose parts contributed to the strength of the whole.

Power, capital investment, battle and sport were the province of the men of Empire. India seen through the eyes of the women who served the Empire was rather different. Although girls' papers of the era tended to devote many of their pages to tips on self-improvement and domestic life, or the vagaries of romance, there remained an important space for the experiences of those who served abroad. The roles filled by Englishwomen working in India were mainly those of medical missionaries or teachers, a transference of the domestic virtues to those in need. In the accounts of their labours, the native population became victims of 'dirt, squalor, ignorance and indifference'. This was fertile ground for the good works of Mrs Emily Kinnaird and the 'Loving Service League', who recounted her experiences and sought new recruits in the *Girl's Own Annual* of

1891. For the sensibilities of girl readers, India was fashioned into a powerless, dependent world of schoolchildren and infirmary patients. Romance was also an integral part of the scene. Not of course the personalised encounter, but rather the abstract attachment which might be forged with the primitive physical beauty of a novel landscape. Mrs Kinnaird explained to the reader that she was often prompted to 'get out a sketchbook and immortalise these picturesque beings' in her time away from the hospital. A woman without official responsibilities could allow herself the indulgence of the romantic view in her encounter with India that was seldom possible within the 'serious' province of the Englishman.[8]

Although women might appreciate the spirit of place, 'softer' sensibilities had to be subsumed in carrying out their daily tasks. The influence of the medical missionaries was seen to work miracles, transforming 'urchins' into pupils whose 'little brown eyes glistened with pleasure in their little English garments', and in restoring health to the victims of urban squalor. The rewards, she noted, for working in such conditions, came from the gratitude of one's charges. In the mission and the hospital the steady, quiet advance of Empire, described in the textbooks, was brought to life in the interaction between charitable workers and the 'masses'. Here was the India served so well by the agents of progress, dispensing medicines and education to alleviate the sufferings of a country immobilised by poverty and ignorance.[9]

Of course, one might argue, these women did represent the 'mothering' of the Empire, the humanitarian impulses of selfless care with little in the way of material reward. While not denying either their devotion to duty or the positive contributions of medicine, one can question the impact on the reader of the stark contrast drawn between the energy and resolve of the British figures and the passive, apathetic poor. There is little real sympathy in the narrative for the conditions within India; bravery was reserved for the white women workers, with no mention of the human fortitude necessary to endure such suffering by the victims themselves. The impression which counterbalanced the 'service' to India was of a subcontinent manifestly feeble and helpless without the intervention of the good servants of Empire.[10]

The image of India as a society indifferent to its own people's suffering was reinforced in other 'true' stories. *Young England* in 1899 told the story of 'The grain merchant of Jubbelore', a man who hoarded grain in the midst of famine to 'sell at an immense profit'. While his neighbours starved he was pictured on a bamboo mat casually smoking his hookah. These images stood in clear contrast to the charitable spirit claimed by the English, and suggested two very different ideas of social responsibility. In addition, the competence of locally trained 'professionals' was questioned. When the grain merchant's child became ill the 'child's ailment, in the hands of the Hindu doctor, became serious'. Only the summoning of the resident English surgeon ensured the child's recovery. While the rich man possessed no social conscience and was unresponsive to distress outside the needs of his immediate family, the local doctor was both unskilled and unreliable.[11] Here was a picture of India failed by its own middle classes, which allowed an argument for the introduction of British standards of social and professional ethics. In *Indian Memories*, Lord Baden-Powell gave his reading of this 'flawed' society:

> In the training of the average Indian there is not yet any discipline nor any attempt to inculcate in him a sense of honour, of fair play, of honesty, truth and self-discipline and other attributes which go to make a reliable man of character.[12]

Images of the Indian in the contemporary Empire, such as those above, appeared in the more 'respectable' annuals, and were therefore directed at a readership from the upper to the lower middle classes. It is clear that the norms which were in operation to judge and mediate the characteristics of the 'other' in this context were derived from values evolved out of the 'go ahead' energy of the middle class and the 'new' public-school ethos. While the textbooks had described the sense of duty and service which informed the post-Mutiny Raj, the annuals identified its allies and 'burdens'. While British men and women from Queen Victoria to the medical missionaries fulfilled their obligations within the imperial connection, India was brought forward where necessary to confirm the structures of power, the civilising impact of British civil servants, and the humanitarian deeds of missionaries and nurses. Princes show their loyalty in deference to the monarchy and an assimilation of British codes of behaviour on the cricket pitch and in the jungle. Middle-class Indians are saved from their own incompetence by the intervention of an English doctor. The Indian 'masses', including women and children, respond gratefully to the ministrations of the 'Loving Service League'. In these images of contemporary relations with British India, the annuals stressed the harmony and mutual benefits of upper-class solidarity, and the 'civilising' effect this had on the rest of society, a message for young Britons which reverberated in both imperial and domestic contexts.

It is telling that few dangerous or hostile Indian subjects were allowed into the non-fiction of contemporary Empire. However, this was more than compensated for when the publications turned to the 'heroic past'. Milestones of the advance of British power in India were very popular features in the magazines and annuals, combining history and characterisation in a formula which both instructed and entertained. Based on events which the child might know from his or her textbooks, in style resembling an 'advanced' version of the historical readers, these articles infused life and adventure into the classroom fare. Described with great detail and colourful images, the historical narratives offered an undeniably attractive complement to the textbook.[13]

When reading this 'popular history' one can imagine how the 'reality' of events from the past could blur into the imaginative detail of 'adventure'. Indeed, authors often pointed out to the reader that few countries could claim such exciting examples of national expansion.

> The realm over which Queen Victoria rules is so wide and includes so many savage or semi-civilised races, that it would be strange if her representatives did not meet with stirring adventures....[14]

It was with this advice to the reader that the *Girl's School Magazine* introduced 'Mrs Grimwood, the heroine of Manipur'. Hers was a story which would demonstrate that 'the Anglo Saxon race still retains those characteristics which have made England what she is', a revealing assumption about history's relevance to the present concerns. While these attitudes would have been shared by most publications, the treatment of a woman's role in the imperial past does reveal signs of a tension between 'acceptable' women's roles and the qualities demanded from imperial women. As a consequence the narrative moves back and forward from traditional gender behaviour to some exchange of roles between Mrs Grimwood and her husband, in the 'extraordinary' circumstances after his death. As roles shift for Mrs Grimwood and the situation worsens, it is interesting to see how the image of India which she holds changes as well.[15] At the outset she is careful to distinguish between official judgements made by her husband in the conduct of his duties, and the picture she draws from the sidelines. Her husband, the Resident, might need to 'warn or admonish the native ruler, should his rule be unjust or tyrannical'. She could 'cultivate the acquaintance of the princes and princesses and learn the language'. She was well aware of restricting her initial impressions to those deemed suitable for the sensibilities of the Resident's wife. In her semi-official capacities Mrs Grimwood found herself very attracted to the beauty and manners of the 'girl royals', pictured as 'very much like English girls in their love of novelties'. Her appreciation of the 'picturesque' echoes the sentiments of the medical missionaries. Apart from the fact that it was her job to cultivate good relations with the local ruling class and that these were Indian women of cultured habits and conspicuous wealth, there was also a feeling of women enjoying the novelty of each others' company. Without the burdens of directing 'serious matters' or complications of direct power relations, one gets a glimpse of real curiosity and interest in the interaction.[16]

When it came to describing the male royals, the tone changed markedly. Three of the princely brothers were treated very dismissively. Neither mentally nor physically did they measure up to the image of the 'good ruler'. Contempt and disapproval were clearly expressed:

> short, fat, ugly and lazy, they indulged themselves in every way, and showed themselves to be wretched cowards.[17]

The picture of pampered, ill-tempered and weak-minded princes echoed the history textbooks' criticism of those local leaders who were both volatile and corrupt. It was quarrels between the three brothers which led to the revolution in Manipur. There was one brother, however, who was 'a man of a different stamp'. His description was closer to the 'respectable' adversary whom historians had found in men like Haidar Ali.

> the strongest man in Manipur ... an ardent sportsman and excellent player at polo ... fairer in complexion than most of his countrymen ... with a more vigorous mind....

Of course, there were dangers inherent in the 'manly' prince as well, for although Mrs Grimwood found him 'particularly amiable in organising shooting and hunting parties', she was well aware these same qualities could turn him into a 'remorseless enemy'. This was the 'old elite' of India, with some good qualities, but without the reliability of the contemporary princes. While these characters were useful in highlighting the unpredictable and often dangerous environment in which Empire had been forged, they were confined to the narrative of the past.[18]

Mrs Grimwood's suspicions were to prove well grounded. She knew her lessons of history, remembering 'the horrible story of Nana Sahib's fiendish cruelty at Cawnpore'. The threat of betrayal would become real when her husband was 'cruelly murdered by execution in the palace yard'. Details of the uprising are rather vague, but centred on a succession crisis in which the Indian populace backed a candidate the British would not countenance. Now 'true character' emerged. Mrs Grimwood, casting aside her secondary role, became the 'heroine', while the Indian, now with no exceptions, became the enemy. While Mrs G displays her reserves of 'courage and constancy', the locals reveal their depths of duplicity.

The dynamics of this story are particularly interesting in what they reveal about attitudes toward both Indian character and the position of women in Empire. The woman, because she is 'Anglo-Saxon', can assume under fire those traditionally male attributes which 'have made England what she is'. When the chips are down, racial inheritance over-rides gender constraints for the imperial woman. Meanwhile, her extraordinary heroism is contrasted with the cowardly actions of her former friends. Indeed, the 'enemy' is discredited partly by his lack of 'manly' characteristics, in contrast to Mrs G's 'readiness of resource and pluck'. This image of women in British India added to the Empress (mother) and the victims of outrage to provide, in the Resident's wife, an active participant absent from the textbooks. In this role, Mrs Grimwood literally, however, steps into her husband's shoes, and assumes the role of caretaker of the men's Empire. She 'holds the fort' until an English officer arrives with his faithful Gurkhas, at which point she is rescued and sent home. The messages to the reader mix contemporary views on class, race and gender. Women have, as Anglo-Saxons, the racial inheritance to show superior character traits in an emergency, even if this moves them beyond traditional notions of gender behaviour. While in peacetime they can embody the higher feelings of Empire and enjoy their relations with girl royals, once 'under fire' Mrs G acts for the Empire until the relief force arrives and returns her to England and 'normal life'. In the crisis, characteristics attached to women move away from Mrs G and are used to denigrate the 'unmanly' princes. However, the conservative values which supported Empire could not allow a rising of women any more than a mutiny in Manipur. Once the crisis is past, Mrs Grimwood returns to her domestic sphere and accepted place in the imperial hierarchy. In the 'natural' resolution of her 'adventure', both she and the Indian mutineers have been safely contained by the superior fortitude of an Empire where 'womanly' traits, whoever displayed them, demanded a dominant response.[19]

Stories of famous defences made good reading, and India provided many examples for the children's papers. At the turn of the century *Young England* ran a series of articles whose subject matter and style of writing give the flavour of this kind of periodical 'history'. One was set in the years of the Indian Mutiny, retelling the tale of Sir Henry Lawrence and the defenders of Lucknow, in a narrative clearly constructed to appeal to the young audience. Night after night, men of 'fortitude' and women of 'self-forgetfulness' faced the spectre of enemy encirclement. The reader was invited to identify with one of the Martiniere college boys caught up in the events:

> We think no end of our own troops and feel quite certain that they will be able to beat back every assault ... but the strain of the ceaseless vigilance and the awful sense of responsibility were telling on us all.[20]

Having ensured that the readers' sympathies were firmly aligned with the defenders, the Indian rebels appeared to supply all that was menacing and evil in the grim tale. Descriptions of the enemy force employed a wealth of natural imagery. In the 'tempest' threatening the Empire mutineers became 'angry waves hissing in the wake of some boat that has cloven them for a moment on its way to shore'. For the ship of state this was no more than a momentary peril, and the actions of the Indians became the manifestation of a nature both unpredictable and without human sensibilities.[21]

As the siege progressed the image of the Indian as a contemptible adversary became stronger. There were long periods of waiting and watching for the faceless enemy to show themselves, while the landscape seemed infused with a sense of nameless terror. Slowly, while the tension built, there were signs and sounds of burrowing under the walls. Children could easily identify with the fears felt by the young boys trapped inside, listening for clues to where the unseen menace might surface. But a faceless opponent, scrabbling like rats in a cellar, was hardly the model of heroic combat. The mutineers at Lucknow were both dehumanised and placed outside the norms of 'civilised' engagement. This unwillingness to engage in a 'fair fight' only increased the narrator's contemptuous attitude toward the Indian assailant.[22]

When the annuals recreated great moments from the history of Empire, the textbook view of India was both enhanced and expanded. Names familiar from the classroom – Clive, Hastings, and Lawrence – were augmented by the experiences of lesser figures like Mrs Grimwood, bringing history closer to the world of the reader. The episodes which periodicals found appropriate for their ends needed to involve action, and this was usually found in relating the 'conflicts' which had secured India. History as conquest therefore relegated the Indian in most cases to the role of adversary, a recycling of the 'oriental' tyrant or the 'murderous sepoy'. Although essentially presented as informative, editors knew that thrills and danger would enliven the 'dry' facts, giving a much freer rein to the descriptive powers of their authors.[23]

In retelling the story of Mutiny or siege, the 'treacherous' Indian of the textbooks became more fully realised. Details of glinting eyes and cruel smiles were added, while the tactics of the rebels were more fully explained, with remorseless battering at fortifications and burrowing in subterranean tunnels. Words that historians could not find to describe their actions flowed easily. Indians now were characterised as lower life forms – the rats, snakes and insects of the natural world. For the British soldier, these were less worthy opponents than the tiger or the elephant of the hunt, and made of such encounters a 'dirty' business, robbing military men of the glory of battle. Indian allies were not missing altogether, for they proved the ability of the British to secure loyalty even in the most hopeless of circumstances, but it was the cruel face of India which most directly proved the superior 'character' of Empire.[24]

History, throughout the period, and increasingly in the years before the First World War, was used to exemplify the strength of national character and the military. The Mutiny, the siege of Lucknow, Cawnpore, the Sikh Wars – all were replayed many times in the children's papers, and each time the disloyal Indian, no matter how menacing, was defeated. While this was an 'imperial India' more diverse, more animated, and more detailed than the textbooks', in essence the characterisation of India was remarkably similar in school and popular history. Both served the same imperative – to stir patriotism and enlist the 'subject' in defence of Britain's glorious past. The nature of the adversary, clearly destined to submit to superior military and moral force, was drawn to justify and ennoble the power used against them. Accorded the 'legitimacy' of historical 'fact', while simultaneously providing the thrills and adventure of fiction, the annuals' highly selective view of British military successes in India endorsed the continuity of British power while constraining the 'reality' of rebellion to the past.

Not all the young of Britain might have agreed with the author of 'Terror from the East' when he observed that history 'was a dry and desolate region in which to forage', but many must have enjoyed moving from real life, however exciting, into the fictional world of the periodicals.[25] Worthy adult role models in the 'improving' papers might elicit respect and awe from the reader, but for true excitement the adventure stories were unsurpassed. Recognising this fact, the editors put illustrations from these tales on the covers of each issue, placed to catch the eye and the pocket money of the boys and girls who anxiously awaited the latest instalment of a long-running serial. Here unfolded a new cast of characters to place in the arena of British–Indian relations. To the exploits of historical figures were added the deeds of Dick Darling, Stanley Merridew, the Collingwood brothers, and a host of others. Both at home and abroad they encountered figures like Prince Rhadama, the priests of Kali, Sudoo the snake charmer, Thugs, and a variety of other Indians brought to life within these stories.

India featured prominently in the adventure fiction. The author of an article in *Blackwood's Magazine* explained why the episodes of the Indian Mutiny had 'taken the firmest hold on the public imagination':

> The events of the time seemed to provide every element of romance that could be desired in a story – valour and heroism, cruelty and treachery, sharp agony and long endurance, satiated vengeance and bloodthirsty hatred.[26]

Ralph Rollington, publisher of the *Boys' World* for many years, recalled a typical day at the office, which included the visit of a Mr Holloway.

> H: I have spent so many years in India, served in the ranks throughout the defence of Lucknow, and witnessed such terrible sights during the Mutiny – my dear wife being murdered by the Sepoys, that it will be quite a relief to be able to sit down quietly and do a little literary work. I've never got over the shock.
>
> R: Here's an idea! Write it up, it would make a grand boys' story.[27]

Both public and private memories created in India a spirit of place ideal for the setting of adventure fiction. This spirit could be found wherever the Indian appeared, including settings less exotic than the subcontinent. Public-school stories were a very popular genre in the children's literature of the nineteenth and twentieth centuries. By the 1890s these familiar serials in the periodicals often featured a 'dusky' chum.[28] One of the most famous popularisers of the form, Frank Richards (one of the pseudonyms used by Charles Hamilton), created the memorable figure of Hurree Jamset Ram Singh, who lived for years within the walls of Greyfriars School. Reflecting on Hurree's career with the *Gem* and the *Magnet* in the years between 1908 and 1940, Hamilton wrote in his autobiography:

> By making an Indian boy a comrade on equal terms with English schoolboys, Frank felt he was contributing a mite toward the unity of

the commonwealth, and helping rid the youthful mind of colour prejudice.[29]

Although Hurree became a permanent member of the Greyfriars' Famous Five and shared endless adventures with Bunter, Bulstrode, Wharton and Nugent, the 'equal terms' on which he operated should be examined. Although the Indian schoolboy was well liked by the English boys, and indeed protected by them from the racial slurs of other pupils, the outline of his character rests upon stereotypical assumptions. One of the main factors in Hurree's acceptance into the life of the school and the affection of his friends was the Indian youth's familiarity with the public-school ethos and his desire to 'belong' to the fraternity. When he arrives at the school with other 'aliens', French and German boys, he assures the Greyfriars lads that he belongs to the 'English party'. While the troublesome foreigners inaugurate their arrival by fist fights with the boys of the 'Remove', Hurree shows his loyalty by siding with Bunter and co., and stressing his willingness to defend the 'Empire'. While part of the appeal of the stories was the chums' somewhat subversive attitude toward local authority, the code of behaviour in their own world did not challenge the conventions of Empire. The Indian upper classes had often moved freely within the boundaries of the imperial world, and Hurree no less represented the possibilities of acceptance.[30]

In the stories, the English public-school boys represent aspects of an imperial ethos which encouraged the mutually beneficial relationship with Hurree. Harry Wharton was the character who had most explicitly taken up the 'White Man's Burden'. It was he who first described Hurree for the reader, and demonstrated a working knowledge of Indian racial characteristics, observational powers usually accorded to an 'old hand' in India.

> a complexion of the deepest, richest olive showed him to be a native of an oriental clime, and though he was clad in the ordinary Eton garb of the schoolboy, there was a grace and suppleness about his figure that betrayed the Hindu.[31]

Wharton is the defender of 'fair play', who strongly objects to other boys using the word 'nigger' to address his new friend, and 'thrashes' Bulstrode in defence of Hurree's sensibilities. Wharton's reward is leadership within the school, Hurree's undying gratitude, and a large diamond produced from the prince's pocket. No imperial advocate could ask for more.

Hurree is a complex character, accorded both strengths and weaknesses, and his popularity in the annuals no doubt did encourage more positive attitudes toward certain aspects of India. One can go some way with Richards in claiming a commonwealth 'unity' at the school, and it would not be accurate to suggest that Hurree was only a crude stereotype. There was real affection displayed among the chums. However, in the descriptions of Hurree, Richards could be seen to reinforce some of the more denigrating images of the upper-class Hindu.

> He had never lost the beautiful variety of English his Bengal instructor had imparted to him. His good nature was as boundless as the floweriness of his language and the fact that he received a fabulous sum of pocket money did not diminish his growing popularity.[32]

The chums delighted in many aspects of Hurree's alien character. Although all foreigners in the annuals 'speak funny', readers would recognise that the English lessons of the High Bengal School were rich with humorous malapropisms, which were the prince's speciality. Hurree's use of English is a key source of the stories' humour and was a standard way of distancing all foreigners, particularly those with 'aspirations' to join the dominant culture. But in this case the young prince is smart enough to understand the dynamics of British arrogance, and endears himself to the Remove by self-consciously mocking the pretensions of his native education. Despite a 'soft' appearance he can also produce extraordinary sleights of hand, throwing Bulstrode off his feet with an old Indian wrestling trick. Finally, up his sleeves rests a succession of diamonds, useful in cementing his friendships and buying their way out of tight places.[33]

Certainly the reader laughed just as often at Bunter, and appreciated Hurree's superiority to the school bully. But the terms of his acceptance involved a complex negotiation of his own identity. He is incorporated within the Remove partly through his rejection of the other foreigners and does not fight as they do for a recognition of national identity. He claims to be 'English', but the boys' descriptions of him emphasise his 'Indianness'. He is the only character for whom wealth plays any part in negotiating his position. The humour provoked by his use of English is deprecating. Once inside the world of the public school, Hurree could only stay there by accepting certain rules, set by the English boys. Bunter and co. would have scoffed at the idea that they were waving the flag, yet they implicitly endorse imperial imagery and control in their relations with the Indian prince. Their acceptance of Hurree was not an improvement on the standard 'terms' for Indian entry into the upper orders of imperial society.[34]

Although the *Magnet*'s 'Famous Five' were the most popular and long-lived example of British schoolboys befriending an Indian prince, most journals used this formula in feature stories. These were essentially 'co-operative' figures, who bolstered the idea of an Empire where the young reproduced the patterns of their elders. Prince Rhadama in the *Boy's Comic Journal* (1897) was to prove a useful contact for his chums from boarding school. Ten years later Ralph Readypenny travels to the kingdom which Rhadama now rules, and successfully persuades him to protect his trading enterprise from French competition. It is suggested that this is a fair deal for the service which Ralph had offered the young Indian by 'protecting' him during his school days. Fair play brings real rewards in this story. Ralph cannot resist mocking the pretensions of the king's marching band, describing as farcical their attempts to recreate the British model. His friendship with Rhadama does not extend his tolerance to other members of the kingdom. This typical story suggests that fostering alliances with wealthy young Indians at school could pay off, while reminding the reader that this was, despite practical considerations, an 'unequal' partnership.[35]

Friendship with representatives of 'modern' India could also work in discrediting undesirable political or class enemies. In 'Why Revel stole the image', the protection of British schoolboys assists Prince Chunder Dhuree to escape the clutches of Jusel Singh, emissary of the conservative religionists 'who did not favour cooperation'.[36] *Chums* in 1911 featured 'The green diamond', in which an Indian fire-eater attempts to steal the emeralds of the Rajah of Bandustan. The Driftwood boys recognise the 'common' thief as a princely imposter, pursue him and return the emeralds to the rightful owner. For this the boys received a considerable reward.[37]

In Britain Indian fictional characters operated within fairly restricted boundaries. Their roles were partly set by the conventions of the story formulae, and partly by the limits of society at large. All were clearly temporary visitors, whether at school or on some exceptional errand from their home country. They lent an 'exotic' element to the domestic setting, while operating as second players to the exploits of English boys. Wealth, particularly fantastic jewels, played an important part in their relations with the British characters. While monetary gain was never the explicit aim of British action toward the alien, the riches of the princely visitors were crucial in cementing alliances and providing just rewards. Concerns about the 'temptations' which fabulous wealth had placed in the way of British servants of Empire seemed irrelevant, as the young Britons had to earn their access to it by good deeds. These were not boys who would expect duty to go unrewarded, but who, like Ralph Readypenny, could combine the 'fair play' of the public-school ethos with a keen 'merchant' instinct.[38] These stories suggested a model of reciprocity between Indian and British interests, and a fair exchange of 'acceptance' or 'privilege' for money. In its way it presents a more honest view of middle-class values and racial snobbery than some of the blood and thunder adventure serials. Crude and overt racism was rejected, and the possibility of mutually beneficial relations taken for granted. Nonetheless, the price paid by the young Indians for this friendship was the rejection of their own culture – education, traditions, and fellow countrymen. And the acceptance was always with reservations – for there was no suggestion that it was either possible or desirable for any Indian to settle in Britain and become a permanent member of the host society.

Conversely, in stories set within the subcontinent, young imperial heroes moved freely through the Indian landscape. These young English characters were of necessity more explicitly allied with the imperial ethos than their counterparts in the school stories. Although generally operating independently of the official set, nonetheless the hero's progress was closely allied with the advancement of British interest. Jack Hinton's appearance in the court of the Emir illustrates the connection between individual adventure and national service quite explicitly:

> he used his opportunities to such good effect that he managed to dispel all the prejudice which the Emir entertained against British rule; and ultimately the Emir and his people petitioned the government to be incorporated in the Indian Empire.[39]

While the boys were drawn as 'manly' and independent characters, the maintenance of honourable behaviour in India was a given. Prospective members of the Boys' Empire League, advertised in the papers, were sworn to observe certain standards:

> Every member promises to treat all foreigners with Christian courtesy, and in the spirit of noblesse oblige to try to do nothing that would lower his country in their eyes....[40]

In India this was both an imperial and a personal imperative. Lord Curzon voiced the prevailing view of those who served in the post-Mutiny era, in phrases redolent of the imperial boys' papers:

> We can only hold this country by our superior standards of honour and virtue and by getting the natives to recognise them as such.[41]

[47]

In later years George Orwell would express, rather less solemnly, the demands made upon the British in India.

> It is a condition of his rule that he shall spend his life in trying to impress the 'natives' and so in every crisis he has got to do what the 'natives' expect of him ... my whole life, every white man's life in the East, is one long struggle not to be laughed at.[42]

Just as these concerns helped to shape the actions of the British, in life and in fiction, they also circumscribed the roles played by their subjects. This was particularly true in India, where the cast of characters played out not just the story at hand but also the dynamics of Empire itself.[43]

One of the challenges familiar to the successful adventurers abroad was a test of their ability to establish alliances with friendly locals. The Indian ally in the adventure story could be drawn either from the elite or from the ranks of ordinary soldiery, and occasionally took the form of a faithful servant. In each case, the emergence of loyalty to the British involved an explicit rejection of countervailing pressures within their own society. A story set on the North-West Frontier illustrates the tensions of divided loyalties. A young British soldier introduces the reader to the Indian prince in their ranks:

> His native name was Shija-ul-Mulk, but we British spoke of the chap as 'Sugar and Milk'. It was so much easier to remember and pronounce than the name with which his princely parents had burdened him. It suited his sweet and girlish nature.[44]

Other positive attributes included 'a lighter skin than most of his kinsmen' and 'a generous heart'. The extent to which the young prince has been 'won over' becomes a key factor in the story, for when his brother turns 'traitor' on the English, 'Sugar and Milk' in turn kills his mutinous sibling.[45]

There are many messages in this story. Only the most extraordinary of circumstances could provide the possibility for a reader to applaud the murder of one's brother. However, this was India, and the bonds of Indian brotherhood were clearly of a different order than those enjoyed by their Western counterparts. The triumph of Shija was presented as his ability to transcend even the ties of blood when convinced of a greater morality. The power of British standards vindicated, the story both allowed admiration of Shija's enlightenment and the example set him by the British. Like the Indian public-school boy, the price paid was an extreme example of a willingness to subsume national and family membership and internalise the ethos of British values.

Other members of the ruling classes also seemed willing to aid the British, if only in contrast to a less acceptable competitor or successor. In 'Terror from the East' Cyril Collingwood compares the current ruler of Baroda with his father:

> His immediate predecessor had been one of the best of his breed: in all but the colour of his skin he was an Englishman ... loyal to the white race ... a keen sportsman ... the new Galkwar was not built in the heroic mould.[46]

Young Jack Hinton, in another story, was 'pleasantly surprised' to find in the court of the Emir,

> a tall, fine man, clean shaven, no suggestion of the debauchee but a warrior, proud, strong ... not a man addicted to vice....[47]

Here was a leader whom Jack could admire, and who treated him with respect. The story involves a test of character for both Englishman and Indian. Jack is approached by a competitor to the throne, 'Ali', and promised safe passage from the Emir's court in return for British aid. Jack, recognising a dangerous conspirator, refuses, even to save his own life. His contempt for the offer prompts 'sixteen good kicks' to drive home the point. When Jack informs the Emir, 'Ali' is sentenced to death for treason, and the grateful ruler becomes not only a friend but also an ally. Later the Emir confesses that it was he who masqueraded as the traitor to test the young Englishman. Both men emerge as honourable, and the evil face of India is vanquished.

It is clear in these stories that the presence of the British provides a yardstick and an example for Indian standards of appearance and behaviour. It is the young hero who enables the best to emerge in the Indian character as he breaks away from competing values in his own environment. Transfer of allegiance to the 'British way' is then followed by the reader's recognition of positive possibilities within the relationship. However, it is questionable whether the audience accorded any intrinsic worth to the Indian character in this process. Certainly both Shija and the Emir make extraordinary sacrifices, one abandoning his family, the other his empire, and these stories were played out repeatedly in the periodicals, by royals and servants. Were these positive images of India? Yes, insofar as it showed the ability of India to absorb Britishness, as this was not something

[49]

all native peoples were believed capable of achieving. But if one asks whether this kind of story would produce a respect for *Indian* characteristics, the answer is clearly no. Admiration of the alien often rested on a capacity to improve under European tutelage. Like Hurree and the Indian public-school boys, native rulers, even at home, could be secured within the British orbit, and the credit for this transformation distributed rather unequally between intrinsic abilities and external progressive influences. If the stories suggested too strongly that the rulers could behave to these standards on their own, why keep the British there?[48]

One facet of India which appears only in the adventure fiction is the mysterious or inscrutable figure. The image of India as a land of mystery, alien customs, exotic scenery, and strange religions was one which had found its place in the textbooks, but only in generalised descriptions of the subcontinent. It is in the imaginative world of adventure fiction that these aspects of India took human form. Young readers were most likely both attracted and repelled by these figures – the excitement of the unfamiliar balanced against fear of the unknown.

A meeting with strange 'religious cults' set the stage for an unusual adventure.

> We had fallen among Thugs, members of that awful Indian race of whom we even still know so little, save that they come and go like a pestilence, that their sole mission in life is to kill ... a satanic creed that teaches ... murder each month or be doomed to endless perdition himself.[49]

Full of inaccuracies and excessive claims, this description is more than a little muddled and misleading. They were hardly a separate race, and the conflation of murder with religious beliefs serves to distance them beyond the pale of Christian experience. Here is the India of extremes, a people with the most primitive of instincts – 'worse than either snake or beast'. Those who believed in 'murder or go to hell' lived in a world ruled by forces of the changeless, old India.

Thugs appeared quite frequently as agents of death and destruction, and for young heroes they were a formidable challenge. These were hardly conventional adversaries, and their excesses have kept this 'type' appearing in adventure films down to the present day. However, then as now, British/Western heroes have proved equal to the task of undermining these villains and countering their compulsion to destroy. With superhuman powers and magical skills, these Indian figures pushed the resourcefulness of the British to the limits. Often young heroes showed a rare ability to turn local superstitions against their attackers. The ability to tame and direct the energies of tiger agents of Siva was only one sign of the latent skills summoned by the British abroad. And, while the reader knew that this 'power' rests upon the English affinity with animals, the Thugs, less astute, believed the goddess had delivered a 'sign of mercy'.[50]

Thugs had to be handled quite carefully in the fiction. They were not to be over-romanticised, for history had clearly consigned them to the criminal class. On the other hand it was just their danger and unpredictability which made them attractive adversaries in the popular press. Thugs were presented as beyond redemption, certainly, and British characters tended to 'teach them a lesson' and move on. As the 'outlaws' of the Indian frontier, they were indispensable in providing a source of opposition beyond the law and the limits of civilised society. Young audiences must have greatly enjoyed the fictional encounters in which the young heroes fought like with like, beyond the rules of the battlefield and with fantastical weapons at their disposal.

The 'man of mystery' might also be without affiliation to a particular cult or deity. In 'The treaty of Tibet' young Lieutenant Merridew witnessed the simultaneous appearance in his cell of both a luminous message and Raj Dhas, an unknown 'Hindoo'. The old man's eyes 'glittered inscrutably' as he offered to guide Stanley to a stolen treaty. Both Merridew and the reader share doubts throughout the story about the Indian's true intentions. Although Raj seemed quite prepared to let Stanley fall to his death from a treacherous bridge, he also used his power as a snake charmer to save him from hostile servants of Kali.

> The man of mystery had come back to aid Stanley ... as he glided in at the door of the temple his glittering eyes were like balls of fire in their hollow sockets ... quite inhuman....[51]

In the end it was Raj's magical powers which ensured the success of the mission, when his explosives inexplicably appeared at a critical point. Stanley was left to explain to the reader.

> Old Raj Dhas helped to save us in spite of himself! It was impossible to discover the full truth about him.[52]

Raj, although clearly more trustworthy than the Thugs, also represented a power which could not be fully comprehended by the outsider in India. Although the British characters mocked superstitious folly and realised no sustained loyalty could be expected from such mercurial characters, neither could they discount the assistance freely given in moments of danger. These Indians brought alive in a most vivid manner an India untouched by the influences of a Western government and its culture. While the texts and the 'improving' journals painted the subcontinent as emerging from the 'darkness' of primitive existence, the fictional heroes thrived upon this interaction with the 'perilous' East. In the non-fiction these elements of the Indian landscape had to be either reformed or eliminated as a threat to order and good government. Safely placed within fiction, however, they remained free to answer the imaginative needs of the audience.

The villain encountered within India bore similarities to the one who roamed the world and found a place in British sideshows and circuses. These characteristics also resembled the famous 'evildoers' of history, Siraj ud Daula and Nana Sahib, although the fictional context allowed greater scope for recasting a 'malign influence'. As in the history texts, local rulers were portrayed as enemies of their own peoples and of the imperial presence, displaying the tyrant's abuse of power and helping to build the image of an exploited local peasantry. These rulers were presented as 'natural' oppressors, wielding arbitrary powers 'a hundred times more severe than the rule of the English'.[53] Again, the voluntary transfer of loyalty became a significant element in building an unfavourable comparison between British and local rule.

> Gradually ... the natives came back to their own allegiances realising how just and generous was the rule of the English, far excelling the tyranny of the native born princes, who thrived on cruelty and avarice. In the famine districts the people began to remember the kindly rule of the English.[54]

It was also possible for the Indian peasantry to take their own revenge on a particularly cruel ruler, with a revealing use of British hunting imagery. In a frenzy in which the scent of blood had replaced reason, the citizens swarmed 'like hounds after a fox, eager to be in at the death'.[55] It is interesting to note that although the authors portrayed their heroes showing little reluctance in disposing of mutineers or marauding robbers, there was a marked hesitation in effecting ultimate retribution on a member of India's ruling classes. Although the English protagonists were instrumental in creating a conflict which can be resolved only by the elimination of the royal, the deed was generally left to the hand of his own subjects. As with Shija on the North-West Frontier, internal retribution joined the 'best' instincts of the locals with the ambitions of the imperial powers, exhibiting by 'sacrifice' the transition to British rule.[56]

Characteristics ascribed to 'evil' rulers more than justified their fall from power. Descriptions revealed the antithesis of the British upper-class ideal. They were unjust, unscrupulous, and tyrannical – leading from intimidation rather than respect. There was no orderly succession to the throne, nor conventions of diplomacy, rather suggestions of 'poisoned' competition and 'atrocities' against neighbouring states.[57] In personal appearance and actions they were clearly not of the 'heroic mould'. Often seen as cowardly, vice-ridden, and effeminate, their immorality and 'softness' distanced them from the muscular Christianity of the better sort in England.[58] Young heroes felt honour-bound to redress the injustices of their rule and remove them from power. Fiction here was directly re-enacting the textbooks' rationale for British intervention in India.

While the 'masses' could be allied to British interests against a hated tyrant, not all of India waited to be saved by the young hero of fiction. If one wished to provide an adventure with a host of dangerous adversaries, an attack of rebels or mutineers could easily be set within the Indian context. History of course provided the archetypal 'Red Years' of '57, and the adventure stories invented many more, featuring 'uncounted missions of natives, armed and lusting for blood'. Some of the most lurid detail found in the juvenile fiction attached to the mutineer:

> With smiles on their faces and black treachery in their hearts, they lured confiding men to death ... all were alike, not one of them but his hands were dyed in innocent blood. No mercy must be shown to such stuff.
>
> One native, severely wounded, heard the groans of a wounded Hussar and contrived to crawl to his side. With his knife he cut the white soldier's throat ... the fatigue party cut the native to pieces; and if they killed some of the wounded, is it to be wondered at....[59]

The extremity of the language and the harshness of the image, reminiscent of modern video nasties, was quite normal in the periodical fiction of the era. The licence of fiction seemed to release the long-harboured bitterness of betrayal in India, tempered in history and the non-fiction. In the fiercely competitive world of juvenile papers, however, editors encouraged writers to enthral and horrify the reader with details of the 'indescribable horrors' hinted at by historians and servants of Empire. This somewhat belies their stated intentions to provide 'healthy' alternatives to their 'blood and gore' predecessors. Or it may suggest that they eschewed the portrayal of violence only in the domestic context, believing that readers would know that maiming and killing 'natives' abroad was within the realm of imperial self-defence.

Bloodthirsty detail built upon the foundations of folk memory and familiar analogies. Calling its readers to the ranks of battling British boyhood, one author referred to the 'great, grim game' in progress on the battlefield where, unfortunately, stealth and dishonourable tactics became the only possibilities for a British force meeting an enemy for whom the fair fight had no meaning. Only when the Indians greatly outnumbered the British would they chance a frontal attack, and then meet the 'small but disciplined band who blew dozens of them to shapeless pulp'. Looking across the masses in rebellion, authors fell back on the familiar conventions of the faceless, inhuman swarms of the Mutiny. The repeated reference to 'nameless' terrors and a 'nightmare' experience suggest that the mass attack represented the limits of fear and anxiety under fire. There was no possibility of negotiation, incorporation or compromise with the irrational assailants, intent when aroused only to destroy and dismember the Empire.[60]

Joining the corrupt ruler and the mutineers was another aspect of India, the subject of Empire whose contact with Western values had produced not incorporation but dangerous liberation.[61] There had been some mention of the 'subversive' educated classes in the textbooks, but the tone had been generally confident that their demands could be met within the framework of imperial rule. In the popular press this 'babu' figure was incorporated into the cast of villains, often crudely drawn and denounced as Indians of 'mixed blood' and 'cunning intelligence'. Their skill in disguise and subterfuge might initially fool the British protagonist into believing them allies, but such impressions could be quickly abandoned. In 'The snake charmer's secret', the main action of the story was Jack Hinton's bettering of the wily Sudoo.

> They no longer wondered at their unwilling host's intelligent and sane appearance ... snake charming was but a blind to cover his true trade ... writer and printer of the seditious papers that permeate so mysteriously through India, keeping the natives in a ferment with the cunningly fanned flame of suppositious wrongs.[62]

Like the snake in the grass or the garden, beguiling unsuspecting mortals with falsehood, the agitator was both clever and poisonous.

Imperial boys needed 'all their wits and agility' to achieve his downfall, see him 'convicted of treason, and transported'.[63]

When the Collingwood brothers encountered a 'leering babu', they observed that his arrival 'removed all traces of the heroic' from the encounter. The reader was reminded repeatedly that the brothers particularly despised this Indian for mocking their concern with heroism and romanticism. The 'babu's' mimicry of British language and behaviour was particularly galling.

'Hello, you chaps', began the babu familiarly, 'This is what I call a bully find for us, eh, what'.[64]

Between two worlds, the 'babu' was presented as a charlatan in both, criminally misleading his fellow Indian while perverting the message of British India. Unlike the good-natured prince at English public school, these characters showed no gratitude toward their 'benefactors', using their education as a weapon to sow discontent and reap rebellion. Brave only on the printed page, in direct confrontation with the young British hero the subversive was unmasked as both coward and liar, betraying the interests of East and West. This hostility toward the educated and politically aware Indian was an attitude suggested in the textbooks and fully articulated in the adventure fiction. The antipathy this engendered in the schoolchild seems particularly important, given the reluctance of the British imperialist to acknowledge the 'babu' as a voice of nationalist aspirations. By drawing the figure with characteristics particularly unappealing to youth – intellectual pretensions, a mocking demeanour, cowardice and cringing duplicity, the fictional adventures ensured that the rising imperialist would feel little sympathy for his position, indeed would join with the hero's decision that removal from the community was a fitting punishment for the 'troublemaker'.[65]

The adventure stories of the weekly papers are closely allied to the novels of those writers who had made such a success of the formula, and subsequently lent their talents to the editors of the weekly magazines. Henty in particular, 'the Boy's Own historian', exemplified the ethos of the new imperialism, and glorified its military successes.[66] For Henty and his many imitators, India, as all imperial outposts, offered the setting for 'testing' the character of the hero, mainly through conflict. And, unlike in the school stories, there were few opportunities for friendship, although the issue of loyalty was always to the fore. Even potential allies had to pass remarkable tests of their allegiance, destroying family members and forfeiting their kingdoms. There were, of course, faithful servants who served their

British masters and mistresses, but these examples of imperial fidelity were far outnumbered by the cast of villains. In order for the boy heroes to be successful and to validate imperial values within the adventure narrative, the adversary was an essential representation of the unacceptable 'character' of India.[67]

Did the girl hero in India meet a different Indian? The *Girl's Empire* did provide some examples of 'adventures' for girls abroad and their interaction with Indian figures. In general, the roles they played displayed the same limitations which had held for figures like Mrs Grimwood in the historical pieces, a temporary assumption of the heroic and a rescue by their fathers or brothers. Honoria Brandon in 'The mate of King Cobra' showed both her amusement at the 'quaint grandiloquence' of the educated 'natives' and the ability to command her 'Oriental surroundings'. She also mocked the 'religious scruples' of the Hindu in the story. This reflects the girl's assumption of imperial attitudes as a condition of her access to the adventure narrative. In 'A ride for life', Fanny Barklay finds herself cut off from her brothers as the stirrings of Mutiny come closer. She is aided by 'faithful servants' and the loyal Indians of her brothers' detachment. However, on her ride for help she encounters the Gujars, a group of highwaymen known for their 'savage predatory instincts'. They insult her, and she narrowly escapes without harm. While these villains are in essence not much different from the Indian mutineer or Thug as drawn in boys' stories, there is the added danger of potential 'violation' of the white woman. The need to protect women from the 'depravity' of the 'oriental' grew as part of the post-Mutiny hardening of attitudes toward the Indian, and in these stories adds to the threatening aspects of the Indian imagery. In both fact and fiction, this aspect of Indian 'character' was often used to justify strict controls over inter-racial contacts in India.[68]

It is possible to see in the adventure stories those aspects of the Indian Empire which continued to demand control, despite the self-confident rhetoric of the post-Mutiny Raj. The textbooks have shown how the long shadow of the Mutiny continued to shape perceptions of India's people, and how these anxieties could be fanned by the fears of a European war. While the periodicals carried substantial proof of Indian regiments preparing to defend British interests, the fiction continued to replay the capture of India itself. On the one hand these stories were meant to build the confidence of youth in the defensive capacity of the nation, but in the process they kept alive the image of a hostile and potentially mutinous subject people. A great moral indignation and swift retaliation met the cruel mutineer and the duplicitous leader, matching the history texts' increasing harshness toward those who impeded the course of Empire.[69] The 'educated' classes, whose role had been criticised in the non-fiction, became in the fictionalised 'babu' an object for revulsion. Thugs and robbers, and wily men of mystery, carried the image of an India where English realism and a vision of law and order could not be abandoned.

It was a 'bloodstained' landscape, despite the claims for peace and prosperity made elsewhere, and the Indian subjects, while shown ultimately to respect the control of their 'betters', had reached this conclusion in a contest where the force of arms was as important as the force of character. This fiction kept alive, in its desire to show an active, prepared, superior British hero, an India where trust was at a premium and watchfulness an imperative. While history and non-fiction dealt with the loyal elites and the grateful masses, the adventure stories sustained the military arm of Empire through its action against the subversive elements. This priority, and the needs of a 'thrilling' encounter, kept the image of an ungrateful, treacherous, and cruel India in the reader's imagination, defeated each week, but ready to rise again.

The creation of 'imperial India' in the juvenile periodicals is a good example of the process by which subject peoples were co-opted to confirm both the external Empire and the status quo at home. While a primary function was to 'sell' the Empire to the young, and employ the Empire as a strong selling point, the children's press was also answering critical questions about race, class and gender. The image of the Indian helps us to understand not only current prejudices about peoples of the subcontinent, but also the preoccupations and anxieties which the adult world in Britain held about the future. All of the peoples in this study fulfilled this imperial function, and shared some common characteristics, but each arguably fitted certain parts of the role better than others, and carried some parts of the message more convincingly.

India offered the best example of the 'official' Empire, the realm in which British institutions – civil, legal and military – had been exported halfway round the globe. This made India the most directly ruled, and the most useful point of comparison between local traditions and Western 'civilisation'. While the analysis was simplified for the young reader, one can see in the criticisms of the Indian the echo of long-held views about the 'oriental', which had moved from the romantic and academic into the bureaucratic lexicon of the imperial defender.[70] One particularly common manifestation of these views was the 'oriental despot', whose methods proved the merits of Britain's democratic tradition and benevolent monarchy. By the same standards, Westernised Indian princes also provided proof that the

Empire was welcomed by the more 'enlightened' sectors of society. The Indian Army (post-Mutiny) was described in terms which stressed its loyalty and the discipline which prevailed under British commanders, thereby drawing the conclusion that the 'hopeless sepoy' could be transformed by European intervention. The masses of India became an 'exploited peasantry' under the old order and grateful recipients of reform under the new. For all the Indians encountered, it was British 'service' which was needed, and in the new imperialism it was just this responsibility which a rising generation needed to assume.[71] Elites and 'masses' aside, the middle orders in India also helped to validate the British presence. It was this group who needed to be educated into assuming the modernisation of the country, but at a pace determined by the ruling powers. At this moment in history, they were clearly not ready. The proof was found in fiction and non-fiction, in the underskilled professional classes and in the 'half educated', irresponsible journalists and local politicians. This India remained still only half emerged from the chaos and anarchy which had initially prompted British expansion, and carried the message that the civilising mission was only partially completed.

The Indian image represents quite complex cross-currents on issues of race and class, although on the surface the 'lesson' for the young reader was reasonably clear. The content of the periodicals, whether directed at middle- or working-class youth, reflected the existing class structure within Britain. The Indian figure can be shown to support these conservative views about the necessity of hierarchy and order. While highly critical of the confusion of races and languages in India, the juvenile press approved the function of a princely elite who share upper-class values and pastimes with the English, as well as giving material support to their rule. That class loyalty is an important factor can be seen in the change of heart toward the Muslims in India, for having used their militarism as a reason to step in and protect the Hindu, by the late nineteenth century the Raj supported the Muslim princes and mistrust centred on the Bengali intelligentsia. This has less to do with ideas about colour than it does with who supports a code of militarism and continued British rule. Class arrogance can also be seen in the ridicule attached to those, whether working-class English or Indian 'babus', who attempt to climb beyond their station by an imperfect mimicry of the upper orders. The poor in India enjoy the same paternalism extended to the labouring classes in England, and the suggestion that 'laziness and improvidence' have something to do with their conditions. The 'good' Indians are those who get closer to the target, sportsmen like Ranji, public-school boys like Hurree, or the rajahs of the hunting establishment. These individuals lend their support to the permeation through the papers of values and activities associated with Britain's upper classes, and their reward is to be considered very nearly English gentlemen.[72]

Material on India also carried the prevailing messages about gender. Whereas there was some admiration for the martial races of the subcontinent, there was a clear contempt felt for a weakness and softness observed in some sectors of the population. Both princes and 'babu conspirators' were described as pampered, petulant, volatile, and slight of stature. British boys appeared 'manly' in comparison. Ridicule of the educated Indian, which the 'flowery' language of Hurree illustrates, showed the anti-intellectual bias which was central to this era's image of the healthy, active schoolboy. These images suggested the 'undeveloped' or 'underdeveloped' state of India, childlike, rather womanly, and offering superiority to the young British male. This imperial boy and his needs dominated the papers, and influenced the role of women, both English and Indian. In fact, there are almost no images of Indian women, with the exception of the girl princesses or the 'urchins' of the mission schools. The poor girls blend into the 'teeming millions', while the princesses get 'royal merit' but are purely of ornamental value. Relations between British women and their Indian counterparts show support for traditional gender roles. The story of Mrs Grimwood illustrates the limits of an energised imperial role for women, and the more likely image of the English-woman abroad is in the caring professions, carrying the maternal instincts of Empire to the grateful child-subjects. This 'service' is offered as a more worthwhile occupation than fruitless political agitating at home.[73]

The image of the imperial Indian offered the reader more than the lessons of racial supremacy, and satisfied a larger number of social needs than just the maintenance of Empire. The standards brought to judge the qualities of India's character clearly reflected the Anglo-centric, chauvinistic, conservative outlook of those who published, edited and wrote the weekly editions, but the picture of India also reflected unacknowledged sentiments. The hatred shown by the mutineer and the deference of the cowardly sepoy were projections of a hostility and fear which separated the races in British India and produced these arrogant, self-serving and sterile images of the 'other'. What the images also betray is the insecurity which lay behind this assertion of 'knowing' the other, so crucial to maintaining control in India. What the British knew of India represented, in Edward Said's words, 'a form of displacement and incorporation by which one voice becomes a whole history, and for the White Westerner, as reader or writer – the only kind of oriental it is possible to know'.[74]

Notes

1 W. W. Hunter, *The India of the Queen*, London, 1908, p. 74; 'Family life', *Girl's Own Annual*, vol. XXII, 3 November, 1900, p. 69.

2 'Queen Victoria at her Hindustani lessons', *Girl's School Magazine*, vol. 1, no. 236, 1 February, 1893, p. 30; for images of Queen Victoria see J. Trollope, *Britannia's Daughters*, London, 1983, pp. 14–15.

3 M. F. Billington, 'Imperial Delhi', *Girl's Own Annual*, vol. XXXV, 1912, pp. 353–5.

4 Col. J. Fitzgerald, 'A brave man', *Boy's Own Annual*, vol. XXIX, 1906–7, pp. 574–5; 'Story of the Gurkhas', *Young England*, vol. XXXVI, 1913–14, p. 260; 'A Sikh soldier', *Boy's Own Annual*, vol. XXXVII, 1914–15, p. 284; 'The Indian Camel Corps', *Boy's Own Annual*, vol. XXXVII, 1914–15, p. 416.

5 H. Keble, 'How I cornered Ranji', *Captain*, vol. I, 1899, pp. 339–43; 'Ranji's book', *Public School Magazine*, vol. I, 1898, pp. 85–7; J. A. Mangan, *The Cultural Bond: Sport, Empire and Society*, London, 1992, prologue, p. 6; H. Perkin, 'Teaching the nations how to play', in J. A. Mangan, ed., *The Cultural Bond*, London, 1992, p. 217.

6 'An elephant hunt worth watching', *Young England*, vol. 35, 1913–14, p. 402; 'Out for the jungle pig', *Young England*, vol. 35, 1913–14, pp. 185–7; J. MacKenzie, *The Empire of Nature*, Manchester, 1988, pp. 169–95.

7 'Shall I go out to the Colonies?', *Young England*, vol. XXI, September, 1899, pp. 40–3.

8 'The question of ageing too soon', 'Fancy stitchery', and 'Martha's marriage' in *Girl's Own Annual*, vol. XXXV, 1912; E. Kinnaird, 'In India with medical missionaries', *Girl's Own Annual*, vol. XIII, 1891, p. 687; P. Barr, *The Memsahibs*, London, 1976, pp. 178–80.

9 E. Kinnaird, *ibid.*, p. 686.

10 Annuals such as *The Girl's Empire*, *Girl's School Magazine*, *Girl's Realm*, and *Girl's Own Annual* featured articles on the 'caring professions' at home and abroad throughout the period; see A. Davin, 'Imperialism and motherhood', *History Workshop Journal*, vol. 5, 1978, pp. 9–65; Trollope, *Britannia's Daughters*, pp. 86–92.

11 'The grain merchant of Jubbelore', *Young England*, vol. XXI, 1899, p. 373.

12 R. Baden-Powell, *Indian Memories*, London, 1915, p. 17.

13 Famous defences were a feature of *Young England*, in particular, appearing in issues from 1899 to 1914.

14 'Mrs. Grimwood, the heroine of Manipur', *Girl's School Magazine*, vol. I, nos 1–2, March, April, 1892, pp. 1–4, 17–20.

15 *Ibid.*, p. 2; on gender roles see V. Ware, *Beyond the Pale*, London, 1992, p. 237; Davin, 'Imperialism and motherhood', pp. 9–21.

16 'Mrs. Grimwood', pp. 2–3.

17 *Ibid.*, p. 1.

18 *Ibid.*, pp. 1–2.

19 Ware, *Beyond the Pale*, pp. 123–59; K. Reynolds, *Girls Only*, London, 1990, p. 79; J. S. Bratton, 'British imperialism and the reproduction of femininity in girls' fiction', in J. Richards, ed., *Imperialism and Juvenile Literature*, Manchester, 1989.

20 H. Groser, 'How the British held Lucknow in '57', *Young England*, vol. XXI, 1899, pp. 5–8, 85–8.

21 *Ibid.*, p. 8.

22 *Ibid.*, p. 86.

23 This was particularly true of stories which blended fact and fiction, setting young characters alongside 'great heroes'; 'How the British held Lucknow in '57'; 'The beleaguered garrison', *Pluck*, vol. 2, no. 30, 1895, pp. 1–4; 'For Queen and country', *Pluck*, vol. 2, no. 44, 1895, pp. 1–3.

24 For 'animal hierarchy' see J. M. MacKenzie, 'Hunting and the natural world in juvenile literature', in J. Richards, ed., *Imperialism and Juvenile Literature*, Manchester, 1989, pp. 169–70.

25 'Terror from the East', *Chums*, vol. XII, nos 944–60, September 1910 – February 1911, p. 157.
26 'The Indian Mutiny in fiction', *Blackwood's Magazine*, vol. CLXI, 1897, p. 219.
27 R. Rollington, *The Old Boys' Book*, Leicester, 1913, pp. 44–5.
28 I. Quigley, *The Heirs of Tom Brown*, London, 1982, p. 98.
29 F. Richards, *Autobiography*, London, 1952, p. 38.
30 F. Richards, 'Aliens at Greyfriars', *Magnet*, vol. 1, no. 6, 21 March, 1908, pp. 1–4.
31 *Ibid.*, p. 2.
32 *Ibid.*, p. 11.
33 *Ibid.*, p. 3; the *Boy's Own Annual* illustrated the comic nature of the educated 'babu' in a series of short comic features in vol. XXXVI, 1913–14.
34 On class and race in India see P. Mason, *Prospero's Magic*, Milton Keynes, 1962, pp. 2–29.
35 'England's glory', *Boy's Comic Journal*, vol. XXVII, no. 724, January, 1897, pp. 1–5; see also 'Four men in a mousetrap', *Public School Magazine*, vol. 1, 1898, p. 542.
36 'Why Revel stole the image', *Chums*, vol. XV, no. 732, 9 September, 1906, pp. 108–9.
37 'The green diamond', *Chums*, vol. XIX, no. 965, 8 March, 1911, pp. 481–3.
38 For the new 'type' of boy hero see J. Bristow, *Empire Boys*, London, 1991; see also J. A. Mangan and J. Walvin, *Manliness and Morality*, Manchester, 1987; K. Boyd, 'Knowing your place', in J. Tosh and M. Roper, eds, *Manful Assertions*, London, 1991, pp. 145–68; M. Green, *Dreams of Adventure, Deeds of Empire*, London, 1980, p. 220; L. James, 'Tom Brown's imperialist sons', *Victorian Studies*, vol. 18, 1973, pp. 89–99.
39 'An emir from the East', *Chums*, vol. XIX, no. 977, 31 May, 1911, p. 698.
40 *Boys of the Empire*, vol. 1, no. 1, 27 October, 1900, p. 19.
41 Lord Curzon, quoted in K. Rose, *Superior Person*, London, 1969, p. 345.
42 G. Orwell, 'Shooting the elephant', *Selected Essays*, London, 1957.
43 On the British abroad see P. Howarth, *Play Up and Play the Game*, London, 1973, p. 5; J. A. Mangan, 'The concept of duty and the prospect of adventure', *Journal of Educational Administration and History*, vol. 12, no. 1, 1980, pp. 31–9; J. A. Mangan, *Athleticism in the Victorian and Edwardian Public School*, London, 1981, pp. 202–3.
44 'Sugar and Milk: an incident in a frontier siege', *Boys' Own Empire*, vol. 1, no. 11, 1 January, 1901, pp. 256–7.
45 *Ibid.*, p. 256–7.
46 'Terror from the East', p. 223.
47 'An Emir from the East', p. 697.
48 See R. Visram, *Ayahs, Lascars and Princes*, London, 1986, chapter 5, for the debate over the 'suitability' of Indian representation in Parliament; see also Hunter, *The India of the Queen*, pp. 73–4; A. J. Greenberger, *The British Image of India*, Oxford, 1969, p. 45.
49 'Fallen among Thugs', *Boy's Comic Journal*, vol. XXVIII, nos 721–3, 1897, p. 411.
50 'Captured by Thugs', *Chums*, vol. 1, no. 2, 1892, pp. 182–3; 'Running down the Thugs' decoy', *Chums*, vol. VIII, no. 376, 1899, pp. 215–16.
51 'The treaty of Tibet', *Chums*, vol. XIX, no. 942, 28 September, 1910, p. 75.
52 *Ibid.*, p. 76.
53 See J. R. Seeley, *The Expansion of England*, London, 1883, p. 196.
54 'Terror from the East', p. 284.
55 *Ibid.*, p. 366; for hunting and war see MacKenzie 'Hunting and the natural world in juvenile literature', p. 189.
56 See 'Sugar and Milk', p. 257; 'Terror from the East', p. 345; 'The brother of the Rajah', *Boy's Own Annual*, vol. XXXVI, 1913, pp. 218–21.
57 Sir A. Lyall, *Asiatic Studies*, London, 1882, p. 302.
58 K. Ballhatchet, *Race, Sex and Class under the Raj*, London, 1980, pp. 116–21.

59 'Terror from the East', pp. 34, 157.
60 See A. Leigh, 'Adventures of Jack Alderson, VC', *Boy's Own Annual*, vol. XXVIII, 1905–6, p. 424–6; 'For Queen and country'; 'The beleaguered garrison', *Pluck*, vol. 2, no. 130, 1895, pp. 1–4; 'The boy garrison', *Chums*, vol. 1, no. 2, 1895, pp. 164–5.
61 F. Anstey, *Baboo Jabberjee, B.A.*, London, 1897; V. Chirol, *Indian Unrest*, London, 1910, pp. 15–16; E. Said, *Culture and Imperialism*, London, 1993, pp. 247–9; V. G. Kiernan, *The Lords of Human Kind*, London, 1969, pp. 50–1.
62 'The snake charmer's secret', *Chums*, vol. 1, no. 2, pp. 1–14.
63 *Ibid.*, p. 14.
64 'Terror from the East', p. 176.
65 See P. Mudford, *Birds of a Different Plumage*, London, 1974, p. 74.
66 For Henty as contributor to imagery see J. Richards, 'With Henty to Africa', in J. Richards, ed., *Imperialism and Juvenile Literature*, Manchester, 1989, pp. 72–106; G. Arnold, *Hold Fast for England*, London, 1980.
67 For the need for adversaries see K. Boyd, 'Knowing your place', p. 146–50, G. Avery, 'The manly boy', in *Childhood's Pattern*, London, 1975.
68 'The mate of King Cobra', *Girl's Empire*, vol. III, 1903–4, pp. 330–2; 'A ride for life', *ibid.*, pp. 231–4; for rape fears see Ware, *Beyond the Pale*, p. 39; Ballhatchet, *Race, Sex and Class under the Raj*, pp. 119–20.
69 See 'Why Revel stole the image', p. 108; 'Tuppence Coloured's revenge', *Chums*, vol. XV, no. 788, 1906, p. 1022; 'The search for the mystic opal', *Boy's Comic Journal*, vol. XXVII, no. 726, 1897, pp. 114–16.
70 E. Said, *Orientalism*, London, 1991, pp. 44, 238–41.
71 See J. Springhall, *Youth and Empire: A Study of the Propagation of Imperialism to the Young in Edwardian England*, unpublished PhD, University of Sussex, 1968; also, by same author, *Youth, Empire and Society*, London, 1977; H. E. Cooper, *British Education, Public and Private, and the British Empire, 1850–1930*, unpublished PhD thesis, University of Edinburgh, 1979; also J. Field, *Toward a Programme of Imperial Life*, Westport, 1982, pp. 26–31.
72 On class and caste in India, see, Ware, *Beyond the Pale*, p. 187; Mackenzie, *The Empire of Nature*, pp. 167–99; Kiernan, *The Lords of Human Kind*, pp. 45–54; Green, *Dreams of Adventure, Deeds of Empire*, pp. 289–96.
73 Mangan and Walvin, eds, *Manliness and Morality*, p. 10; L. Bland, *Banishing the Beast*, London, 1995, pp. 70–2; for relations between British women reformers and India see Ware, *Beyond the Pale*, pp. 119–69.
74 Said, *Orientalism*, p. 243.

CHAPTER THREE

The unknown continent:
Africa in history textbooks

A Two Man-Power Wireless Transmitter
By J. HARRISON. A.M.I.A.E.

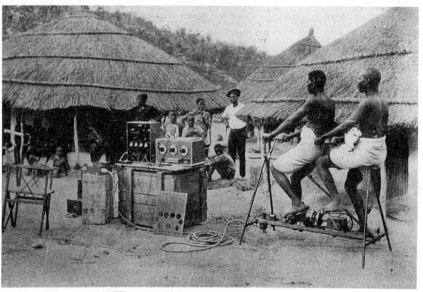

Power for the Wireless Set in Rhodesia.   *Photo: Marconi Co.*

Africa did not merit much attention in the history textbooks until the Boer War entered the public consciousness. The history of Britain's imperial interests was devoted mainly to the Indian subcontinent, and Africa as a secondary concern for textbook authors reflected the view that India was the centre of Empire. In addition, Africa, unlike India, was not the setting for great power rivalries until the 'scramble' for territory in the late nineteenth century. When one adds to this the common perception that Africa had no 'recorded past' accessible to the historian, apart from sporadic European contacts and the slave trade, it becomes clearer why in the late nineteenth century British historians gave relatively less space and attention to developments on the 'Dark Continent'.[1]

When Africa did take its place in the history texts, however, the narrative approach followed the form historians had used in the colonial history of British India. An introduction to the subject usually included general comments about the continent, but explained little more than that these 'dark regions' remained a mystery. Across the texts there was a striking uniformity in the events chosen to illustrate a history of British involvement in these areas. While little was written of the era predating the nineteenth century, textbook authors looked to a 'relevant' past which included the slave trade, 'little wars' of the nineteenth century, and the Anglo-Boer War.

In introducing Africa as an area of imperial concern most texts felt the need to offer at least a brief explanation of how Britain had developed links with this part of the world. Initially the contact had been unofficial, but once interest had been awakened at the official level, the textbooks moved to endorse a 'right of intervention' in the region. This militated against any suggestion that Britain had joined an opportunistic and undignified 'scramble' for territory.

> Missionaries, traders, men of science and adventurers have all been working since the eighteenth century to get a clear knowledge of the unknown continent.[2]

Bright (1901) stressed that Britain had 'begun the job of civilisation' in Africa before 1876, although it was 'slow to take advantage of the mercantile considerations'. Other texts supported the picture of a mainly altruistic presence throughout most of the nineteenth century, involving little 'appreciation of the possibility of British extension into South and East Africa'. The characterisation of the pre-imperial intervention gave the student a number of useful impressions, which helped to lay the foundations for the images of 'imperial Africa'. Reading the textbooks one can feel very strongly the desire to convey 'goodwill' toward the African, and to play down the motivation of self-interest or profit in the connection. The British are presented in search of 'knowledge' rather than material wealth from this uncharted territory.[3]

However, once the 'race' had begun among the European powers, authors noted 'the realisation of the importance to England of the country ... had not come one moment too soon'. A number of historians reassured the reader that England would not be left behind, that a 'full share of the spoils was hers ... due to the higher colonising, ruling and adventurous qualities of the British race'. Students were encouraged to view the exercise of such powers as natural and inevitable.[4]

> No one could have expected that the Dark Continent of Africa would not be explored, largely by British men, but also portioned out among Europeans, among whom the British would be not the least successful.[5]

Unlike the conflict with the French in eighteenth-century India, however, little space was given to European contests over possession of Africa. A diplomatic 'carve up' did not lend itself to the heroic school of history, and consequently was not pursued in any detail. Difficulties or encroachments might be referred to, but they merited only the vaguest of references.

> Needless to say, the scramble led to considerable diplomatic complications ... these were gradually overcome.[6]

The textbooks strongly supported the idea of Britain taking its place among the imperial powers in Africa. To do otherwise would have been a sign of weakness. Although textbooks written later in the period did explicitly mention the gold and riches to be gained in the increasingly lucrative ventures in Southern Africa, earlier works seldom went beyond mentioning the 'value' of the spoils. In general, there seemed less of a need to explain why Britain moved into Africa. Whereas in India the instability of local government had been brought forward to rationalise intervention, the historian's idea of tribalism was a far remove from the image of the nation state, and a violation of sovereignty less of an issue. The more 'primitive' the society the historian dealt with, the less of a case was made for imperial advancement.[7]

Probably the most important element of the African image emerged from the imperial view of the slave trade and its abolition. Like the Mutiny in India, this was the 'knowledge' of Africa which had most strongly permeated the public consciousness and conditioned society's attitudes. The images from an 'era of humanitarianism' persisted as assumptions into the imperial age.[8] Certainly the history textbooks suggest that slavery as institution and trade was the significant determinant in shaping attitudes toward Africa. Their approach to the topic showed a consensus around certain points. Authors universally condemned the institution of slavery and the 'private' commercial interest which had encouraged its expansion. The consideration of slavery's role in building Britain's national wealth was not critically addressed, while national interest was firmly attached to the campaign for abolition.[9]

History for schools, not surprisingly, consistently took the 'higher ground'. Readers were reminded of the sufferings of those transported from homelands against their will.

> The poor wretches suffered horrible torments, being packed almost as closely as the sufferers in the Black Hole of Calcutta, in nearly as stifling an atmosphere, so that large numbers died on the way.[10]

The comparison with the Black Hole came from the pen of S. R. Gardiner, one of the most eminent historians of his day. Students most likely believed that he knew, but we are tempted to ask how he knew that the English suffered more in Calcutta than the Africans in the middle passage. In a section which engages in criticism of a dehumanising trade, Gardiner suggests that the loss of hundreds of thousands of black lives can somehow be understood or balanced by an 'atrocity' against the English in a time of war. It may be just the use of a familiar reference point to summon an appropriate degree of indignation, but in such a balancing of horrors and numbers there is a familiar undercurrent of the 'relative value' of lives lost.

Gardiner's reference to Indian 'atrocities' might also work to place the traders' actions beyond the limits of behaviour acceptable in British society. Their disregard for humanity became comparable to the 'cruel disregard' of Nana Sahib. Most historians sought to distance the slave trade from the legitimate commercial transactions of Empire.

> The slave trade was not a commerce, but a crime ... pillage and murder.[11]

Finally, the responsibility for the pernicious trade was placed partially upon the African peoples themselves, in the textbooks' assertion that the compliance of the West African tribes was critical to the supply of the human cargo. While the reader might just about accept the notion of selling one's enemies in times of war, schoolchildren must have been rather shocked to learn that African rulers might also sell their loyal subjects. This straightforward summation for junior pupils held the note of a cautionary tale:

> The African chiefs, in time of war, sold their captives. In times of peace they sold their subjects.[12]

One can see the concern of the history textbooks to express moral revulsion toward the trade while ensuring that the reader placed the individuals responsible, European and African, outside the province of 'civilised' society. What was incorporated into the history of Britain was 'the great act of justice ... Britain's abolition of the trade and her efforts to end its existence in other parts of the world'. As V. G. Kiernan has observed, these efforts of Britain in working to free the enslaved and transported African invested the European with a 'treasury of merit', which helped to justify extending control over the African at home.[13] In 1911 Fletcher and Kipling explained for the senior pupil:

> The natives everywhere welcome the mercy and justice of our rule, and they are no longer liable, as they were before we came, to be carried off as slaves by Arab slave dealers.[14]

In the history textbooks of the late nineteenth and early twentieth century, Britain was absolved of responsibility for the slave trade, became the major force in its abolition, was identified as the protector of the African, and extended its presence in Africa to effect 'mercy and justice'. The image of the African people in the narrative works toward acceptance of this view of British relations with the 'Dark Continent'. As the passive 'victims' they were powerless to prevent the loss of their own freedom; as 'aggressors' they illustrated the disregard for human life endemic in primitive society, consigning their own peoples to a life in bondage. Underlying these images was the assumption that it was in part the African's own nature which allowed slavery to develop and flourish. To a contempt for those who traded in human life was added the covert assumption that only a people who did not understand the concept of 'freedom' would allow it to be taken away without a struggle. Here was the 'ignoble' as opposed to the 'noble' savage. This tendency to blame the victim for lacking the courage to resist placed the African at the centre of the process of enslavement, and is resonant of hidden texts in history's treatment of oppression and genocide. Placing a major part of the responsibility for enslavement on the Africans who supplied the slaves, while telling little of the demand, cast further doubt on the 'character' of Africa and supported the unassailable 'high ground' claimed by British historians in the slavery question.[15]

The image of Africans 'enslaved' by their own nature persisted in the description of the freed slaves. Reference to the conditions of newly emancipated Africans in the West Indies reflected the contradictory impulses of morality and material progress, particularly in areas where slavery had been the major source of enforced labour.

> Now they refused to work more than they chose and squatted on small patches of garden ground where the bounty of sun and soil gave them enough for their simple wants, preferring to live an idle, happy, helpless animal existence to working hard for comforts and rewards they were quite contented to do without ... negroes settle down in happy sloth.[16]

Fletcher and Kipling's popular textbook contained a rather extreme expression of the same sentiments.

> The population is lazy, vicious and incapable of any serious improvement or of work except under compulsion. In such a climate a few bananas will sustain the life of a negro quite sufficiently; why should he work to get more than this? He is quite happy and quite useless, and spends any extra wages he may earn upon finery.[17]

The authors of the history textbooks had improved little upon the reflections of Thomas Carlyle in the 1840s, whose description of the 'idle black gentleman, rum bottle in hand, pumpkin at discretion' provided a prototype for the image of 'idle' and 'useless' black subjects in post-emancipation Empire.[18]

Young readers were being exposed here to some of the prevailing myths which had grown from racial theories of the eighteenth and nineteenth centuries. The ideas of men like Dr Robert Knox had become common currency by the end of the nineteenth century. In *The Races of Man* he articulated and helped to popularise the pseudo-scientific racism which claimed that the dark races were in a relatively stagnant state, quite incapable of attaining civilisation as the European knew it. Incorporated into his thesis was the assertion that climate played a large part in producing an endemic indolence, just as the Western European climate encouraged a vigorous, if somewhat dour race. 'Simple wants' and 'happy sloth' were the signs of the 'degenerate' state and contained the African at the bottom of the evolutionary scale. Signs of cultural divergence, such as structures of social organisation, constructs of time and sexual practice, articulated by the racial theorists, were viewed by Victorian technocrats as inferior to the progressive, family-orientated, work-directed values of England. Historians accepted that these differences, racially discrete and determined, helped to explain phenomena in the post-emancipation period and passed their conclusions, without question, to a new generation.[19]

When integrating the images of the slave with the post-emancipation African, historians were suggesting that the lessons of slavery produced a sense of moral indignation mixed with contempt for peoples unable either to protect themselves or to effect necessary change in their conditions. This was an image which helped to promote the idea of subsequent 'benevolent intervention'. Given Britain's role in the abolition of the slave trade, the nation's conscience was clear of any but the best motives, indeed granted evangelical fervour in the struggle for freedom. Having exercised such moral leadership, was it not then a duty to continue to protect and guide weaker mortals? For most of the nineteenth century this task was performed by the Christian missions, but once rivalry over Africa surfaced among European governments, the same sentiments could and would be marshalled in the history textbooks to justify the extension of more formal British controls.

While slavery was a dominant theme in the presentation of West Africa, there were also military conflicts which entered the textbooks and provided examples of another kind of relationship. The 'glorious little wars' of Queen Victoria's reign were commonly included as examples of the extension of British power, and it was in the context of building admiration for successive policing operations in 'trouble spots' of Empire that the 'fighting tribes' emerged. These operations were described as 'irritating' episodes, as this description of the action against the Asante in 1864 illustrates:

One of those little wars consequent on the widespread character of the Empire, from which Great Britain is seldom free....[20]

'Little wars' was clearly a loaded description of what represented a major turning point in the history of African peoples, yet in the texts these episodes could appear as a mere listing of recurrent clashes, just 'another little war with a warlike tribe', the natural by-product of expanding British interests overseas. There was a sense of both pride and inevitability as the texts recorded each increase in imperial aggrandisement. Warner and Marten explained tensions in West Africa as emerging from the 'grab for Africa', which involved 'various little wars in Uganda, Nigeria, and with the Ashantees'. Apart from rather vague allusions to a defence of trade and coastal forts, there was little explanation of what specific issues created the resort to arms. Arguably, students, secured in the view that 'little wars' of conquest were inevitable, absorbed the casual attitude toward their causes and did not need to be persuaded of the rights or wrongs in each case.[21]

The nineteenth century was a period of recurrent hostilities between the British and the Asante people. As a counterpoint to the slave image of the West African the textbooks presented the view of the Asante as a 'powerful and warlike race'. As with the Sikhs in British India, subject peoples who displayed a willingness and ability to contest the British were accorded a degree of respect. Histories which cited the 'gallantry' and 'skill' of British troops in combat might also note the bravery of the Asante warrior. Junior readers had their own explanation of the warrior kingdom:

> The English had a good deal of fighting with the black king of Ashanti before he would allow them to enter his country.[22]

While recognised as formidable adversaries, the Asante were also characterised as 'barbarous' and 'untrustworthy', terms which helped to justify subjection. Bright was, typically, one of the few authors who reflected upon a 'somewhat nasty assertion of British rights against a semi-barbarous people'. The majority of texts agreed with the need for punitive action to restore peace to the region. 'Tribal claims' were rejected as just cause for disturbing trade relations and, as was so often the case in the history texts, the pupil was left with the impression that warlike peoples by their nature, rather than their reason, engaged in combat. A desire to heighten the 'heroics' of the British defenders led to descriptions of sudden, unpredictable peril when a 'host of barbarians swooped down on the coast and threatened British settlements'.[23]

When textbooks did place responsibility for the outbreak of war beyond a 'warlike' temperament, African chiefs were usually found to be culpable. One such 'irresponsible' figure was the Asante Prempeh, who led his people against the British in 1896. Bright stated clearly who was at fault for the deteriorating situation:

> He had fallen out with the British authorities ... by his slave trading, human sacrifices and refusal to pay indemnities and vexatious interference with trade.... The British called for remonstrance which he disregarded and defied.[24]

For the younger pupil, the behaviour of Prempeh was put in simple moralistic terms. In 1913 Lady Callcott suggested that the King 'was treating his people so cruelly that the Queen felt she must interfere'. The British use of force needed to show cause and provocation, unlike the adversary's. In this case Prempeh became the archetypal 'bad ruler', whose people needed saving from his inhuman practices. Once the student had read that he was engaged in slaving and human sacrifice, British actions were clearly vindicated.[25]

Textbooks offered the student two contrasting, but ultimately complementary, images of the African of the West Coast. One was the victim of slavery, prey to the greed of a few Europeans and of her or his own people, and rescued by the enlightened actions of Britain. The Asante represented the savage warrior, fierce and brave, but beyond the pale of civilised behaviour and a potential menace to peaceful British traders. The 'character' of both the slave and the 'barbarian' shared the primitive incapacity for self-respect or self-control and this justified an assumption of power on the grounds of both benevolence and self-defence. Rulers like Prempeh were criticised for preferring the benefits of the 'slave trade' to the regenerative influences of legitimate imperial transactions. Both 'little wars' to protect coastal trading interests and the commitment to a 'civilising mission' were justified in the texts by the image of the West African.[26]

What was omitted from the narrative of Africa's past is also part of the process of imperial myth-making. Then, as through most of the twentieth century, the achievements of ancient civilisations in Africa and the Americas had not been incorporated into textbook history. The artefacts produced by these sophisticated cultures did occasionally enter the texts, but in a manner which reveals the bias and arrogance clustered around any notions of 'native culture'. The 'mysterious golden stool' of the Asante was occasionally inserted in the narrative in relation to the 1896 war, but with no explanation of its significance as an 'emblem of rule', either culturally or in the course of this conflict. While the great national museums of Britain were building their ethnographic collections, including African items like the Benin bronzes, historians focused on evidence of 'degeneracy' in the West African peoples. This reflected the way in which the scientists and the museums of the era resolved the apparent discrepancy between high standards of cultural production and 'savagery', that is, by stressing the degenerate status of these societies in the imperial era.[27]

By far the greatest interest for the historian was the white settlement colonies in Southern Africa, and it would be there that the British Empire faced its greatest challenge between 1890 and 1914. One might expect, therefore, a reasonable number of references to the 'natives' of the region. Certainly, in introducing the history of British India there had been some attempt to describe the 'races' of the subcontinent. With few exceptions, however, in Africa the 'native' was just a 'native'. In a particularly uninformative introduction to the peoples of South Africa, S. R. Gardiner advised the reader of 'the enormous preponderance of a native population ... five persons out of six being natives'. York-Powell and Tout felt it necessary to assert that South Africa was a 'genuine colony', despite the fact that 'native races will remain the great majority of the population'.[28]

Historians not only exhibited a reluctance to acknowledge more than the numerical evidence of the African, but also to find any positive aspects of their interaction with the European. Oman and Oman attributed the slow growth of the Cape Colony to the existence of the 'troublesome Kaffir', a derogatory term taken from the Arabic for infidel, which was commonplace in the texts to describe any black South African. Others equated the 'native' and the Boer as the two long-standing obstacles to peaceful and orderly settlement. The suggestion was that if only there were not so many Africans settled on good land and contesting boundaries life would have been much easier for the British in the area. The image of a great mass of people, rather like the herds of wild beasts, peripheral yet potentially destructive, dominated the general views of the 'native' presence in the south. By reducing the identity of the African inhabitants to wandering figures in the landscape, the familiar justification of the conqueror, that of improving a land not used productively by its inhabitants, supported the idea of white settlement.[29]

At times the actions of certain groups did compel the authors to translate 'native problems' in Southern Africa into specific encounters. The Zulu nation, like the Asante, was singled out for attention in the textbooks. Their image as a proud fighting people has been long-lived.[30] In this case, the context for the introduction of the Zulu warrior was usually the Zulu War of 1879. It was acknowledged that they had evolved a 'powerful' and 'remarkable' military nation, capable of forming a standing army, and led by a succession of strong despotic rulers. Both junior and senior texts mentioned King Cetchwayo, who emerges as one of the few African leaders meriting admiration. The *Raleigh History Reader* illustrates a common assessment of the man:

> a man of huge stature and admirable physique, who was one of the most remarkable of the native chiefs in regard to his cunning, valour, and powers of organisation.[31]

Like the Asante, the Zulus could be admired only within limits, for whatever their skill and discipline, they could not be allowed to produce an unacceptable level of insecurity for local Britons. Historians presented British interests in Natal as directly threatened, and no responsible official could accept 'the constant menace to neighbouring tribes'.[32] Simplistic explanations of a resort to arms centred culpability on Zulu leadership:

> The refusal of the Zulu king to disband his army led to the invasion and conquest of Zululand. Cetewayo's refusal to accept a British resident and reform his barbarous military system led to war.[33]

In the absence of an exploration of British intentions in the region or of the impact of confederation plans on the Zulu nation, the student was left with the impression that another warlike nation with intransigent, unreasonable leaders provoked Britain into war. Indeed, the British invasion was viewed as essential to the maintenance of peace.[34]

Textbook descriptions of the scenes of battle reinforced the image of an enemy 'skilled in all the arts of savage warfare'. At Isandlwana, a critical point, the Zulu showed a 'wild bravery', and their victory was accompanied by 'fearful scenes of slaughter' of the British forces. The ferocity of the onslaught brought great loss of life, an imperial force 'cut to pieces'. The battle lost prompted the authors to conclude that the British had under-rated their adversaries, a 'lamentable' error, rectified by the dispatch of thousands of troops to break the Zulu power. The subsequent division of the Zulu nation into districts ruled by friendly chiefs was briefly mentioned as the solution to the 'Zulu problem', but no consideration was given to the impact of these changes upon the 'troublemakers'. Once subdued, the Zulu disappeared from the textbooks and the attention of British history.[35]

The Zulu nation, like the Asante of West Africa, appeared in the context of war, were defeated, and became irrelevant in the subsequent history of Africa as Empire. The Zulu was granted a greater measure of respect than the West Africans, however, for apart from showing qualities of martial skill and discipline, the Southern African nation was not associated with the slave trade. Like the Sikh, who was set apart from other Indian subjects, the Zulu image of a 'singularly fine and brave race' was to endure. Although they could not be trusted to make the transition to allies or comrades at arms, the Zulu fitted well the archetype of the noble primitive, whose submission could evoke both a pride in imperial strength and a pity for the inevitable casualty of progress. The elevation of the Zulu in the eyes of the historian and the society at large shows clearly that conflict had become the central interest of textbook history, and that the Zulu had become the adversary whose defeat confirmed an imperial supremacy. The defeat of the Zulu, in patriotic terms, contained the best 'tragic heroic' components of the imperial story, similar to the testing times of the Indian Mutiny and the Sikh Wars. As a proud, virile and disciplined people, unlike the pitiable slave, the Zulu commanded an admiration from textbook historians singular in the history of British Africa.[36]

Innes in 1907 advised the student that in the Boer War 'they had before them not one of the familiar "little wars" but a "big one"'. Bosworth and Meiklejohn echoed the 'anxiety' which events at the Cape had produced, in an area where 'the wave of Anglo-Saxon advance' exemplified the dynamic of Empire. The racial dimension of the historical narrative here takes on an interesting twist. Reflecting the rhetoric of the times, the texts stressed that in this instance the 'race problem' was not with the African, but with the Boers. Bright helped by explaining that the 'uncivilised' condition of the Boer had emerged from his 'contact with only inferior races'. In other words, their Dutch origins were no longer enough to connect them to the progressive Anglo-Saxon virtues, now exclusively defended in the area by the British forces. In this case it was no longer expedient to identify racial difference by physical characteristics alone, as the Boers had forfeited their right to inclusion in the Anglo-Saxon ranks. Ascribing to the 'enemy' a racial difference made the resort to arms against fellow Europeans in Africa a more natural and acceptable development, in selling the war to both the public and the schoolchild.[37]

Meanwhile the Africans were relegated to the role of spectators, outside the arena in which the future of the region would be decided. Only occasionally, and then indirectly, was the African brought 'on stage', to illustrate some aspect of the quarrels between Boer and British. Criticism of the Dutch might focus on their inability to deal constructively with the 'native problem'. Textbooks attributed to the Boers the most negative of attitudes toward the locals, including the damning indictment of 'slaveholders'.

> The natives were regarded by the Boers as belonging to an inferior race, destined to be for all time hewers of wood ... for the white races.[38]

In contrast, the British settlers were pictured as more enlightened and protective of 'native interests', 'looking upon the natives as peaceful tribes bullied by the Boers'. Even Fletcher and Kipling, hardly racial progressives, felt the Dutch 'treated the Kaffirs very badly and objected when we tried to protect them'. The African enters the narrative in order to assist in portraying the Boer as reactionary and inhumane, the British as better intentioned. Students might be left with the impression that a primary reason for the British argument with the Boers was their treatment of local tribes, and that British control of the region would stop the exploitation. Here, again, 'patriotic' authors delivered as 'history' much of the propaganda which was circulated to sell the war to the public, in particular the idea that the British were fighting to protect the African from harsh treatment.[39]

There was no suggestion that the African was more directly involved. This reflected the official policy toward the non-mobilisation of black troops. After protracted public and private debate, Milner and Chamberlain at the Colonial Office had agreed by 1899 to a 'white man's war', and Balfour in the Commons argued for no 'reasonable analogy' between India and Africa in the raising of local troops. While historians now admit to a considerable support and combatant role played by African people in the war, history texts shortly after the event dealt neither with the debate nor with the evidence of participation. By ignoring Africans in events central to the future of their homelands, they became not only passive observers of the European power struggle, but also an irrelevant factor in the outcome.[40]

The 'invisibility' of the South African was strongly reinforced in the textbook treatment of the Boer War. In summarising the 'lessons' learned from the war, the consequences involved only the white participants. Loyal support was noted from other British colonies, but no mention of African activity in the British camp. The implication was not that the African was either disloyal or hostile, but rather unequal to the burdens of imperial defence. The triumph of 'imperial sentiment' rested with the British. The martial tribes could not be trusted and the peaceful tribes could not be disciplined into a fighting force. Victory over the Boers was viewed as a positive development for the African, replacing the 'bullying' Dutch regime with the benevolent British presence.[41]

When compared with India, Africa clearly did not have as much to offer the historian seeking proof of the 'course of Empire', but examining these texts does offer important pointers toward those aspects of British history which informed the image of the African peoples. While there was contempt expressed in the texts for all civilisations which blocked the course of British power, in a sense the African escaped this by being denied a usable past. While the student knew that India had a history, even if it was manipulated into a justification for Empire, the impression of Africa was that there had been no historical development at all, and that this was typical of societies without the identity of nation states. To some degree the Zulu was seen as having 'evolved' into a superb fighting force, but this was a refining of 'brute characteristics' under warrior despots rather than a model of historical change. In terms of significant political or social evolution, as seen in Western states, there was none. This in itself diminished the African in European eyes, and helped to reinforce the image of a continent in primitive stasis, unconnected to the dynamic of nineteenth-century progress. In general, the African leaders were viewed as beyond the boundaries of diplomatic or military alliance, although 'noble warriors' could capture the imagination of the British public.[42]

The central images of the history texts, and those which were seen as most important to the schoolchild, were those of the slave and the 'noble savage'. Both answered the primary considerations of illustrating the benevolence and wisdom of British policy. In order to highlight the humanity of the British, the African peoples appeared not in their own story of slavery and freedom, but as the object of abolitionist 'fervour' and official protection. However, while the British valued their freedoms, and each schoolchild learned of the history of these hard-earned rights in their own country, the African was portrayed equating its arrival with rum and bananas. Historians who removed from the African core values of British society, independence and enterprise, and put no alternative guiding principles in their place, left the impression of primitive, unorganised beings, whose hope lay only in placing themselves under the protection of friendly powers.

'Little wars' in Africa demonstrated another facet of the need for control, and exhibited the 'savage' tendency for volatile and unpredictable behaviour. In these cases there was some ennoblement of the warrior, particularly fine physical specimens like the Zulu. But the texts were just as likely to refer to the Asante as 'barbarians', placing their actions outside any modern notions of warfare. Such virtues as these peoples possessed were seen as relics of a primitive past, long since abandoned by northern races, and unequal to the force of British arms.

There was no suggestion that their opposition to the British rested upon any appreciation of rational self-interest, or a defence of homelands. For the British, 'tribal peoples' had no property rights in the commonly held sense of individual titles or national boundaries, and this view obviated any need for the historian to construct arguments for Europeans acquiring land or mineral wealth. Once troublesome 'tribes' had been subdued, they joined the vast majority of Africans on the periphery of the imperial drama, which for the historian was being played out most successfully in Southern Africa. They then could concentrate on the exploits of men like Cecil Rhodes, whose 'energy and foresight' had placed its mark on the valuable British possessions. The 'boldness' of his actions placed in even greater contrast the image of a continent seeking external organisation and leadership, and whose resistance was shown as minimal. There was a sense in which the textbooks reassured the student that without an abuse of power, and with proper concern for 'native' protection, there was ample room for the British in Africa, without the complications posed by the more 'advanced' societies of India or China.[43]

Notes

1 H. A. Cairns, *Prelude to Imperialism*, London, 1965, chapter IX; R. Robinson and J. Gallagher, *Africa and the Victorians*, London, 1981 edn, pp. 24–5; R. Oliver and A. Atmore, *Africa Since 1800*, Cambridge, 1981, p. 111; C. Oman and M. Oman, *A Junior History of England*, London, 1904; G. Bosworth, *A History of the British Empire*, London, 1905; A. Hassall, *A Classbook of English History*, London, 1901; C. S. Fearenside, *A School History of England*, London, 1904.

2 R. York-Powell and T. Tout, *History of England*, London, 1900, p. 1027.

3 J. F. Bright, *A History of England for Public Schools*, London, 1887–1901, p. 151; Hassall, *A Classbook of English History*, p. 547.

4 C. Oman, *History of England*, London, 1895, p. 738; A. Hassall, *The Making of the British Empire*, London, 1896, 1910, p. 161; see also York-Powell and Tout, *History of England*, p. 1028; M. W. Keatinge and N. L. Frazer, *A History of England for Schools*, London, 1911, p. 519; Bright, *A History of England for Public Schools*, p. 151; J. Meiklejohn and M. J. C. Meiklejohn, *A School History of England*, London, 1901, p. 459; G. Warner and C. H. K. Marten, *Groundwork of British History*, London, 1912, p. 680.

5 Fearenside, *A School History of England*, p. 312.

6 Warner and Marten, *Groundwork of British History*, p. 680; see also Hassall, *A Classbook of English History*, p. 580; T. Livesey, *Granville History Readers*, London, 1902, p. 198.

7 Hassall, *The Making of the British Empire*, p. 161; Bright, *A History of England for Public Schools*, p. 255; Keatinge and Frazer, *A History of England for Schools*, p. 530; Oman, *History of England*, p. 737; R. Rait, *A School History of England*, Oxford, 1911, p. 187; Warner and Marten, *Groundwork of British History*, p. 681.

8 P. Curtin, *The Image of Africa*, London, 1965, p. vi; V. G. Kiernan, *The Lords of Human Kind*, London, 1969, p. 213; Cairns, *Prelude to Imperialism*, p. 182; A. J. Barker, *The African Link: British Attitudes to the Negro in the Era of the Slave Trade, 1550–1807*, London, 1978.

9 S. R. Gardiner, *A Student's History of England*, London, 1892, p. 823; see also Bright, *A History of England for Public Schools*, p. 798, Warner and Marten, *Groundwork of British History*, p. 765.

10 Gardiner, *A Student's History of England*, p. 823; see also Warner and Marten, *Groundwork of British History*, p. 705; Bright, *A History of England for Public Schools*, p. 1142.

11 *Avon Historical Readers*, London, 1895, p. 139.

12 Bright, *A History of England for Public Schools*, p. 1445; see also Oman, *History of England*, p. 609; Rait, *A School History of England*, p. 123.

13 'Treasury of merit', Kiernan, *The Lords of Human Kind*, p. 213.

14 C. R. L. Fletcher and R. Kipling, *A School History of England*, Oxford, 1911, p. 239.
15 Gardiner, *A Student's History of England*, p. 823; *Avon Historical Readers*, p. 139; Warner and Marten, *Groundwork of British History*, p. 705; A. Buckley, *History of England for Beginners*, London, 1904, p. 351; G. Bosworth, *Cambridge History Readers*, Cambridge, 1911, p. 212; T. Carlyle, 'Discourse upon the nigger question', in *Critical and Miscellaneous Essays*, London, 1905 edn, pp. 370–83; R. Knox, *The Races of Man*, London, 1862, p. 222; both Carlyle and Knox considered it the 'natural' tendency of the African to enslavement.
16 York-Powell and Tout, *History of England*, p. 1030.
17 Fletcher and Kipling, *A School History of England*, p. 240.
18 Carlyle, 'Discourse upon the nigger question', p. 356; see also J. Haller, *Outcasts from Evolution*, New York, 1975, p. 41; Sir H. Johnston, *The Backwards Peoples and Our Relations with Them*, London, 1920, p. 42.
19 Knox, *The Races of Man*, pp. 220–30; Johnston, *The Backwards Peoples and Our Relations with Them*, pp. 56–7; Cairns, *Prelude to Imperialism*, pp. 8–18; R. Lewis and Y. Foy, *The British in Africa*, London, 1971, pp. 57–81; B. Kidd, *The Control of the Tropics*, London, 1898, chapter 3.
20 *Graphic History of the British Empire*, London, 1890, p. 744; see also T. F. Tout, *A Short Analysis of English History*, London, 1891, as an example of a text on 'little wars'.
21 Warner and Marten, *Groundwork of British History*, p. 682; see also Bright, *A History of England for Public Schools*, p. 498; J. C. Curtis, *Outlines of English History*, London, 1901, p. 70; T. Livesey and B. Besonthorp, *History of England*, London, 1908, p. 169.
22 Lady Callcott, *Little Arthur's History of England*, London, 1913, p. 284.
23 Bright, *A History of England for Public Schools*, p. 372; *Graphic History of the British Empire*, p. 774; see also R. S. Pringle, *Local Examination History*, London, 1907, p. 144; Carter, *History of England*, pp. 179, 229; Livesey, *Granville History Readers*, p. 198; A. Buckley, *A History of England for Beginners*, London, 1904, p. 354.
24 Bright, *A History of England for Public Schools*, p. 187.
25 Callcott, *Little Arthur's History of England*, p. 284; see also Buckley, *A History of England for Beginners*, p. 369.
26 F. Glendenning, 'School history textbooks and racial attitudes, 1804–1911', *Journal of Educational Administration and History*, vol. 5, 1973, pp. 37–8.
27 A. Coombes, *Reinventing Africa*, New Haven, 1994, pp. 17–39, 85–105.
28 Gardiner, *A Student's History of England*, p. 969; Bright, *A History of England for Public Schools*, p. 545; see also Oman, *History of England*, p. 737; A. Innes, *History of England*, Cambridge, 1907, p. 514; York-Powell and Tout, *History of England*, p. 1039.
29 Oman and Oman, *A Junior History of England*, pp. 234, 247; J. Meiklejohn and M. J. C. Meiklejohn, *A School History of England*, p. 459; Keatinge and Frazer, *A History of England for Schools*, p. 519; York-Powell and Tout, *History of England*, p. 1040; Hassall, *A Classbook of English History*, p. 571.
30 'The fighting power of the negro', *The Spectator*, 12 November, 1898, p. 680; Kiernan, *The Lords of Human Kind*, pp. 231–3; R. Postgate and A. Vallance, *Those Foreigners*, London, 1937, p. 174; Sir C. Dilke, *Problems of Greater Britain*, London, 1890, p. 527.
31 *Raleigh History Reader*, vol. 8, London, 1898, p. 202; see also Innes, *History of England*, p. 501; York-Powell and Tout, *History of England*, p. 1040; Bright, *A History of England for Public Schools*, p. 545; *Avon Historical Reader*, p. 215.
32 H. Ince and J. Gilbert, *Outlines of English History*, London, 1906, p. 128; Carter, *History of England*, p. 233; Hassall, *A Classbook of English History*, p. 572.
33 R. Walker and G. Carter, *Local Examination History of England*, p. 171; see also Keatinge and Frazer, *A History of England for Schools*, p. 524.
34 Innes, *History of England*, p. 501; there was no suggestion that the invasion of Zululand was related to Lord Carnarvon's confederation plans, nor of British

economic interests in the area; see J. Guy, *The Destruction of the Zulu Kingdom*, London, 1979, pp. 41–50.

35 On Isandlwana, see T. Livesey and B. Besonthorp, *Macmillan's History Readers*, London, 1891–95, p. 200; Oman and Oman, *A Junior History of England*, p. 248; Hassall, *A Classbook of English History*, p. 572; Innes, *History of England*, p. 501; Livesey, *Granville History Readers*, p. 199; Bright, *A History of England for Public Schools*, p. 549; on its aftermath, see York-Powell and Tout, *History of England*, p. 1040; Bosworth, *A History of the British Empire*, p. 295; Curtis, *Outlines of English History*, p. 70; Keatinge and Frazer, *A History of England for Schools*, p. 525.

36 For the Zulu image, see Kiernan, *The Lords of Human Kind*, pp. 231–2; C. Bolt, *Victorian Attitudes to Race*, London, 1971, p. 144; Cairns, *Prelude to Imperialism*, p. 108; see also Carter, *History of England*, p. 233; Bright, *A History of England for Public Schools*, p. 545.

37 Innes, *History of England*, p. 512; Bosworth, *A History of the British Empire*, p. 293; Meiklejohn and Meiklejohn, *A School History of England*, p. 444; Bright, *A History of England for Public Schools*, p. 234; Buckley, *A History of England for Beginners*, p. 346; York-Powell and Tout, *History of England*, p. 1040; Warner and Marten, *Groundwork of British History*, p. 705; Fletcher and Kipling, *A School History of England*, p. 238.

38 Warner and Marten, *Groundwork of British History*, p. 705.

39 Fletcher and Kipling, *A School History of England*, p. 239; see also Hassall, *A Classbook of English History*, p. 176; Meiklejohn and Meiklejohn, *A School History of England*, p. 460; Curtis, *Outlines of English History*, p. 72; E. Spalding, *Piers Plowman Histories*, London, 1913, p. 267; Rait, *A School History of England*, p. 187; Keatinge and Frazer, *A History of England for Schools*, p. 530.

40 P. Warwick, *Black People and the South African War 1899–1902*, Cambridge, 1983, pp. 15–18.

41 Meiklejohn and Meiklejohn, *A School History of England*, p. 461; Hassall, *A Classbook of English History*, p. 585; Livesey, *Granville History Readers*, p. 200; York-Powell and Tout, *History of England*, p. 1049; Innes, *History of England*, p. 515; Keatinge and Frazer, *A History of England for Schools*, p. 530; Warner and Marten, *Groundwork of British History*, p. 715; Oman and Oman, *A Junior History of England*, p. 238.

42 V. Chancellor, *History for their Masters*, Bath, 1970, p. 124; C. L. Hannam, 'Prejudice and the teaching of history', in M. Ballard, ed., *New Movements in the Study and Teaching of History*, London, 1971, p. 31; Glendenning, 'School history textbooks and racial attitudes, 1804–1911', p. 38; Bright, *A History of England for Public Schools*, p. 277; Bosworth, *A History of the British Empire*, p. 264; Warner and Marten, *Groundwork of British History*, p. 706; Fletcher and Kipling, *A School History of England*, p. 239; Livesey and Besonthorp, *Macmillan's History Readers*, p. 208; Keatinge and Frazer, *A History of England for Schools*, p. 530.

43 For Cecil Rhodes see Bright, *A History of England for Public Schools*, pp. 238, 242; Hassall, *A Classbook of English History*, p. 580; Meiklejohn and Meiklejohn, *A School History of England*, p. 459; Keatinge and Frazer, *A History of England for Schools*, p. 530.

CHAPTER FOUR

The goodfellows: Africa in the children's periodicals

With the exception of the Zulu, it is doubtful if history textbooks worked to increase children's positive interest in the peoples of Africa. The information given was not only highly selective but carried the impression that this was a less significant part of the imperial world, certainly in comparison with British India. While Africa's relevance to British history lessons may have been in question, there was little doubt that the popular press of the day found the image of Africa a strong selling point. In children's periodicals and magazines a black figure was frequently found in non-fiction, fiction, comic insets and advertising. The versatility and accessibility of the image was not matched by other subjects of Empire.

Where the African did and did not appear is instructive in understanding the imagery and its relation to other 'alien' characterisations. There was a notable lack of interest in the 'official' relationship between the British and the African. Queen Victoria was not pictured at work learning African languages, nor were tribal chiefs brought forward to demonstrate publicly their loyalty to the crown. In this sense the popular press reflects the reality of indirect rule and white settlement in this part of the world. No complex administrative structure to parallel India's was ever envisaged. In Africa official duties could easily give way to recreation. The safari was an essential component of any royal visit, and the children's papers provided ample space for evidence of imperial dominance over the natural world. These excursions were in interesting contrast to the 'hunt' in India, particularly in terms of the social dynamics between visitor and local peoples. The crown recognised no elite in Africa which corresponded to the Indian princes, so the hunt there was not a mediating ground for the upper orders. Africans who joined the safari were in demonstrably inferior social roles, as guides, scouts or bearers. The 'service' of their secured loyalty was less about governance than a facilitating of the ritualised dominance of the hunt. The Queen's response to the unveiling of her statue in the public park at Durban was to send a 'gracious message of thanks to her loyal white colonists', a clear sign that in South Africa, at least, the presence of European settlers shifted the burden of overt patriotism away from the African. Signs of imperial solidarity were expected only from the white settlers; the closest the African came to contact with visiting imperial elites was carrying the shooting party into the jungle or sighting the game.[1]

In extraordinary circumstances the notion of imperial service could be expanded to include military support, but not without reservations. For most of the era there was a reluctance to employ African soldiers as empire troops. *Chums* in 1900 addressed the issue, discussing the pros and cons, including the useful actions of the Hausa in defeating the Asante in the late nineteenth century. On the negative side, black recruits could prove problematic for white officers:

> That the recruits are more difficult to lick into shape than intelligent white men can easily be conceived.[2]

Ability rather than loyalty was in question. Unlike the sepoy, the Africans' tribal loyalties were not believed to be an obstacle in supporting the British. The Hausa veterans of the Asante wars were pictured as securely in the imperial camp.

> When the time comes Tommy Atkins' black comrades in arms will be ready to fight as gallantly as they have done in the past for the honour of the Great White Queen....[3]

The language here betrays the different appreciation of these troops' allegiance. There is a greater confidence in the assumption of winning them over; Victoria has become the awe-inspiring white queen of the adventure stories. While there was little fear of mutiny among such troops, there was a concern over the appropriate skills and discipline needed to form an effective fighting force.

The uncertainty of the British nation over the potential of the African as 'soldier of Empire' had been aired in a *Spectator* article of 1898. While acknowledging that it would be a 'wise policy' to incorporate peoples who had 'no caste, ceremonials, or prohibitions to complicate arrangements', it was felt that 'slower' peoples posed their own difficulties. On the positive side of the argument, it would provide an outlet for the 'fighting tribes', whose energies must be either exterminated or redirected into an 'imperial outlet'. The article concluded with sentiments echoed in material for the young reader.

> Experience points to the fact that the African of the fighting tribe, when entirely free from European influence, is brave as a man can be; that the African who has fairly settled down among Europeans is not less brave, but that the negro, when just touched with civilisation, is very hard to train.[4]

The periodicals showed this ambivalence toward the African as soldier. Without the control and guidance of British officers, or the experience of European practice, the results could be problematic. In 1913 the *Boy's Own Paper* carried an article on 'A one ship navy', which explored the state of naval preparedness in the independent state of Liberia. The tone of the narrative was set in the opening paragraph, as the President and his ministers arrived to inspect the single vessel recently arrived from London.

> The President and his minister came on board to inspect her, and were greatly delighted with their new acquisition, or one might say, new toy.

The crew were pictured as hopelessly incompetent, ignorant even of the compass. When asked in what capacity they wished 'to ship', the responses read like a pantomime farce.

> No.1 Blue Peter, Sir. No.2, Prince of Wales, Sir. No.3: Brandy and Soda, Sir.

The fate of the crew was to be 'caught, tortured, killed and eaten' by the cannibals they were pursuing on the coastal patrol. The 'message' of the article was clearly dismissive of any notion of an independent African navy. In the hands of the Liberians the British warship became a useless bit of hardware, an expensive toy, whose potential they could neither understand nor master, and in their ignorance would destroy. The reader was advised that, even with the modern apparatus of warfare, the Africans could not or would not assume an adult perspective on the question of self-defence. This view supported a paternalistic, if not directly interventionist position toward this nation of ex-slaves.[5]

Although there was no equivalent of the Indian Mutiny to be refought on the African battlefield, the martial aspect of Africa's peoples did feature in the 'stories of famous defences'. The encounter with the Zulu nation at Rorke's Drift served to illustrate the African presence in the great events of national expansion. Unlike the contemporary view of African military skills, here was the enemy 'who gave no quarter'. The Zulu's was an 'impetuous valour' unmatched on the continent. While the periodicals stressed their submission as essential to the safety of homesteads in the Natal, the 'romance' of the last stand of the noble warrior evoked admiration, echoing the sentiments of the history textbooks. Arguably the Zulus did not present the same kind of threat to imperial interests as the mutinous Indian, nor were they considered 'treacherous' agents of betrayal. The absence of these factors allowed for appreciation of warriors who engaged in a savage, but, on their own terms, fair fight.[6]

Public debate over the Boer War found its way into the popular press for the juvenile market, and brought another contribution to Africa's profile. While the *Boy's Own Paper* expressed its reservations

[83]

over the conflict by maintaining a profound silence during the war years, more bellicose publications gave full coverage to the events and personalities of the time. *Chums* in particular identified with the British war aims and displayed a notable anti-Boer stance. A competition in 1900 posed the question 'Which British leader, now fighting the Boers, do you most admire?'. The winner was Baden-Powell, 'Hero of Mafeking', the 'soldier that every Briton loves'. When Lord Roberts' 'March to Pretoria' was chosen as one of the 'Pictures from the Book of Empire' in *Young England*, the 'difficult and protracted' struggle in South Africa became the setting. Those publications which did provide 'reports' on the course of the war or reflected later on its significance to the British nation, whatever stance was taken on the course of the conflict, agreed in portraying a 'white man's war'. The history of events for popular consumption, like that in the textbooks, did not consider the role of the Africans or its impact upon them. *Young England*'s description of the 'natives' as a 'motley crowd of spectators' expressed the view of all.[7]

So far the non-fiction of contemporary events and recycled history suggests Africans whose relations with the Empire are on the one hand tangential, as peripheral subjects in the administrative sense, and yet clearly of untapped potential as the raw material of imperial defence. It did boost the confidence of the Empire to recognise their loyalty, yet the problem remained of how to focus and direct a primitive energy into constructive 'imperial' channels. Once the 'fighting tribes' had been subdued, and British interests secured, there was no 'job' for the African within the imperial establishment, neither a bureaucracy or a standing colonial regiment. Yet, if left alone, the result could look like Liberia's naval preparedness. 'Guardianship' appeared the best course for the foreseeable future in terms of British official policy. The periodicals clearly supported this relationship, and illustrated its appropriateness through the images of Africa's connection to the crown, to the armed forces and the agencies of Empire.

The non-fiction of the periodicals also featured stories and factual reports on the 'spirit of enterprise' which individual Europeans had brought to the African territories. Profit may have been the motive force, but the descriptions of the business people, farmers and traders who worked there were careful to include the alleged humanitarian aspects in their exploitation of African resources. Cecil Rhodes was pictured as a man who both 'changed the map of the world' and used his money to fund clubs for 'ragamuffins' of the London street.[8] Private enterprise was imbued with romantic and visionary sentiments. In 1913 the *Boy's Own Paper* offered a story of 'The romance of track-laying in the wilds', where the 'dream of the great Empire builder is rapidly being realised'. Rhodes' vision was seen to incorporate white and African alike, as they worked together against the elephants, crocodiles, leopards and swarms of white ants. The labour of the African was pictured as totally voluntary and the benefits of increased trade open to all. Local chiefs were reassured by the engineers, while curious tribespeople enjoyed demonstrations of the steam traction engine. Families were compensated when a predatory lion claimed the lives of railway workers.[9]

The image of African workers on large-scale projects, supervised in military style, was positive and also reflected well on their employers. In other pursuits a black workforce might pose problems. The small-scale entrepreneur in South Africa raised another voice in offering his view of African labour.

> What sort of labourers do these kaffirs make? Well, they're not good for much, except in the way of minding cattle ... for most other work they're no use at all, not a bit. The only thing is that they're cheap.[10]

The transportation of Indian workers to Natal in 1899 seems to reinforce this judgement, suggesting that for daily toil, the African was 'unreliable'. *Chums* in the same year carried a picture of local magistrates in the area disciplining black workers found 'wandering out of bounds'. In South Africa the local government had also found it necessary to enforce a special code of laws to control local labour. The 'spirit' of these laws, as explained in the papers, was to enable smooth economic development and support the Anglo-Saxon colonists' idea that South Africa must be maintained as far as possible as a 'white man's country'.[11]

The value of South Africa to the British rested in no small part upon the wealth extracted from the diamond mines. When the *Public School Magazine* followed the Corinthians on a rugby tour in 1898, the sportsmen took an opportunity to visit the DeBeers Mine and glimpse the 'native' compound. The narrator was keen to emphasise the benevolent practices of the operators and overseers. Although it appeared necessary to enclose living quarters with barbed wire to avert 'native trickery', workers were 'shouting, whistling and singing as happy as could be'.[12] Another visit, reported in the *Girl's School Magazine* of 1893, commented on the 'comfort' and 'happiness' of those locals employed in the diamond mines.

> The good treatment of the natives is shown in the fact that when many of these kaffirs come to offer their services every rib stands out, and

their whole body skeleton is more or less visible. When their six months is over they waddle away without a rib showing, and with rolls of double chin.[13]

Writers did admit, however, that employing large numbers of local workers did pose problems, mainly with new-found wealth. Those working in the gold and diamond mines did have to be watched very carefully to prevent temptation. The manager of DeBeers explained to his visitors the precautions taken against theft:

> The watchers are now armed, and before their inferiors are allowed to leave the compound, their eyelids, toenails, and any cuts about them are strictly examined.[14]

Despite these precautions, the African labourer was shown as clearly benefiting from the presence of foreign capital. Wages 'went toward the sustenance of the population, filtering through the whole of the country'. While some articles did acknowledge salary differentials between black and white workers, the authors were at pains to point out the 'extras' (food, churches, swimming baths and so on were provided within the compound) and that white workers had to pay for such things from their own wages. The reader was left in little doubt that the African worker was fortunate to enjoy the security and opportunities afforded by European capital ventures.[15]

At times the 'natives' were also pictured turning their 'natural' abilities toward productive work, without external intervention. The Zulu traits of endurance and speed could find them pulling a rickshaw on the streets of Durban. Another job which suited their talents was delivering post on the veldt:

> Up to the inn door came standing a real Zulu postman, tall, muscular, nothing on but the postbag itself. In his huge bony fists the postman clutches a 'knob kerrie' or heavy wooden club, and an 'assegai', without which no respectable Zulu can go anywhere or do anything.[16]

As in all the occupations mentioned, the qualities stressed were those of strength and agility, or 'native skills', as with the Africans who served as guides, scouts and porters for the European visitor. Both private and official imperial interests acknowledged the usefulness of 'primitive' people, with their keen eyesight, stamina, speed, quick reactions and knowledge of local terrain. These proved invaluable for jobs unsuited to the white settlers, and essential in maintaining services for white emigrants and travellers.

[86]

The periodicals offered numerous examples of the African worker, both on large-scale projects and in private employment. This suggests how important the economic factor was in the African context, particularly in Southern Africa, and the need for local labour. Africa represented raw materials and untapped wealth, but exploitation of the African was not an acceptable part of the picture: it was important to fashion a positive image of the lives of the imperial workforce. It was also important to sustain the concurrent image of Britain as a people opposed to coerced labour and conducting their imperial business in a benevolent spirit. Therefore articles which dealt with African labour in the diamond or gold mines emphasised the voluntary nature of employment and the 'fair' conditions which prevailed. Any problems with a local workforce were seen to arise from the Africans' own nature, unadapted to the norms of a European work ethic. Their needs were simple, like those of the freed slave, and this relaxed attitude toward work required strict discipline and close supervision. 'Experts' advised that it would be a long time before the African would be ready for more than unskilled or heavy labour. There was no image of an alternative tribal economy in which Africans played a fruitful or responsible role, and once outside the white settlements they were viewed as returning to a 'state of nature'. Those locals who wished to work were treated well, and those who did not were tolerated. The investor and settler, within this landscape, were pictured not as usurpers of local resources but rather as generators of wealth in areas outside the province of 'native' concern.[17]

Another important view of the African was contained in the reports from overseas missions. These accounts appeared most often in the 'improving' journals, those aimed at a middle-class readership and sponsored by religious interests. The picture of the African which emerged from the missionary perspective reflected a number of ambitions particular to the Christian Empire. One was the desire of the authors to inspire the readership to support the missions both financially and through new recruits. This need prompted an optimistic approach to the work in Africa and presented the African as a fertile field for sowing the seeds of change and regeneration. Another concern was support for the social gospel, at work in both foreign climes and the streets of British cities. Not only the Africans' souls but also their social structures and living habits were targeted by Christian reformers. Many missionaries in this period were products of the 'muscular Christianity' pervasive in public schooling, and this bold, energised and aggressive approach was a popular aspect of the missionary story. The responsive 'native' convert helped to validate these methods. Finally, there was the legacy of Britain saving the African from the horrors of slavery, and this memory worked in the missionary narrative to encourage the readers' continued commitment to the uplifting and improvement of a vulnerable people.[18]

The relationship between the African and the missionary was often illustrated in the 'before and after' comparison of those touched by the mission spirit. An outstanding Christian agent like David Livingstone might elicit a 'respect and love' which 'transformed the natives with whom he lived and worked'. The 'devoted conduct' of Livingstone's followers was illustrated in the story of 'A Livingstone relic', when for 'nine long months they carried and guarded the sun-dried, bark-swathed body' on the long trek to Zanzibar. Even more than the physical effort involved was the ability of the African to overcome 'superstitious fear of a corpse' on the long journey. This devotion aligns partly to the figure of the loyal servant found throughout Empire, who would risk life, limb and the alienation from her or his own natural allegiances to serve the exemplary Briton. The Livingstone narrative makes clear that such sacrifice was inspired by the strength of the exemplary Christian adventurer.[19]

The force of a certain kind of British character to effect change was further explored in 'A biography of Arthur Fraser Sim: athlete and missionary'. His mission in Central Africa had been 'peopled by varsity men from Oxford and Cambridge' for over thirty years. Sim had come to the station from another 'savage' environment, an inner-city mission in Britain, where he had dealt with the 'roughest specimens' of urban life. He records a vivid impression of his first contacts at the mission. The 'raw material' did not look promising. Around him were creatures of idleness, easily tempted into 'evil ways' and exhibiting 'no conscience for sin'. He had been warned of the 'soft, cowardly natures of central Africa' and was prepared for those who 'lacked the courage of true Christianity'. Sim described for the reader those traits which identified the street and jungle 'savage'.

> Sensitive to a degree ... yet depths of child depression over trifles, quick to regain the almost abnormal buoyancy of animal spirits ... disgracefully casual ... keen enough when his interest is aroused but a creature full of obvious shallows and unsuspected depths ... superficially very sharp, though seldom clever; not yet self-reliant, exasperatingly suspicious, with that odd mixture of incredulity and credulity both equally misplaced, which makes him so difficult to teach.[20]

Sim's first step was to establish a sports programme. If one could catch them at an early age the rules of the game would be theirs for life. 'Taming' the wild creatures was the necessary precursor to engaging them in scholarly pursuits. Childhood was to be a longer period than for British youth, as the transition to adulthood was more difficult and involved a greater danger of 'uppitiness'. Short trousers were the rule for mission boys. Sim echoed the prevailing view that the African would take longer to emerge from the child state, and require a greater patience and perseverance than that employed with inner-city urchins. However, the athletic prowess of the African was to his advantage, and Sim's confident description of eager initiates helped to build a promising picture of missionary endeavours on the continent.

In girls' annuals the missionary message was given a tone more fitting to 'female needs'. While Sim concentrated his efforts on athletic avenues to heaven, Mrs Hartsock aimed to provide the 'heathen' with 'higher aspirations' in the schoolroom. Her work in the Congo, written up in the *Girl's Empire* (1902), emphasised the bringing of the 'word':

> The Bobangi language was not written till the missionaries undertook to do so. Now they have a few school books, a hundred or more hymns, a translation of the Book of Matthew, and several other chapters of the New Testament.[21]

Apart from the judgement on 'backwardness' associated with oral cultures, her observations on tribal life are interesting for their reflection of a woman's point of view. While decrying the lack of an 'intellectual and moral training' in the African family, she also commented upon the joy which accompanied the birth of a child, 'kindly welcomed by all the relatives and friends'. The openness and affection between parents and children she found most gratifying, although the continued practice of inter-tribal enslavement was deplored. She, like all missionaries, was writing with an eye to new recruits and wished to present her experience in a manner appealing to potential volunteers. But beyond these considerations, her narrative shows again that women could respond to a shared experience, in this case childbirth, with an empathy which could over-ride the strictures of the imperial or Christian mission.[22]

While all impressions of the 'other' filtered through the perspective of the 'redeemer' must be questioned, the message which missionaries gave to the readers of the periodicals did move beyond a simple dismissal of tribal life and custom. That the African did appear a better prospect for conversion than other 'heathen' was made clear, partially because there appeared no religion to displace. Unlike 'complex' societies with a more formal religious observance, tribal societies had, in the missionary view, only the superstitious power and fear represented by witch doctors. Success in undermining their controls and freeing their subjects, enslaved in ignorance, spoke well 'for the effects of true Christianity'. What the African needed, and what the missionaries' social gospel could provide, were the parental guidance and humane discipline appropriate to wayward children. The connections made between the settlement house movement in Britain and the mission stations in Africa confirmed this. While this view of the African was on the one hand contributing to the damaging stereotype of the childlike African, and fostering support for the colonisation of souls in the imperial world, it also gave the young reader a sense that understanding, if not respect, was possible. The view that the African had a redeemable soul open to the Christian message was, in terms of early-twentieth-century society, a positive assessment.[23]

Non-fiction in the children's press also reflected public interest in the African 'expert', whether traveller, hunter or pseudo-scientist. A good example of the kind of information provided lies in the interview with Mary Kingsley in *Chums* (1899). The tone of the introduction gives some idea of the attraction such features held for young readers.

> Without a single white friend to keep her company she goes out to the wilds of Western Africa and heedless of all risks, positively 'chums up' to all the bloodthirsty savages she can find. Some people there are who express surprise that Miss Kingsley has not been made a meal of ... solicitous savages have offered her choice portions of man, but so far as her own person is concerned, it remains intact.[24]

While Miss Kingsley attempted to speak seriously and 'in an informed manner', the interviewer constantly interjected questions on cannibalism. Her collections of artefacts are described as 'strange trophies', and less valuable than the booty of the game hunter. Her trained eye offered an interesting observation for the budding scientist:

> If you were to grow black men under glass cases for ten thousand years you couldn't turn them into white men; but for all that, the African is a good fellow, gentle, kindly, hospitable and very reasonable.[25]

Other 'scientific' observers also offered their classification of African characteristics. Herbert Ward, FRGS, related his visit to the 'barbarians' of Bolobo in the Congo Free State.

> Although not cannibals, they are notoriously cruel as a tribe – frequently torturing and killing their slaves in a most barbarous and inhuman

fashion. In appearance the people of Bolobo represent a somewhat higher form of the negro type – they are avaricious, cunning and ever ready to take advantage of others' weakness and inferiority.[26]

Although the muddling of racial characteristics with social and culturally determined behaviour was endemic in the British view of all foreigners in this period, its practice by the pseudo-scientist embedded the pernicious error with particular effectiveness. In publications which showed the readership how to compile collections of many diverse objects, isolating the attributes of human groupings was a familiar kind of exercise. But, by subjecting subject peoples to 'scientific' method, which might 'grow' Africans 'under glass' or sort 'negro types' in the post-Darwinian world, juvenile papers encouraged children to view the African as a 'specimen' of the natural world, a dehumanising and alienating perspective.[27]

'Facts' offered to the reader emphasised the 'strangeness' of African life. A tribal chief merited attention for his false teeth and fifty-nine children. Attendance at a native funeral stressed the 'peculiar and ghastly obsequies'. With the exception of the missionaries, few turned their 'expert' gaze on the ordinary family or domestic relations in their pursuit of striking contrasts with the familiar. When the *Boy's Own Paper* featured two articles on West African 'culture' in 1906 the full blast of European arrogance was felt. Tribal masks became 'most interesting as a sample of what they can turn out in the way of funny faces when he makes up his mind to do something out of the common'. Excursions into the realms of literature were 'just as interesting and much funnier'. Art as a medium in Africa was relegated to a means of lightening the 'mortal terror' of the primitive world.[28]

The contribution of the 'expert' in building the image of Africa is a particularly acute example of securing the rising generation into the ignorance of the old. The blend of entertainment with professional expertise produced a particular kind of information, selective, distorted and misleading. Under the guise of enlightening the audience, Africans were relegated to a position of cultural and social inferiority. Their culture was treated as laughable and its artefacts as grotesque manifestations of backwardness. African society became interesting only when bizarre, shocking or contemptible. The approach was closer to the experience of a 'freak show' than a studied exposition of African life. Juvenile periodicals were reflecting here a growing trend toward 'experiencing' the Empire which found popular expression in the colonial exhibitions of the era, where 'science' and entertainment merged in the spectacle of African life. They too treated material culture as a 'curiosity' or 'trophy' of the imperial connection, co-opting the authority of 'scientific' judgement to authenticate the mythologising of the 'other'.[29]

Another authority on Africa and its peoples was the hunter, whose knowledge came from years of first-hand, thrilling adventures in the wild. The admiration for these romantic figures was evident in the annuals:

> No boy with a drop of British blood in his veins requires to be reminded that Mr. F. C. Selous the great African traveller, is far and away the mightiest hunter of our time.[30]

Selous spoke with an easy familiarity of 'native life'. He could provide the reader with Lobengula's favourite expression, 'give him to the hyenas', as well as other little-known aspects of local lore. He remembered many characters from his travels and was willing to share his memories of their 'savage' practices. The annuals abounded with pictures of these men posing with their trophies in the bush. One of the features of the 'great' hunters, apart from a high body count, was their proven ability to establish a good working relationship with locals. They often repaid loyalty with protection, removing man-killing game which menaced local tribespeople.[31]

Central to the hunters' contacts in Africa was the guide. Without the guide's keen physical faculties and knowledge of the terrain it would have been impossible for hunters to 'test' themselves against the natural forces of the wild. Many authors noted with admiration the natural abilities of those whose presence was essential to the success of expeditions, and reflected on qualities lost to 'soft' British boyhood. Baden-Powell's scouting would combine military discipline with survival skills to address these concerns. Although 'scared and superstitious' at times, the tracker who deserted was more than balanced by portrayals of 'noble savages' who gave their services willingly to the great white hunter. The acute sensory skills attributed to Africans did, however, place them closer to the noble beasts than to the 'advanced' races and, in this sense, confirmed their inferior position on the evolutionary scale. When English people wished, temporarily, to re-experience the dangers of the wild and confirm their character on the perimeters of civilisation, the African had something to teach them. That the successful 'kill' confirmed the dominance of the European over Africa was also apparent, and the assistance of the local guide conveyed a tacit acceptance of the acts of supremacy.[32]

There was, undeniably, an attraction in the life close to nature which these real-life adventures underscored. An article in the *Boy's*

Own Annual expressed some concern that this aspect of the image of Africa might prove rather too appealing to the readership. The author, determined to set the record straight, sought to establish a correct attitude toward 'savagery'. 'Could British boys ever go back and become savages?' The African, in his view, was not a noble or happy child of nature, but rather 'poor, sordid and bloodthirsty waifs, the strays of humanity'.[33] This desire to play down the attractions of uncivilised behaviour may reflect the serious concerns felt at the time over the 'degeneracy' of British youth. A year earlier, in 1904, the Toynbee Trust, in a study of city children, had made the analogy between antisocial habits and savagery:

> It is a mere commonplace that savages are children, and must be treated as such. Perhaps it is less generally recognised that children are savages, and can only by training be brought up to the level of contemporary civilisation.[34]

The annuals instructed the reader for 'signs' in appearance and behaviour – neglect of clothes, person, manners, eating habits and mode of speech. One would know that the situation was out of hand when youth 'came at last to say only "Quash ma boo" or even "Ugh, Waow and Oa"'. When British boys and girls encountered the African one 'must not go down but go up'.

> Move upward, working out the beast and let the ape and tiger die.[35]

Here was a warning for the impressionable fan of the annuals, wishing to escape the constrictions of home or school and turn to the happy, carefree life of unregulated society. Africa was not an alternative to the serious business of adult life, but rather to serve as a yardstick by which to measure one's progress. Those who had been born into 'a higher order of being' might admire the exploits of the British in the wilds, but were reminded that their task was to subdue, not to join, the savage world.[36]

While the history textbooks had suggested that Africa was not a primary concern for the schoolchild, the annuals more than compensated for this lack of attention by providing information in a variety of non-fictional pieces. The juvenile press of the period found much that was interesting in British relations, past and present, with the continent. War in South Africa and the expansion of commercial and business interests encouraged the editors to offer a 'working' knowledge of the African peoples to a new generation of potential settlers, missionaries, investors and travellers. When combined with the entertainment value of the unknown and the exotic, and complemented by the comic possibilities of 'strangeness', children's papers brought the African before the reader in a variety of roles.

Most of the 'history' which found its way into the periodicals drew upon the military exploits of imperial forces, stories of battles fought and defences mounted. Africa was no exception to this rule, but as seen in the texts, offered fewer opportunities than India to view the 'sinews' of Empire. There were 'true tales' from the Zulu and Asante campaigns, replete with detailed description of 'savage bloodlust' and fierce combat. Expeditions against 'slavers' were also fairly common historical pieces, offering both action and morality. And, in keeping with the textbooks' definition of 'useful' topics, the popular press frequently found itself recycling episodes from the Boer War. When the annuals and 'respectable' papers turned their hand to offering 'popular' history, they followed the textbook lead, while adding detail to the slave victim, the fierce warrior and the loyal, if detached, observer in Southern Africa.

The 'real-life' African was portrayed as a slow but not unwilling participant in the advance and defence of British interests. Reservations about the fighting powers of African troops could be subsumed in the need for imperial unity as war in Europe came closer. The physical strength of the African was recognised both in the warrior nations and in a workforce co-opted to build railways and extract mineral wealth. While somewhat prone to 'mischief' and 'laziness', a lack of motivation could also support the imperial case, for it rationalised European exploitation of local resources and diminished the spectre of subversion.

All who commented upon African peoples felt compelled to note their 'savage' state. This was described in various ways, as primitive, heathen, natural or uncivilised. For those who needed to enlist the African in armies, work, or Christianity, the patterns of 'savage life' were an obstacle, and attention was centred on modifying behaviour. For the scientist, explorer or hunter, savagery was more useful, both for study and for guidance through the landscape. Viewing this 'primitive' being as in a childlike state, or as an earlier stage of human evolution, allowed the European to view the tribes as educable and incapable of the malign intentions of more advanced societies.[37]

While paternalism did allow a more benign attitude toward the individual, the judgement remained that the African had no indigenous history, no culture and no observable social structures. When custom or local practice was brought to the reader's attention, whether slavery or funeral rituals, the intention was to condemn or to ridicule, with only the infrequent attempt to appreciate cultural difference. Africans were viewed as incapable of any interest in or ability for self-directed change. They did not, in these materials, build cities, write books, generate wealth or possess a recognisable religion. On the 'evolutionary scale' they remained much lower than the other peoples within the imperial orbit, and centuries away from the British.[38]

The British presence in Africa was presented, however, as less problematic than that in other parts of the world. The African could become a loyal friend and companion, even while representing the antithesis of progress. The 'reality' of the continent, unlike other parts of the imperial world, was not as weighed down by the apparatus of imperial administration nor so infused with the burden of imperial power. The 'experience' of Africa was viewed as accessible in a way that neither India nor China was, and a sense of adventure and freedom echoed in the stories of explorers and hunters. The African was seen to 'step aside' and allow the European to 'play at savages'. It appeared from these articles that the British could trample through bush and jungle with impunity, eased by the perception that there were no settled peoples to displace or culture to confront. Neither was there a troublesome professional or educated class who came forward to question British intentions. Children must have believed that taming the natives was no more problematic than subduing the beasts of the wild. For the young reader of the periodicals, the African became at one with the landscape, which both created a more 'natural' imagery and a dehumanising one.

While historians and non-fiction writers provided information and advice in their professed 'educative' role, the fiction of the popular press allowed the freedom to escape into a world of adventure and imaginative exploits. In the pre-war years many African characters would appear as friends and adversaries of the British heroes. Some, like Pete in the *Marvel*, would remain for many years in the public eye. These characters were an indispensable part of the attraction of the annuals, and a significant addition to the youthful impression of Africa.

Children's familiarity with the 'savage life', and the appeal it generated, was a popular theme in stories of the era. The action might involve running off into the 'wilds' or the acting out of African characters. While warnings might be voiced elsewhere of the dangers of savagery, the fiction illustrated the fun one might have in 'going native'. A boring Sunday afternoon prompted the following exchange between two boys in a paper of 1898:

M: Let's go and live like wild savages.
A: Savages is black.

M: We might grow black if people let us alone....
A: What do savages live on?
M: On hunting and fishing ... when we're savages we mustn't speak to anybody, but only make signs ... you wave your hands about a little and crook your fingers and waggle your head, and those is signs.
A: What do savages make them for?
M: Why, of course, so people mayn't understand what they mean. Savages is uncommonly cunning.[39]

Here was a potential escape from the adult world and its demands. In this imaginative world one could transgress the rules of cleanliness and polite conversation and hide one's thoughts from the prying eyes of authority. The 'savage' waited as an ally, beckoning children away from the constrictions of middle-class morality and conventions.[40]

This detailed 'knowledge' of the habits of savages could be found in both the popular journals and the entertainments of the day. Fiction in the annuals encouraged the young to mimic 'black behaviour' in their own play and home amusements. One story featured a lively game of charades, in which the three young characters enacted the word 'blackamoor'. This they appeared to do without any difficulty:

> Wilfred and Madge were to black their faces with burnt cork, and have some black horsehair put over their heads to represent the woolly pates for negroes and negresses. I was to be the slave owner ... the two niggers were to speak as in *Uncle Tom's Cabin* ... Me no lub nigger, me lub white man....[41]

One of the most popular forms of entertainment in both Britain and America in this period was the Black and White Minstrel Show. Max Pemberton, editor of *Chums* for many years, records in his memoirs the many visits he and his fellow members of the 'Savage Club' made to watch the productions. It is not surprising that aspects of black minstrelsy should appear in the fiction of his and other juvenile papers.[42] School stories were often the setting for the staged 'Nigger Show'. In 1898 the 'public school' annual, *The Captain*, featured a story on 'How we blacked up', in which the lads decide to break with tradition and abandon 'legitimate drama' for the night. There was great excitement in the school as preparations commenced, and a good deal of effort expended in providing correct details of appearance:

> The boys were much annoyed, when instead of the correct nigger wigs, black things with short plumes, you know, we received a parcel of powdered perukes. They didn't go at all well with nigger faces....[43]

[96]

Schoolchildren not only knew the details of dress but also seemed to possess the talents of 'coon dancing' and familiarity with the lyrics of minstrel songs. 'Pompey' Brass was able to 'act just like a minstrel'. Greyfriars boys were no different. In 'Fun by the sea' in 1908, Frank Richards extended the talents of Hurree Singh to include the singing of minstrel ditties. In 'Our Christy minstrel show', a young schoolboy introduces the audience to his dramatic companions:

> I cannot say much in favour of the features of my companions (unrest among the minstrels) but their faces are honest, if ugly; and I ask you to remember that the black will come off in the morning, as they are all cleanly animals.[44]

The usefulness of the minstrel image could extend beyond the school walls as well. In 'The deep game Inky played', a newspaper apprentice adopted 'minstrel disguise' to pursue an Indian prince missing in London. Already covered in printer's ink, he needed only to adopt the rhythms of 'nigger speech' to effect the transformation. The ruse, which was an attempt to hide the serious nature of his quest, was successful. No one suspected a black-face minstrel could be engaged in detection.[45]

The African of the minstrel image reflected many of the deepest-held views about 'blackness' in the late nineteenth and early twentieth centuries. The characterisation rested upon the American experience of slavery and its aftermath, and had served in the United States to neutralise the threat of freed blacks after the Civil War.[46] That these images transferred effortlessly to the British context testifies to the universal appeal of the kind of black character which minstrelsy portrayed and also to its social usefulness. In the juvenile papers 'blacking up' became an experience even the young could adopt in harmless fun. The stereotypes were so familiar that the African was effortlessly within the reach and control of the least gifted of thespians. Within this process the African identity was reduced to burnt cork, speech patterns, and physical mannerisms which the child could master, summon at will, and then discard. As one story advised the eager players – 'All you've got to do is to be as idiotic as possible'.[47]

What the popularity of the form and its assumption by juvenile players suggest is a highly influential strand of the image of Africa. On stage, acted out by whites, the minstrels could sing, dance, tell jokes and reassure the white audience that they were happily subservient to their needs and wishes. In the papers effortless supremacy was granted to the child in the assumption of the minstrel role. Control was complete over the threatening spectre of 'free blacks', reduced to caricatures of incompetence in encounters with the modern world. These were productions which established and popularised long-lived stereotypes of the African persona, and the annuals clearly expected their readers to be familiar with its content and form. Projecting the image of the happy, singing 'darky' was both an attractive release for schoolchildren and a means of controlling and neutralising the possibility of vengeance from a freed slave.[48]

Public schools not only acted out their ideas of colour, but also incorporated in their ranks the African pupil. Here he or she joined the Indian prince, the heathen 'Chinee' and the quarrelsome French and Germans as stock characters in the story papers. When a 'nigger stowaway' is discovered by a group of chums at their local railway station, his introduction to the reader is a characteristic one.

'Ise picaninny Sambo!' he said, with a slight lisp and in the liquid tone peculiar to negroes. 'Blackin brush is only frien'!'[49]

Unlike other foreigners, young Africans who appeared in school stories usually operated with no given name, no specific country, no relatives and in a role confined to the amusement of those who befriended him. Unlike the Indian prince, there was no admittance of the African to scholarly pursuits or to the sportsfield, and his position within the school was maintained through the pity taken upon him by pupils and staff. Sambo was pictured as too simple and unsophisticated to share the other boys' interests in science or games. As a vulnerable initiate, Sambo can only offer his services as a mimic and ventriloquist, and earns his acceptance by a constant stream of self-deprecating jokes.[50] His terms of acceptance, and position in the racial hierarchy, were made clear in the *Captain* of 1898.

There was a negro of sorts, from some part of Africa, a good-natured fellow who got on very well with us, as he did not in the least mind being called Sambo, and having waggish whites peep into his basin to see 'if it came off'. We had two dusky Eurasians who were by way of looking down on this frankly black brother.[51]

Whereas 'uppity' or troublesome black boys were not part of the public-school world, the same was not always true of African schoolgirls. Coosha, the daughter of a Zulu chieftain, made regular appearances in the *Girl's Friend* in the early years of this century. While she owed her arrival in England and the educational opportunities she experienced to the kindly General Burgham, she clearly represented a different 'type' of African than Sambo. As befitted a Zulu, she was endowed with both the pride and the quick wit to counter the discrimination she met at her college. Although she was not spared the 'nigger' English of her male counterparts, she could put it to effective use. She was most likely speaking the words disallowed to her fellow students when responding to the racial taunts of a young German, 'dat you am de uglies woman I eber did see'.[52]

The message for the reader was that young Africans, contained within the walls of English institutions, should be accepted within the prevailing code of 'fair play' and paternalism. Sambo, in particular, as a homeless 'stray', made the bullying of the prefect intolerable, especially against such a harmless and amenable 'pet' of the form. Coosha, on the other hand, represented a 'higher' stage of development, with her Zulu inheritance and candid character. The stories were careful to cast less enlightened foreigners as her detractors. Both these figures fell into the stereotyped casting of the helpless or 'noble' savage, and both merited acceptance because of their apparent eagerness to embrace the opportunities at hand. As penniless arrivals, their treatment was much more an act of charity than the reciprocal deals struck with well endowed princes. Their apparent dependence on the good services of English benefactors made for an image of a non-threatening arrival on English soil.[53]

Once the action of the stories moved beyond the school walls, however, the image of the African underwent significant changes. The Indian, the African and the Chinese were not presented as leading 'normal' lives within Britain, appearing only in the transient contexts of the underworld or travelling shows. The resident black community in Britain was invisible in both non-fiction and fiction.[54] In the annuals young Britons met Africans who were usually 'passing through'. Circus stories were a popular convention of fiction in the era, and a place to contain unusual and potentially dangerous figures. 'Temple, Squeaker and Co.', which appeared in *Chums* in 1910, showed the contrast between 'good' and 'bad' Africans in the camp of a travelling show. The story begins with 'Snowball' meeting a group of schoolboys who kindly show him the route back to his circus quarters. His gratitude was quickly expressed:

> And with the quick change from gay to grave which these children of nature have born in them, tears rolled down the great, black cheeks and he put out a huge black paw to each of the boys in turn. The slightest thing seemed to make him laugh, and the boys already felt a liking for this jovial creature.[55]

Snowball's job in the circus was as a lion tamer, for which his strength, 'huge paws' and attraction to costume were well suited.

Pericles, the villain of the piece, was the violent and thieving presence in the black quarter. His manner toward the white boys, in direct contrast to Snowball's, was sullen and aggressive. It was the 'type' Pericles represented which justified the need for segregation in the living quarters, showing that 'white men and black do not mix very well together socially'. To prove this point, a razor fight soon breaks out. As violence erupts Snowball shows his capacity for 'majestic dignity' by siding with the forces of law and order and distancing himself from the troublemakers.[56]

The formula of this story is a familiar one. The 'good' African emerges as the emissary sent to track down a fugitive from justice and remove him 'back to his own country'. The exit of Snowball and Pericles effects the disappearance of both the villain and the honest but independent African. The 'worthy' black entertainers are allowed to stay. As 'star turns', if they remained isolated in the circus world and socially segregated, they would not be denied work. When they attacked each other or threatened the order of white society, they would be punished and sent home. As with all Africans outside the school walls, the stories stressed a need for strict discipline. Unlike the wealthy princes or the ingenuous Chinese, Africans had little to offer their benefactors when subservience and entertainment were absent. Without these traits, like Pericles, they became both dangerous and undesirable.[57]

It was possible for the heroes of the adventure stories to meet Africans in every part of the globe, reflecting the legacy of international slavery. As when young Africans materialised on railway stations or were found wandering the roads of Great Britain, there was no explanation of how these rootless persons had arrived at a location nor of the reasons they had left their native land. Again the African was available and quite pliable in accommodating the needs of the story. One popular configuration was a group of white youths expanding to include a favoured black 'chum'. Although many papers copied the formula, the most famous and long-running example of the band of adventurers was found in the Harmsworth stable. Originating in the *Marvel*, but appearing in the *Pluck* and *Magnet* as well, was the trio of Jack, Sam, and Pete. From 1901 until the 1920s the staunch friends enjoyed great success, and Pete represented the 'African' which the readership came to know best.[58]

He became a major selling point of the papers, chosen to 'edit' the Christmas edition of *Pluck* in 1904. It was Pete's face which appeared in the advertisements which extolled the supremacy of Harmsworth in the highly competitive market. Neither Indian nor Chinese characters were co-opted in this fashion, suggesting that there was a particular 'attraction' in the black figure. On the crudest level, of course, the smiling and slightly mischievous persona of Pete activated expectations that here was guaranteed fun. The white artists who drew him ensured that he incorporated the physical mien of the minstrel African – bulging eyes, enormous mouth, wild, woolly hair and perennial smiles. His clothes were typical stage costume, with flapping shoes covering over-large feet, loud checked waistcoats, and incongruous hats.[59]

Because Pete shared such a close and lengthy relationship with Jack and Sam the audience felt that here they were coming to know the 'real' personality of the African. The author was at pains to point out the genuine affection which the three felt for each other, and each character had a clearly defined contribution to the success of their adventures. The easy camaraderie which the three shared in the face of relentless dangers created an appealing image of 'boys together'. While the scene and the villains were constantly changing, the trio remained reassuringly constant, eternally young and frozen into rigidly observed stereotypes.

Jack, the Englishman, was the acknowledged leader of the group, and, as one might expect, serious, fair-minded, quick-witted and decisive. Sam, the American, was good-natured, brave, outspoken and rather naive. Jack's paternalistic role extended to the African and the American, both learning from the example of their former master.[60]

Pete's character involved adopting a variety of roles within the stories, including the faithful servant, the 'wise darky', and the trickster. Pete's willingness to 'perform' for his friends was a central part of his appeal, as was so often the case in the story papers. He was constantly finding himself in comic situations – falling into holes, terrified by the mystery of snow, falling asleep on watch and chronically overeating. Much of the humour in the narrative took place in exchanges between Pete and Sam, who traded jokes and insults. It was Sam who teased Pete for his laziness, unorthodox use of English, and his enormous appetite. Pete in return felt free to refer to the Americans as 'lazy cusses'.[61]

The white youths tolerated Pete's mischief and outspoken ways because they needed him. As often as they rescued the African from some predicament caused by his gullible and unwary actions, Pete equally used his talents to ensure the group's survival. He had many tricks, learned from previous lives on the stage and in the circus, and put them to good use in their predicaments. One of his main talents, often reserved for black characters, was a 'sort ob round de corner voice', a ventriloquism which never failed to confuse the enemy.

It was Pete's voice which often alerted the other two to danger or carried the criticism of an unacceptable foreigner. He could also be brave when required, summoning, like Livingstone's faithful bearers, the ability to overcome native superstitions and play his part. There were limits, however, and in a story where Pete has been instrumental in rescuing Jack, the dialogue can be seen to shift the power relations back to their expected form.

P: We have been looking for you all ober South America and de centre ob Brazil and oder continents.
J: Where did you learn to cook so well Pete?
P: Sah, when I was de Queen ob Great Britain's scullery maid in de House ob Lords.
S: Was that when you killed them jaguars on the Canary Islands?
P: It's a funny thing, when a poor nigger wants to speak the troof ...
S: That he can't.[62]

The strong underlying assumption in these stories was that casting Pete as the 'nigger' character was an affectionate and harmless portrayal. Pete himself was seen to confirm this by referring to himself as 'dis chile' and 'dis pore nigger'. The real racists of the narratives were other foreign nationals, particularly the Germans, the Italians and the Mexicans, who featured in a number of stories. Jack and Sam were quick to come to their chum's defence, and Pete to show his gratitude for their protection. Again, in the stories of Pete, the African is viewed, however sympathetically, as using his strengths and talents to confirm rather than to challenge the assumptions of the Anglo-Saxon code.[63]

Perhaps the strongest appeal of Pete, however, was the fact that the reader could also identify with him. While Jack represented the 'proper' way to conduct oneself as a young Englishman, Pete's presence could also prove reassuring. When Pete misunderstood the adult world and suffered for it, the laughter was also partly identification with his plight. If even Pete could summon the resources to face the evil and menace in the world, there was hope for the most uncertain reader. Pete, like the minstrel, could be relied upon to make the readers feel better about themselves, for he offered them a superiority based on little more than the colour of one's skin. They like Pete because they believed he knew this, and offered freely to them a self who 'knew how to please the white man'. In the character of Pete the author created for the young their very own 'white man's nigger', ostensibly a 'chum' but in reality a servant to their own fears and insecurities. Within the stereotype of Pete, the African became severely circumscribed, in a comradeship based on the white man's needs, and indifferent to the reality of the African experience.[64]

Pete and his fellow Africans abroad projected the image of the African operating in close proximity to whites and introduced the young reader to a character working within narrowly prescribed limits. This was a version of the 'domesticated' savage who seemed to do little beyond entertaining and serving the European. In the stories set on the African's 'home ground', however, the British characters found themselves in alien territory, and often dependent on the knowledge and skills of locals. Encountering a friendly tribal chief, for example, could represent a critical turning point in the marshalling of allies against hostile forces. Finding this African was useful, indeed often indispensable, to a white character's successful advance. Without the need for 'instinctive mastery', bred in India by fears of mutiny, the African experience allowed for a certain 'initiation' into African ways.

'In the power of the Pygmies', a story which appeared in the *Boy's Own Annual* of 1914, Guy Kingston, a young aviator, arrives in Africa for the first time in search of a lost Englishman. He learns quickly the advantage of forging an alliance with friendly tribes. Matama, chief of the Bongos, is quite a different image of the 'good African' from that which operated on English soil. When Guy, through his ignorance, insults the chief, a proud and powerful leader, only the intervention of the seasoned white guide saves his life. Crouch, who speaks from a long friendship with Matama, warns Guy that he must not abuse his welcome in their territory, for these are a 'higher form' of African:

> Compared to the tribes they were to meet later in the forest, the Bongos were highly civilised, skilful workmen in iron ... adept at woodcarving and practical farmers.[65]

Matama was in no sense servile to the white visitors; indeed, it was only by observing his rules that the party could stay within his lands. He was, however, anxious to help in the search for the lost Englishman, and directed three of his best men, Pluto, Jupiter, and Neptune, to assist the passage through cannibal territory. Guy learns from Pluto how to survive in the jungle and returns home a 'wiser' young man.

One of the characteristics of the admired African leader was his ability to distinguish between the intentions of competing European powers. While British characters were pictured as forming relations of 'trust' with local chiefs, the intentions of other white men were suspect. Old Mabula in 'Bushman's reef' refused to disclose the location of a gold mine worked by his friend, John Lancey, to the Portuguese, until Lancey's son arrived to claim his inheritance. While rough justice was meted out to the Portuguese interlopers, Derek was welcomed as 'family', and the mine, worth tens of thousands of pounds, returned to its rightful owner. Clearly, a good chief was one who allowed the British to establish economic interests on their tribal lands, while the convention of 'adoption' by the tribe worked against any notion of exploitation.[66]

The positive image of the African ruler, unlike that of the Indian or the Chinese, was not necessarily of a man 'Westernised' into acceptable behaviour. Whereas other foreign rulers were seen to work within complex and often corrupting local structures, from which they needed to be separated, the British view of the African's essentially primitive state allowed the chief to remain 'African', while still capable of transferring affection and loyalty to the white man. In India the good ruler was often described as 'light skinned' or possessing the 'fine features' of an Aryan inheritance, but there was no attempt, even in fiction, to draw the African closer to the physical model of the European. The description of Matama's tribe illustrated the willingness to leave Africans in their 'blackness':

> The Bongos are very dark of skin – they are really black; whereas the Pygmies and the savage races that live in the forest are never darker than chocolate, and often of a lighter brown. When in health, the sleek black skin of a Central African native has the appearance of satin.[67]

It is interesting that the 'black face' was portrayed as displaying emotions seldom accorded to other aliens: kindness, dignity, gratitude, and trust played across their features and could suggest a people 'white in heart'. Indeed, the ability of white characters to 'see through' the surface of the African to a 'true nature' was the mark of one who 'knew' the people.

> His tribe turned him adrift because he was deformed ... a dwarf ... but he made up for that by his enormous breadth and tremendous strength. In face he was decidedly ugly, not an unpleasant ugliness, for he had keen steady eyes of a brilliant black in which could be read fidelity to those whom he served.[68]

In the mould of Livingstone's faithful native bearers, extraordinary deeds could be performed by the African once loyalty was secured. Djuma, a gun bearer, interposed himself between an inexperienced white hunter and a man-eating lion. Red Assegai, a 'magnificent

Zulu', challenged even King Chaka to secure the release of his British 'comrade and friend'. Not only would this African put his life and local knowledge at the disposal of the British, but he could overcome his irrational terrors. Pluto's ability, with the encouragement of Guy Kingston, to follow the trail toward the 'Spirit of the Mountain', demonstrated he would risk all for his companion. These fears were seen as endemic to tribal society:

> He can cope with mortals, but like all of his race, he is very superstitious ... with a strong belief in ghosts and evil spirits.[69]

This extraordinary service was seldom corrupted by material reward. The 'noble savage' was viewed as working to an archaic, if admirable code of conduct:

> Lincoln: Bangwani scorns the yellow iron and the little stones at present, but I am going to put his share in safe keeping for him. When he is old ...
>
> Bangwani: When I find myself getting too old, baas, to be of any use, I shall take my spear and my shield and die as a man should, fighting his enemies, whoever they may be.[70]

Outside the boundaries of white society, Africans were able to retain qualities of the 'noble savage', uncorrupted by the modern world. Here they lived close to nature, with an integrity which did not allow the adoption of white man's ways, a mimicry so often derided when found in the Indian 'babu' or half-Westernised Chinese. The pride, self-sufficiency, and independence of these characters could be celebrated in the adventure fiction, particularly when they put their 'savage skills' at the disposal of the white heroes. An admiration for the ability of the tribes to survive in the harsh environment of bush or jungle could elicit an unfavourable comparison with those 'back home'. After many years in Africa, the guide Crouch concluded that 'the average dwarf has got more brains in his head than many a member of Parliament'. Certainly there was a sense in which the young Briton, testing himself in the wild, emerged from his experience with invaluable knowledge.

> That's a continent that finds out the nature of a man quicker than a dog. It's a continent that makes a man sort of intimate with himself; in a word, it makes him think.[71]

When contemplating the inevitable march of progress, authors could lament what was lost in the process. The 'romance' of the wilderness was very attractive to the more 'advanced' races, but 'savagery' could not be allowed to continue.

> Though I love the wild, I feel it will be a good thing when all this black ignorance and savagery is stamped out, done with and forgotten.[72]

The other side to the natural world, its potential hostility, was represented by tribal chiefs who did not welcome the British or any white people to their environs. The reasons for this attitude might rest in 'innate' characteristics or previous contacts with unscrupulous Europeans. In 1897 the *Boy's Comic Journal* introduced Wattywam, a West African king, who set his followers upon a British expedition. Unlike the 'good' chief, Wattywam was unwilling to share the wealth of his kingdom with the new arrivals. This part of the world had known the white man before.

> White man make slave of my people. Me great king and show white man how he like de same.[73]

Any potential sympathy for the African point of view was quickly dispelled, however, when Wattywam is revealed as himself a slaver and aggressor. The African had no 'case' against the white man; indeed, it was clear to the Captain leading the expedition that this tribe should be taught a 'wholesome lesson'.

> These black rascals must be taught that the world was not created for them alone.[74]

In the weekly story papers, a harsher attitude toward the African who 'got in the way' of the hero's progress was common. The hero was a less reflective character than in the middle-class annuals and had less patience with 'wretched savages'. When the British were compelled to use force against the Bangkiian leader, Kiltip, in another story, the responsibility was seen to rest solely with the African. Here was the leader who worked against the interests of his own people, a familiar criticism of locals hostile to British interests. His death came at the hands of one faithful to the British, and afterwards one of his followers made clear their 'true' feelings:

> Kiltip was a bad man ... and we are glad that he is dead. Our people would never have planned this evil thing without his influence. We have no enmity against the white man. Go in peace.[75]

A brash character like Singleton the Searcher, popular in the pages of *Chums*, represented views toward the African which bore none of the sensitivity to noble savagery. He was a commercial mercenary who undertook assignments in the service of P. T. Barnum, the 'Yankee Circus King', or the Anglo-Congolese Trading Company. He was not only dismissive of Africans but of all other Europeans he met on his travels. Singleton accepted only the Zulu, who shared his contempt of other native tribes, as a worthy companion. To this adventurer, natives were 'easily fooled', and he had little respect for chiefs he could mislead with 'childish devices':

Nothing like plenty of bluff in dealing with these dusky monarchs.[76]

Here was the hero stripped of all inhibiting sensibilities, and straightforwardly successful in securing the economic advantage. That he appeared in the pages of *Chums*, an annual obsessed with the 'creeping weakness' of contemporary British life, was not surprising. Its articles had often been critical of the instincts of the 'faint-hearted' humanitarians abroad. For Singleton, his dealings with Africa were no more than a means to an end, with a personification, appealing to youth, but too strident for most publications, of might makes right. His was the 'ringing voice which compelled obedience' without any time wasting over the sensibilities of those he encountered. Here was the muscle without the Christianity, and readers watched all but the Zulu pushed aside as he bullied his way through the bush.[77]

Another powerful characterisation of the African was the witch doctor, a symbol of unacceptable barbarism. Portrayed as the enemy of the missionary, the settler, the trader and the adventurer, this figure, like the Indian or Chinese 'priest', represented a malign influence within native society. The narrator of 'In the power of the Pygmies' paused to inform the reader of the witch doctor's role in African life.

They are the powers that be. Great chiefs, even kings, are the slaves of fetish, the puppets of the witch doctors.... They rule by fear. Theirs is a reign of terror and they hold their power by cunning, crafty rogues who base their falsehoods on a stratum of the truth.[78]

Witch doctors' influence was portrayed as particularly malevolent and obstructive to the 'progress' of their people. In the annuals' view they worked for no interest but the consolidation of their own considerable power, were intimately involved in the perpetration of slavery, and uniformly hostile to the 'benefits' of European contact.

The worst of an hereditary priestcraft is that it has everything to lose and nothing to gain by the growth of civilisation.[79]

[107]

Unlike the ordinary tribespeople or the respected ally, witch doctors were seen to possess a cunning and manipulative personality unknown in other Africans. While white people never owned up to fearing them, they needed to be constantly aware of the trouble the witch doctor could stir up. The 'scheming' witch doctor was often at the centre of opposition to British interests. All kinds of local problems and debilitating natural phenomena could be laid at the feet of the interlopers.

In 'Seeking the witchdoctor's juju', Mahika used his priestly power to advance schemes to blow up a British-owned mine. The narrative made light of his access to the spirit world, however, stressing the role of native beer in stilling the conscience of the conspirators. Other stories saw a Swazi priest holding the white settlers accountable for the sickness of tribal oxen, and encouraging the locals to seek their revenge. When a European was captured by an unfriendly tribe, or one which had never seen a white person, it was the witch doctor who encouraged torture and death, stirring the tribe into 'bloodthirsty frenzies'.[80]

The 'religion' of these characters was pictured as a grotesque parody of worship. In the tribal ceremonies they were transformed into 'repulsive' and 'hideous' figures, 'dancing maniacs' who donned 'horrifying disguises'. Their pitiless life-and-death hold over the tribe was manifested in cruel ceremony and blood sacrifices, over which they presided with 'the air of one born to authority, and vindictive in the upholding of it'. Here incarnate was the force of 'darkness' which enslaved the continent, a religious imposter beyond redemption, and a perfidious source of intrigue and reprisal against the British presence.[81]

Although the stories granted no respect to his power, they did recognise how potent a force the superstitions and fears of a primitive society could be. Mastery over these 'false gods' was a key test of the resourcefulness of the adventure hero. Direct physical challenge might unmask the witch doctor as a coward, when faced with the courage of the British characters. Often, however, it was the lone Englishman who fell into the hands of a hostile tribe, and then the young white man needed to show how adept he could be at feigning 'mystic powers'. This process was similar to the strategies employed in encounters with Indian 'Thugs'. It was not only young men, however, who could assume spiritual leadership in these circumstances. The 'She' figure, popularised in the novels of Rider Haggard, was also copied in the story papers of this era. The description of a 'strange queen' in a *Marvel* story illustrated her function in realigning native allegiances.

... the maiden, who, with burning eyes, and wild, streaming hair, stood boldly erect, like some modern Joan of Arc. She sat still and unmoved as a marble saint in a cathedral.[82]

Clothed in pure white, surrounded by a 'weird mass of colour', the girl queen appeared as the antithesis of the witch doctor. While acknowledging that her power rested upon the force of superstition, she used her influence to resist the threat of the slavers, and this embodiment of justice and mercy more than justified the displacement of the tribe's natural leaders. While the witch doctor heightened the thrills and danger of adventure in Africa, he was in truth no match for the forces of enlightenment, whether carried in the challenge of intrepid boy adventurers or the saintly warrior-goddess of the she-queen.

The white woman in Africa represents an idealised picture of both gender and race. Apart from the missionaries or the 'She' figures, there are few 'ordinary' girls who operate as heroes, unlike in British India. They would take their place in the inter-war period. Before the First World War, however, she would remain above the rough life of the African adventurer, embodying a symbol of female authority over lesser races. She rules, but as with all 'imperial women' in this period, defers to white men when they appear. She is on a pedestal, as befits the pure European female, but nonetheless does project a kind of sexual dominance over the natives, and in this position neutralises any sensual 'urges' which the outsider may fear from the 'animalistic' African.[83]

Not all Africans, then, were submissive and friendly, and the action of the adventure stories needed villains as well as heroes. In the main these characters represented the malign influence of savagery and superstition, and the mistrust bred of the slave trade. Confusing the English with other Europeans could create conflict, and fears of enslavement or exploitation. When the witch doctor's power was threatened, he would seek to undermine the British presence. Forays against the Matabele or the Zulu often provided the narrative with the thrills of armed encounter, when heroes turned from hunting beasts to tracking 'natives'. Cannibals remained a menace in the landscape. The 'lower forms' of African life could be ruthlessly suppressed in the hero's course through the adventure.

The comic dimension of the African's image was a strong feature of the juvenile periodicals. A wealth of cartoons, jokes and anecdotes illustrated how central this image was to the characterisation of the African. In the weekly papers, like *Pluck*, comic creations featuring foreigners and the British working class were a stock in trade. One of the most popular figures of fun was the cockney, Cookey Scrubbs. His adventures were shared with 'the Skipper' and 'the Engineer', a trio who found adventure around the world. Cookey's unsophisticated and unrestrained behaviour assured that he related well both to the 'natives' and to the animals who entered the stories. 'Three men in a canoe', set in West Africa, showed the Skipper describing his cook's unique relationship with Africa.

> Cookey Scrubbs has been talking to the monkeys. They've received him like a long-lost relation.[84]

Added to his ability to commune with the animal world was the curious feature of appearing to the natives as their long-lost God, Bilboh. Cookey's sign of supernatural powers seemed to rest in his 'luminous nose' (he assures the reader that it is not due to drink) and ability to speak a common tongue.

> Um-loo-loo-loo-loo, what ho, gadzooks and me ham bone![85]

Cookey's origins seemed to make him a 'natural' intermediary with the 'inferior races'. The working-class character was presented as capable in his own way of dealing with the 'native', but these stories suggest that his 'mastery', unlike that of the middle-class characters, rested upon a certain familiarity with the habits of the 'lower orders'. The underlying assumptions of these popular serial stories carried messages to the reader on both class and race. Cookey was described as a 'middling' man, and that is where the reader finds him, defined by his 'betters' in the white community and his 'lessers' in Africa. He demonstrates the consensus in British society around racial identity, which imperialism offered, and which mediated class antagonism. As long as the working class could share in the subjection of imperial peoples, there was less likelihood of designs on privilege in their own society. The Empire offered Cookey a good time, without the responsibility vested in the 'Captain'. His role, while comic, certified that in the 'new imperialism' all classes in Britain had a vested interest and a part to play. Africans, for their part, and by their 'simple' nature, offered to working-class Britons a superiority they could not as easily claim in relation to subject peoples of 'higher order' in the imperial world.[86]

Opportunities were often taken in the papers to make the African's 'gullible' nature the subject of humour. In an interview Tom Browne, a favoured illustrator of boys' papers, recalled his job of 'looking for models'. He tells the story of meeting a 'negro, a chap who earned a living touring public houses chewing glass'. When Browne asked him to pose for a picture, the exchange provided an easy jibe at the credulity of the sitter:

> He looked at me earnestly for some moments, and then demanded; Will it come off? He thought, said Browne with a chuckle, that we wanted to cover him with paint![87]

The 'wonders' of modern life were also confusing to the 'primitive' mind. *Chums* ran many cartoons between 1898 and 1900 which took the encounter with new technology as a theme. One series showed the arrival of the cinema in a tribal village. The tribespeople believe it is 'real' and attack the screen. A picture of 'before' and 'after' illustrated the 'New Electric Battery Treatment: Selling in the 1000s'. Three Africans were pictured standing in amazement before the billboard. The caption explains:

> It has recently been stated that during electrical treatment for a nervous disorder, a negro's skin was changed from black to white. This fact will not be long lost sight of, and before long, we suppose, the natives of Central Africa will be 'shocked'.[88]

A new gramophone, 'The White Man's Surprise Trumpet', could reduce a family's servants to terror. These cartoons, although set in Africa, were expressing sentiments which were familiar from set pieces on the minstrel stage. A combination of superstition and childishness ensured that Africans consistently displayed an inappropriate set of reactions to the trappings of civilisation. This placed them firmly outside the realms of modern life, and again gave British youth the opportunity to feel a clear advantage over a people demonstrably unfamiliar with technological progress. Neither the Indian nor the Chinese offered the same possibilities, in juvenile papers, for such crudely drawn and slapstick humour, which drew upon the childlike innocence and ignorance attributed to Africa.[89]

Humour also played on the European conception of beauty, closely aligned to skin colour and Aryan features:

> 'Look here, Mose', said one coloured man to another, 'yessel de uglies man I eber seed'.
> 'Den I reckon yer neber seed my brudder, did yer?'
> 'No, was he uglier dan yer is?'
> 'Yes, dat man was so ugly dat he neber tuck no gun when he went huntin! He was so ugly dat he jess skeered 'em ter deff!'[90]

[111]

Cannibalism could also be seen as funny, as long as one was at a safe remove. The *Captain* in 1904 featured an illustration on 'How to Make a Christmas Plum Pudding' with an African cookery class. An English naturalist was the 'suet'. The *Public School Magazine* carried this rhyme as part of a soldier's memories of Africa:

> I was born at Timbuctoo
> Which is close to Killaloo
> And twas there I saw a nigger on the shore;
> For I cut his head in two,
> And I prodded him through and through,
> While he amused himself by cutting me in four.[91]

Hunters, explorers, and even missionaries were able to offer funny stories from their experiences in Africa. Many of these incidents could have interposed any 'ignorant' foreigner, but the frequency with which Africans appeared suggested that they were seen as particularly suited to the role. If a joke required that the subject was ugly, stupid, feckless, careless or gullible, the African was often chosen to play the part. The disdain felt for the African pretending to be otherwise could also find comic expression.

> King Umbo of Boomahland was a very fat monarch, and his stoutness was not much hidden by the bead necklaces, feathers, shells, and pink and blue lady's bathing costume which adorned his portly person. This was his court dress. A crown of emeralds, rubies, glass bottle stoppers, corks, false teeth, padlocks and Noah's Ark animals upon his head, and his face severe and stern.[92]

When one compares this description to the reverence accorded the British royals, the annuals' distancing of the African to the bottom end of the evolutionary spectrum becomes more apparent. Ridicule is a crude form of control, and its frequent appearance in these materials suggests both the arrogance and insecurity which shaped Britain's imperial mythologies. It was clear that adult Britain refused to take the African seriously, and the annuals encouraged the young to feel the same. Comedy as much as adventure was a staple of the juvenile market, and in this representation of 'blackness' rested many of the most enduring images of African people.[93]

Both textbooks and the juvenile popular press supported Britain's imperial role. That much is clear. What is also apparent is that their construction of the African helped to socialise the young into views which encouraged its continuation. The textbooks were concerned with those contacts – slavery, 'little wars', the extension of white settlement in Southern Africa – which were of most importance in validating the extension of Great Britain. By denying the African any significant 'past' outside the contact with Europe, this history also encouraged the view of a primitive, static people, a 'free field' for the colonist, the investor and any who wished to 'explore' this untapped continent. Africa was Britain's 'frontier'; and 'progressive' history viewed the movement into the wilderness as evidence of the industry and initiative of the white man. However, what British history also claimed was a moral imperative, and in the case of Africa this meant balancing expansive desires with the benevolence of the antislavery legacy. Any tension was resolved by casting the opponent as a helplessly doomed barbarian, an archaic throwback to the earlier stages of human society, brave and sometimes noble, but a necessary sacrifice to the march of civilisation.

These 'lessons' from history were accepted and elaborated in the annuals and papers of the juvenile press. They 'recycled' and enlivened episodes from Empire; battles were replayed against the Zulu, the Asante and the Matabele, pitting fierce 'savagery' against the heroics of the British military. Campaigns against 'slavers' throughout Africa and on the high seas provided both excitement and the moral high ground. Scenes from the Boer War completed the annuals' endorsement of imperial history, with action centred as in the texts on the European protagonists. The children's papers, like the textbooks, offered no information on the 'Dark Continent' before the era of imperial interest.

It was clear from the coverage of the periodicals that Africa was a topic of keen contemporary interest. With China closed to most Europeans, and Indian 'memories' mainly those of soldiers or civil servants, Africa seemed open to all – investors, hunters, missionaries, explorers, scientists, sports teams and even the occasional royal. It was the ideal setting for experience and adventure. The image of African people seemed to support these possibilities. They appeared willing converts to the efforts of muscular Christianity. They lent their skills to the hunter's dominance of the wild beast. They could conquer superstition to guide white people into uncharted territory. In Mary Kingsley's view, they were hospitable. These images suggested to the young reader that Africans did not mind sharing their continent with Europeans, and indeed recognised the benefits of their presence.

The economic realities of imperial appropriation were also eased by the image of the African as 'worker'. The criticisms directed to ex-slaves (resorting to a state of nature, improvident and lazy) were applied to the African at home. This could work to the advantage of those who wished to sell the Empire. Annuals suggested that

[113]

Africans had neither the initiative nor the desire to improve the land or to extract wealth below its surface. This justified their 'displacement', if not their coercion. Importation of Indian labour was one answer to leaving African people in their 'natural' state. However, when the papers showed the British employing Africans in the South African mines, they were careful to reassure the reader that these were happy and well fed workers, and that a paternalistic capitalism, while watchful, was providing for their needs. Maintaining the image of peoples as nomadic and without recognisable political or social structures, which was a common rationale for imperialist ambitions, both illustrated the problems of 'native labour', and also eased the assumption of British title to land and wealth.[94] The young reader was assured that men like Cecil Rhodes possessed both the talent for realising great imperial wealth and a social conscience. The portrait of the African touched by the economic arm of imperial life supported what the imperialist wanted the young to believe – the Empire brought benefits to all.

While Africa offered the setting for youth to experience the 'romance' of missionary and capitalist ventures, it also enabled the 'experts' to deliver their version of the continent. Here emerged the overt expression of scientific ideas which informed and underpinned the African characterisation. It was clearly the case that scientists collected 'specimens' of African peoples in the same way that they gathered the flora and fauna from all parts of Empire. Children's familiarity with social Darwinism was fed directly by the evidence from Africa of a people at the bottom of the evolutionary ladder. Again and again in the periodicals, the authors and contributors stressed the distance in the racial hierarchy between these 'creatures of nature', akin to beasts of the wild, and the readers' own Anglo-Saxon heritage. More than with any other subject peoples, the African's 'ranking' in the evolutionary scale was made explicit as a justification for Empire.[95]

Both skin colour and issues of evolutionary status had been deeply involved in the rationalisation for slavery. There was a long history of assessing African people as 'outside' the human condition, and while the abolition of slavery ended the right to maintain their subhuman status in law, racial theories which degraded their position did not lose their currency. When science added its weight, with evolutionary theory, the new anthropology, phrenology and ethnology, the African hardly seemed liberated by the European. For the imperial enthusiast, the case for dominance in the natural and social world had been made, and could be summoned through the testimony of those who lived and travelled in Africa.[96]

But youth needed to be persuaded of something else, for there was an undeniable attraction to the 'savage' life and its freedom from adulthood and responsibility. The African had also to convince the young that there was no future in the wild, without the guiding hand of the strong and wise imperial 'parent'. One might 'play at savages', but it could not be a permanent condition, just as childhood must give way to the realities of adult life. On the level of imperial message, this was an important part of allowing the young to 'enjoy' the wild, while clearly implying that it must also be dominated. As a vehicle of domestic socialisation, using the African to discredit savagery could encourage the stilling of juvenile rebellion and confirm the primacy of respectable middle-class values.

The 'colonisation' of African people in the juvenile press lent their service to pressing needs of Empire and nation. Behind the rhetoric of confident imperialism lay the reality of class discontent stirring at home. If all classes and interests could be seen rallying behind the imperial ethos, internal discontents could be submerged and Britain's social order left unchallenged. To an important degree, it was in relating to the African that all of Britain connected to the Empire. This helps to explain why publishers committed to imperial Britain saw in the African a figure who boosted both patriotism and profits. The juvenile periodicals made it clear that the easy-going, good-natured African persona welcomed the connection, and offered no objection to ridicule, either by Cookey Scrubbs or by schoolboys 'blacking up'. As in popular entertainments of the era, the minstrel show and the colonial exhibitions, the papers fashioned an image of the imperial relationship that could be enjoyed by even the humblest citizen, mediating the tensions of class division among whites with a 'consensus' fashioned from the imagery of racial dominance.[97] The images of the happy, singing darky, of the ventriloquist, the clown, the grave or sentimental 'brute', all were relics of the slave–master relationship transposed into aspects of popular culture. While public-school boys might dream of meeting Ranjit Singh, the vast majority of ordinary readers enjoyed the company of Pete. The proliferation of the African image through the popular press was proof that here rested the most successful vehicle for securing a consensus around race, hierarchy, and nationality.

In many ways, although India was the 'jewel', to be prized and guarded, Africa was the Empire to be enjoyed. It was the most satisfying of relations portrayed between coloniser and subject, without the fears of Mutiny and with the clear conscience of the 'liberator'. The African, whether at home or abroad, in fiction and non-fiction, appeared to bring unqualified support to the stereotyped image.

Britons, unable or unwilling to see behind the mask, believed that the smile told all.[98] With careful tutoring, in time, these children would grow up, but for the foreseeable future it would be the duty of white society to let them play, teach them religion, and prove by example the benefits of 'civilised' society. The youth of Britain learned that Africans were 'creatures' with a heart, an untutored soul, and with a consciousness rooted in the primitive past. Believing they had won their compliance, there was little hesitation in accepting images stripping them of their private or national integrity. Within the confines of the stereotypes which served imperial interests and entertained imperial children, the African became enslaved again.

Notes

1 'Shall I go out to the colonies?', *Young England*, vol. XXI, 1899, p. 42; see also 'The Queen at her Hindustani lessons', *Girl's School Magazine*, vol. 1, no. 236, 1 February, 1893, p. 30; W. M. Armstrong, 'HRH Princess Patricia of Connaught', *Girl's Own Annual*, vol. XXV, 1912, pp. 678–83; on a royal safari see J. M. MacKenzie, *The Empire of Nature*, Manchester, 1988, pp. 309–10.

2 'Under the Queen's flag', *Chums*, vol. VIII, no. 387, 2 February, 1900, p. 396; see also *Young England*, vol. XXXV, 1913–14, *Boy's Own Annual*, vol. XXXVII, 1914–15.

3 'Under the Queen's flag', p. 397.

4 'The fighting power of the negroes', *The Spectator*, 12 November, 1898, p. 680.

5 'A one ship navy', *Boy's Own Annual*, vol. XXXVI, 1913, pp. 554–5.

6 'The defence of Rorke's Drift', *Young England*, vol. XXI, 1899, pp. 360–1; 'Against shield and Assegai', *Chums*, vol. 1, no. 13, December, 1892, p. 198; 'Saving the colours: a romance of the Zulu War', *Pluck*, vol. 1, no. 6, p. 1; 'With spear and shell', *Pluck*, vol. 2, no. 6, p. 1; 'How Umslopogaas held the Stair', in *Longman's British Empire Readers*, 1905, p. 179, demonstrated how Haggard's archetypal Zulu bridged the two sets of materials; p. 179; for the image of the Zulu see A. Sandison, *The Wheel of Empire*, London, 1967, p. 31; B. Street, *The Savage in Literature*, London, 1975, p. 55; T. Jeal, *Baden-Powell*, London, 1989, p. 133.

7 The relief forces at Mafeking were brought copies of the *Boy's Own Paper*; P. Dunae, 'Boys' literature and the idea of Empire, 1870–1914', *Victorian Studies*, vol. 24, no. 1, autumn, 1980, pp. 114–16; J. Cox, *Take a Cold Tub, Sir*, Guildford, 1982, p. 60; *Chums*, vol. VIII, 1900, p. 540; 'Wanted to fight the Boers', *Chums*, vol. VIII, no. 379, 13 December, 1899, p. 389; 'Baden-Powell: hero of Mafeking', *Chums*, vol. VIII, no. 403, 23 May, 1900, p. 631; 'Lord Roberts' march to Pretoria', *Young England*, vol. XXXIV, 1912–13, pp. 468–70.

8 'Cecil Rhodes', *Chums*, vol. VIII, no. 363, 23 August, 1899, p. 11; 'Cecil Rhodes', *Chums*, vol. VIII, no. 373, 1 November, 1899, p. 165.

9 H. Shepstone, 'Railway building in Central Africa', *Boy's Own Annual*, vol. XXXVI, 1913–14, pp. 428–31.

10 'On a South African farm', *Young England*, vol. XXI, 1899, p. 342.

11 'Round about Cape Town', *Young England*, vol. XXI, 1899, p. 183; 'Shall I go out to the colonies?', p. 41; D. Ker, 'Crossing the Tugela', *Young England*, vol. XXI, 1899, p. 414; 'A quaint scene at the Cape', *Chums*, vol. VIII, no. 366, 13 September, 1899, p. 54.

12 'With the Corinthians in South Africa', *Public School Magazine*, vol. 1, no. 2, February, 1898, p. 146.

13 'The Kimberly diamond mines', *Girl's School Magazine*, vol. 2, no. 9, 1 September, 1893, p. 155.

14 'With the Corinthians in South Africa', p. 146.
15 'The making of the Witswatersrand', *Young England*, vol. XXXV, 1913–14, p. 19.
16 'Scene in the streets of Durban', *Chums*, vol. VIII, no. 384, 10 January, 1900, p. 323; see also 'Crossing the Tugela', p. 414; 'A Zulu post carrier', *Chums*, vol. XVI, no. 780, 21 August, 1907, p. 9.
17 J. A. Froude, *Oceana: or England and her Colonies*, London, 1886, p. 34; H. A. Cairns, *Prelude to Imperialism*, London, 1965, p. 84; T. Carlyle, 'Discourse upon the nigger question', in *Critical and Miscellaneous Essays*, London, 1905, pp. 370–83; R. Knox, *The Races of Man*, London, 1862, p. 222.
18 R. Lewis and Y. Foy, *The British in Africa*, London, 1971, p. 57–80; Cairns, *Prelude to Imperialism*, p. 151; D. Lorimer, *Colour, Class and the Victorians*, Leicester, 1978, p. 71; C. Bolt, *Victorian Attitudes to Race*, London, 1971; for muscular Christianity see J. A. Mangan, *Athleticism in the Victorian and Edwardian Public School*, London, 1981, pp. 38–41; H. B. Gray, *The Public Schools and the Empire*, London, 1913; G. Best, 'Militarism and the Victorian public school', in B. Simon and I. Bradley, *The Victorian Public School*, Dublin, 1975, pp. 129–45; E. J. Unwick, *Studies of Boy Life in our Cities*, London, 1904; for missionary accounts see *The Children's World and Church Missionary Instructor*, vol. 3, 1893.
19 'David Livingstone: missionary and explorer', *Young England*, vol. XXXIV, 1912–13, pp. 219–223, 263–66; J. C. Lambert, *The Romance of Missionary Heroism*, London, 1907, pp. 133–47; N. R. Bennet, 'David Livingstone: explorer for Christianity', in R. I. Rotberg, ed., *Africa and the Explorers*, Cambridge, 1970, pp. 41–61; Cairns, *Prelude to Imperialism*, p. 40; 'A Livingstone relic', *Young England*, vol. XXI, 1899, pp. 467–69; T. W. Wilkinson, 'Livingstone: the missionary hero of Darkest Africa', *Boy's Own Annual*, vol. XXXVI, 1913–14, p. 670; J. MacKenzie, *Propaganda and Empire*, Manchester, 1984, p. 215.
20 'A biography of Arthur Fraser Sim: athlete and missionary', *Young England*, vol. XXI, 1899, p. 64; for sport and Africa see R. Jenkins, 'Salvation for the fittest: a West African sportsman in the age of the new imperialism', in J. A. Mangan, ed., *The Cultural Bond*, London, 1992, pp. 47–83; see also A. Odendaal, 'South Africa's black Victorians: sport and society in South Africa in the nineteenth century', in J. A. Mangan, ed., *Pleasure, Profit, Proselytism*, London, 1988, pp. 193–214.
21 R. A. Hartsock, 'Children on the Congo', *Girl's Empire*, vol. 2, 1902, p. 442.
22 'Children on the Congo', pp. 441–2; also see V. Ware, *Beyond the Pale*, New York, 1992, chapter 3.
23 'A negrito wedding', *Girl's Empire*, vol. 3, 1903, p. 196; Street, *The Savage in Literature*, pp. 130–1; Bolt, *Victorian Attitudes to Race*, p. 121; Cairns, *Prelude to Imperialism*, p. 152; 'Athletic sports at Frere Town schools', in *Children's World and Church Missionary Instructor*, vol. 3, 1893, p. 61.
24 'Notable people with private museums: Mary Kingsley', *Chums*, vol. VIII, no. 372, 1899, p. 156.
25 *Ibid.*, p. 157; for women explorers see D. Birkett, *Spinsters Abroad*, London, 1986.
26 H. Ward, 'With savages and slavers', *Chums*, vol. 1, no. 33, 26 April, 1893, p. 532; see also H. Ward, 'Faradji, the slaver', *Chums*, vol. 1, no. 33, 4 April, 1893, pp. 498–99; H. Ward, 'Alaki', *Chums*, vol. 1, no. 46, pp. 658–9.
27 The middle-class annuals, *Chums* and *Boys' Own Annual*, in particular, encouraged these hobbies; see also M. Biddiss, ed., Count de Gobineau, *Selected Political Writings*, London, 1970 edn, pp. 134–76; M. F. Montagu, *The Concept of Race*, London, 1964, p. xv; C. Levi-Strauss, 'Race and history', in L. Kuper, ed., *Race, Science and Society*, London, Paris, 1956; J. Huxley and A. C. Hadden, *We Europeans*, London, 1935, p. 283; N. C. Macnamara, *The Origins and Character of the British People*, London, 1900, p. 212; M. Harris, *The Rise of Anthropological Theory*, London, 1968, p. 2.
28 'Faradji the Slaver: an adventure with African dwarfs', *Chums*, vol. I, no. 33, 4 April, 1893, pp. 498–9; 'Tagonda the charm doctor', *Chums*, vol. I, no. 48, p. 778; S. M. Frame, 'Funny faces from West Africa', 'Funny letters from West Africa', *Chums*, vol. XXVIII, 1905–6, pp. 108–9, 630–1; for contrasting treatment

see 'Chinese civilisation', *Chums*, vol. I, no. 12, 30 November, 1892, p. 351; 'A boy's visit to Kashmir', *Boy's Own Annual*, vol. XXVIII, 1905–6, pp. 28–9.

29 A. Coombes, *Reinventing Africa*, New Haven, 1994; see also B. Shepherd, 'Showbiz imperialism', in J. Mackenzie, ed., *Imperialism and Popular Culture*, Manchester, 1986.

30 'Notable men with private museums: F. C. Selous', *Chums*, vol. VIII, no. 364, 30 August, 1900, p. 28; for Selous see J. MacKenzie, *The Empire of Nature*, Manchester, 1988, pp. 38–9; K. Tidrick, *Empire and the English Character*, London, 1990, pp. 48–87.

31 'An elephant hunt worth watching', *Young England*, vol. XXXV, 1912–13, p. 402; G. Page 'Through the mealies after wild pig', *Boy's Own Annual*, vol. XXIX, 1906–7, p. 601; 'A sportsman's paradise', *Young England*, vol. XXI, 1899, p. 384; 'Lassooing a lioness', *Young England*, vol. XXXIV, 1912–13, p. 404; see also J. MacKenzie, 'The imperial pioneer and hunter and the British masculine stereotype in late Victorian and Edwardian times', in J. Mangan and J. Walvin, eds, *Masculinity and Morality*, Manchester, 1987, pp. 176–98.

32 R. Baden-Powell, 'The Boy Scout', *Boys of the Empire*, vol. 1, no. 3, 10 November, 1900, p. 57; 'A terrible adventure with hyenas', *Boy's Own Annual*, vol. XXVIII, 1905–6, p. 27; ' A narrow escape from a lioness', *Boy's Own Annual*, vol. XXIX, 1906–7, p. 555; F. C. Selous, *Sunshine and Storm in Rhodesia*, London, 1896, p. 31.

33 C. Ken, 'Something about savages', *Boy's Own Annual,*, vol. XXVIII, 1905–6, pp. 28–9.

34 E. J. Unwick, *Studies of Boy Life in our Cities*, p. xiii.

35 'Something about savages', p. 28.

36 J. H. Whitehouse, *Problems of Boy Life*, London, 1912, chapter VI; H. Cunningham, *The Children of the Poor*, Oxford, 1991, pp. 123–32.

37 B. Kidd, *The Control of the Tropics*, London, 1898, p. 53; F. Mannsaker, 'The dog that didn't bark', in D. Dabydeen, ed., *The Black Presence in British Literature*, Manchester, 1985, pp. 118–20; Bolt, *Victorian Attitudes to Race*, p. 211.

38 Sir H. Johnston, *The Backward Peoples and our Relations with Them*, London, 1920, pp. 8–9; J. Haller, *Outcasts from Evolution*, New York, 1971, p. 138.

39 J. Barlow, 'The aunt of the savages', *Girls' Realm*, vol. 1, no. 1, 1898–99, p. 254; 'Something about savages', p. 254; L. James, 'Tom Brown's imperial sons', *Victorian Studies*, vol. 18, 1973, September, p. 98.

40 *Boy's Own Annual*, vol. XXIX, 1906–7, portrayed British boys as primitives in a series entitled 'Good Ole Times'; 'Mills of the lion patrol', *Chums*, vol. XIX, no. 970, 12 April, 1911, p. 577; no. 961 of the same year ran a serial on 'Cave dwellers who ran away from school to live in the woods'.

41 F. Miller, 'Our charades', *Girl's Own Annual*, vol. XII, no. 571, 12 December, 1890, p. 151.

42 M. Pemberton, *Sixty Years Ago and After*, London, 1936, p. 162.

43 'How we blacked up', *Captain*, vol. 1, no. 1, 1898, p. 166; see also C. Bolt, 'Race and the Victorians', in C. Eldridge, ed., *British Imperialism in the 19th Century*, London, 1985, p. 132–3; J. Mackenzie, *Propaganda and Empire*, Manchester, 1984, p. 39–67; R. Toll, *Blacking Up*, London, 1974, p. 226; M. Pickering, 'Mock blacks and racial mockery: the "nigger" minstrel and British imperialism', in J. S. Bratton, et al., eds, *Acts of Supremacy*, Manchester, 1991, pp. 179–236; J. Pieterse, *White on Black*, London, 1995, pp. 132–51.

44 S. Wishing, 'Our Christy Minstrel show', *Captain*, vol. XII, 1905, p. 511; F. Richards, 'Fun by the sea', *Magnet*, vol. 1, no. 22, 7 July, 1908, p. 3; P. G. Wodehouse, 'The head of Kays', *Captain*, vol. XXI, 1905, p. 4; H. B. North, 'Jerry Dodds, millionaire', *Chums*, vol. VIII, no. 403, 30 May, 1900, p. 642.

45 'The deep game Inky played', *Chums*, vol. XV, no. 744, 12 December, 1906, pp. 348–9.

46 See K. Castle, *American Minstrelsy 1879–90*, unpublished MA thesis, University College, London, 1978.

47 'Our Christy Minstrel show', p. 510; A. Daniels, 'The banshee banjo', *Chums*, vol. XVI, no. 807, 26 February, 1908, p. 576.
48 The minstrel song sheets of the era contained many examples of the physical stereotypes associated with the 'happy' minstrel; see the Harding Collection of American Sheet Music, The Bodleian Library, Oxford.
49 M. Merriman, 'The new chum or the three British boys and sambo', *Pluck*, vol. 2, no. 27, 1905, p. 3; for the 'Sambo' figure see J. Boskin, *Sambo: The Rise and Demise of an American Jester*, Oxford, 1986; Pieterse, *White on Black*, pp. 152–6.
50 M. Merriman, 'Chums of Waverly', *Pluck*, vol. 3, no. 59, 1905, p. 29.
51 A. R. Hope, 'Red ram', *Captain*, vol. 1, no. 1, 1898, p. 52.
52 M. St John, 'Pollie Green and Coosha', *Girl's Friend,*, vol. VII, 1908.
53 M. Cadogan and P. Craig, *You're a Brick Angela*, London, 1976, pp. 132–7.
54 See P. Fryer, *Staying Power*, London, 1984; see also the rare reference to black workers in 'Stories of pluck and adventure in the coal mines', *Boy's Own Annual*, vol. XXXIII, 1909–10, pp. 103–6.
55 'Temple, Squeaker and Co', *Chums*, vol. XIX, no. 940, 2 November, 1910, p. 154.
56 *Ibid.*, pp. 154–6; see also S. Smiles, 'The ringmaster's daughter', *Marvel*, vol. XV, no. 383, 1900, p. 2.
57 B. Street, 'Reading the novels of Empire', in D. Dabydeen, ed., *The Black Presence in British Literature*, Manchester, 1985, pp. 95–111.
58 E. S. Turner, *Boys will be Boys*, London, 1948, p. 107.
59 The *Gem*, vol. 1, March–September, 1907, advertised the 'famous trio' on its frontispiece; D. Lorimer, 'Bibles, banjoes and bones: images of the negro in the popular culture of Victorian England', in B. Gough, ed., *In Search of the Visible Past*, London, 1975, pp. 31–50; C. Witte, *Tambo and Bones*, Westport, 1971.
60 S. C. Hooke, 'The eagle of death', *Marvel*, vol. XV, no. 385, 3 March, 1901, p. 3; S. C. Hooke, 'The death sentence', *Marvel*, vol. XV, no. 387, 4 April, 1907, p. 3.
61 'The eagle of death', p. 5; 'The death sentence', p. 4.
62 S. C. Hooke, 'The black horseman', *Marvel*, vol. XV, no. 389, 18 April, 1901, p. 7.
63 'The black horseman', p. 9.
64 *Pluck*, vol. 2, no. 39, 1904, carried a picture of Pete under the caption 'A pressing engagement' – balanced on top of him was a piano loaded with black minstrels; *Pluck*, vol. 2, the endpiece, 1904, described Pete as the 'jolliest of chums'; Lorimer, *Colour, Class and the Victorians*, p. 89–90, Toll, *Blacking Up*, p. 256, L. Levine, *Black Culture and Black Consciousness*, New York, 1977, p. 194.
65 'In the power of the Pygmies', *Boy's Own Annual*, vol. XXXVII, 1914, p. 396.
66 S. P. Hyatt, 'Bushman's Reef', *Boy's Own Annual*, vol. XXXVII, 1914–15, pp. 162–3.
67 'In the power of the Pygmies', p. 396; see also 'Red Assegai', *Chums*, vol. XIX, no. 961, 8 February, 1911, p. 400; 'The flying death', *Chums*, vol. XIX, no. 951, 30 November, 1910, p. 226; and 'The treasure cave adventure', *Chums*, vol. XIX, no. 953, 14 November, 1910, pp. 258–9.
68 'Mataka's hoard', *Chums*, vol. XIX, no. 944, 10 December, 1910, p. 100.
69 *Ibid.*, p. 101; see also 'In the jaws of the lion', *Young England*, vol. XXXIV, 1912–13, pp. 229–30; 'Red Assegai', p. 401; 'A Livingstone relic', p. 469; T. W. Wilkinson, 'Livingstone: the missionary hero of Darkest Africa', *Boy's Own Annual*, vol. XXXVI, 1913–14, p. 670; 'In the power of the Pygmies', p. 152.
70 'Mataka's hoard', p. 101; see also H. N. Fairchild, *The Noble Savage*, New York, 1961, p. 2; H. Baudet, *Paradise on Earth*, New Haven, 1965, pp. 10–11.
71 'In the power of the Pygmies', p. 78; on 'testing oneself' in the wild see MacKenzie, 'The imperial pioneer and hunter and the British masculine stereotype in late Victorian and Edwardian times', pp. 176–98.
72 *Ibid.*, p. 4.
73 'Steady, brave and true', *Boy's Comic Journal*, vol. XXIX, no. 728, 20 February, 1897, p. 107.

74 *Ibid.*, p. 122.
75 'The savage chief', *Boy's Comic Journal*, vol. XXX, no. 774, 8 January, 1898, p. 4; see also A. Grahame, 'The chiefs of the black spear', *Pluck*, vol. 2, no. 48, 1895, p. 15; 'The cunning of the Boer', *Young England*, vol. XXI, 1899, p. 169.
76 'The quest of the veiled king', *Chums*, vol. XIX, no. 970, 12 April, 1911, p. 570; the 'Singleton' figure was in the 'aggressively English' mould of Jack Harkaway – see Turner, *Boys will be Boys*, pp. 78–92; James, 'Tom Brown's imperialist sons', pp. 93–9.
77 Dunae, 'Boys' literature and the idea of Empire', pp. 111–12; R. Rollington, *The Old Boys' Book*, Leicester, 1913, p. 107; M. F. Thwaite, *From Primer to Pleasure*, London, 1963, pp. 228–9; Turner, *Boys will be Boys*, p. 92; 'The quest of the veiled king', p. 112.
78 'In the power of the Pygmies', p. 152.
79 'A daring enterprise', *Boy's Own Annual*, vol. XXIX, 1906–7, p. 458.
80 'A daring enterprise', p. 458; 'Seeking the witch doctor's juju', *Chums*, vol. VIII, no. 384, 17 January, 1900, p. 348; 'The witchdoctor's revenge', *Boy's Own Annual*, vol. XXXVI, 1913, pp. 66–8; 'The little god with moving eyes', *Boy's Own Annual*, vol. XXXVI, 1913, p. 152–5.
81 'A daring enterprise', p. 470; 'The chiefs of the black spear', p. 4; 'Caught by Congo headhunters', *Chums*, vol. XV, no. 728, p. 24; 'Red Assegai', p. 402.
82 'The phantom pilot', *Marvel*, vol. XV, no. 381, 21 February, 1901, p. 9; 'The white slaves', *Pluck*, vol. X, no. 252, 1899, p. 6; 'The crocodile worshippers', *Young England*, vol. XXXIV, 1912–13, pp. 116–18; H. R. Haggard, *She: A History of Adventure*, London, 1887; Turner, *Boys will be Boys*, p. 112–13.
83 On the 'sexuality' of 'She' see J. Bristow, *Empire Boys*, London, 1993, pp. 128–40; see also Ware, *Beyond the Pale*, pp. 37–9; Coombes, *Reinventing Africa*, p. 93; L. Bland, 'Sinning on a tiger skin or keeping the beast at bay', in J. Beckett and D. Cherry, eds, *The Edwardian Era*, London, 1987, pp. 88–99.
84 H. Belbin, 'Three men in a canoe', *Pluck*, vol. 1, no. 9, 1904, p. 15.
85 *Ibid.*, p. 18.
86 Working-class heroes appeared in the story papers, *Pluck*, *Marvel*, *Gem*, and *Magnet*, as central characters; 'Poor but plucky', *Pluck*, vol. X, no. 241, 1899, p. 1; 'Dennis Doyle: bookstall boy', *Pluck*, vol. IX, no. 238, 1899, p. 2; in the 'respectable' papers, like *Chums*, they were the accomplices of middle-class heroes.
87 'An interview with Tom Browne, illustrator', *Captain*, vol. 1, 1898, p. 231.
88 'A study in black and white', *Chums*, vol. VIII, no. 364, 30 August, 1908, p. 31; see also *Chums*, vol. VIII, no. 402, 23 May, 1900, pp. 636–7.
89 *Boy's Own Annual*, vol. XXXII, 1909, p. 245; 'A funny story', *Girls of the Empire*, vol. III, 1903–4, p. 200.
90 'Fun section', *Boy's Comic Journal*, vol. XXXIX, no. 729, p. 208; see also *Captain*, vol. 1, 1898, p. 367, for winners of a joke competition, 'What is the best place to cremate an African? Blackburn.'
91 'My experiences in the British Army', *Public School Magazine*, vol. 1, 1898, p. 30; 'An ingredient', *Captain*, vol. VIII, 1904–5, p. 13.
92 'Three men in a canoe', p. 20; see also 'Jumping to a conclusion', *Chums*, vol. 1, 1892, p. 387; 'It was Sambo!', *Captain*, vol. XII, 1904–5, p. 13; 'No use', *Boy's Own Annual*, vol. XXXVI, 1913–14, p. 128; for comparable comic representations see 'Chinese laundryman', *Boy's Comic Journal*, vol. XXVII, no. 721, p. 208; *Boys of the Empire*, vol. 1, no. 1, p. 41; 'Some comic reminiscences of the morse telegraph in India', *Boy's Own Annual*, vol. XXIX, 1906–7, p. 186.
93 See Pieterse, *White on Black*, pp. 132–51.
94 For image of nomadic people see Cairns, *Prelude to Imperialism*, pp. 39, 165; V. G. Kiernan, *The Lords of Human Kind*, London, 1969, pp. 203–4.
95 For the importance of scientific ranking see P. Curtin, *The Image of Africa*, London, 1971, pp. 36–48, 363–84; Lorimer, *Colour, Class and the Victorians*, p. 207.
96 See J. Richards 'With Henty to Africa', in J. Richards, *Imperialism and Juvenile Literature*, Manchester, 1989, pp. 72–106.

97 Even Bunter went out to Africa; Turner, *Boys will be Boys*, p. 208; for links between class and Africa see Cairns, *Prelude to Imperialism*, pp. 92–3; Lorimer, *Colour, Class and the Victorians*; R. N. Price, *The Imperial War and the British Working Class*, London, 1972, chapter 2.
98 See Paul Dunbar poem 'We wear the mask', 'We smile but O great Christ our cries, To thee from tortured souls arise', 1909, in A. Chapman, ed., *Black Voices*, New York, 1968, p. 355.

CHAPTER FIVE

The sleeping giant: China in history textbooks

History textbooks which appeared in the classrooms of this era offered the Chinese only the most restricted of places. Themes which dominated the presentation of British and imperial history – the growth of liberal democracy and the expansion of overseas power in the eighteenth and nineteenth centuries – touched the Chinese more lightly than the other groups in this study. The best example for the export of British institutions and the extension of power in the wider world was deemed to be India, which dominated the interest expressed in the historical interaction with 'foreign peoples'. Those texts which displayed a strong emphasis on the military advance of British fortunes, irrespective of geographical context, preferred to concentrate on Indian or African expeditions to the exclusion of encounters in China.

Apart from China's lack of appropriateness for illustrating the 'lessons' of imperial history, its absence from the history textbooks also rests upon other assumptions current in Western society. Like India and Africa, China's past did not conform to the European experience:

We have before us the oldest state and yet no past, but a state which exists today as we know it to have been in ancient times. To that extent China has no history.[1]

Chinese history became, in this extract, in itself a kind of mysterious riddle, a state that is old but has no past, a country which passes through time without change. Of course what was meant by these comments was that China did not have a history on the European model, and that its 'static' and 'conservative' nature could not be accommodated within the dynamic and linear development of modern societies. This idea, compounded by the image of China as a 'closed' community, impenetrable to Western eyes, helped to rationalise the exclusion of China from 'useful' study for the rising generation.[2]

Neither did the official relationship between the two countries help to encourage the notion of 'benefit' from a familiarity with Sino-British relations. As China was not expected to become an important area for permanent white settlement or extensive British control, a new generation of potential civil servants or administrators need not be alerted to the duties and responsibilities, nor settlers to the development potential, which China represented. The future of British economic interests, despite an established presence in the treaty ports, remained uncertain. With control effectively limited to Hong Kong and a few cities, China offered less of an opportunity for textbook historians than was the case with Africa and India to link economic penetration with the introduction of progressive reforms, or the expansion of British institutions. The use of imperial history in the training of 'good citizens', who would use their votes, and their wages, to support imperial issues and products, required better examples of British sacrifice and heroics than China could offer. Without a stronger connection to the 'case' for imperial pride and allegiance, and taking their lead from both the academic and the public view that China was essentially 'unknowable', textbooks suggested much the same to the student of history.

Those aspects of the historical relationship with China which did gain admittance to the textbooks, however, were closely linked with the growth of imperial trade. No significant mention of the Chinese occurred before British involvement in the Opium War of 1839–42, and all subsequent references related to the Western ambition of maintaining an 'open door' to the riches of the East. China represented a kind of halfway house between the British commitment to 'free trade' and the desire to control its lucrative sources. That there was a wider European dimension to the unfolding of events in China was passed over lightly, and often contained within a generalised notion of the difficulties posed by Chinese hostility to any 'external influences'. Conflict of interests here as elsewhere in Empire centred not on the notion of a European scramble, but rather on the entrenched resistance of the local power. Those events which were chosen to represent a 'history' with China, the Opium War, the *Arrow* incident, a second Chinese War, 1856–60, and the Boxer Rebellion, focused upon the difficulties which emerged from the reluctance of China to negotiate a 'fair field' for British interests.[3]

> Everything is covered by a veil ... a glimpse just sufficient to set the imagination at work and more likely to mislead than inform.[4]

This quotation from Thomas Macauley expresses well the message of the textbook historians. Despite the difficulties in interpreting China's past, some historians did feel the necessity to comment at least on the undeniable evidence of Chinese civilisation. J. F. Bright characteristically devoted more space to events in China than his contemporaries, and speculated upon the nature of its relations with the outside world. Public-school classes learned from his *History of England* that China was a 'great civilised nation', but one with a 'self-asserting' character, which included an 'extreme dislike of the Chinese to deal with foreign nations upon terms of equality'.[5] The sentiments of Bright's rather restrained prose were echoed throughout the texts, although other historians took greater exception to the 'high-handed' attitudes of Chinese officials:

China boasted of possibly the oldest civilisation in the world, and looked with contempt on the mushroom growth of Europeans.[6]

The Heroic Reader, for younger pupils, put it more simply, informing the reader that 'the Chinese hate the English as they hate all foreigners'.[7]

The texts clearly were of the opinion that these attitudes were not acceptable in the modern world, and particularly not when held toward Europeans, whose own 'self-asserting' character demanded a reasonable response. Even Bright, who noted Britain's 'self-complacent assertion of authority' in the region, questioned whether China really had the right 'to deprive itself and the world of the advantages of commercial intercourse'. Against the vigour and enterprise of the West, and after its defeat at the hands of Japan in 1894, China was adjudged by 1900 to be 'in decline', and exhibiting the 'decadence of a venerable but worn out civilisation'. Age was no match for the energy of the British nation, and like other great empires which had refused to adapt to change or emerge from their protective but stultifying isolation, China would have either to 'wake up' or to succumb to its torpor.[8]

Behind the 'arrogance' in China's attitude toward the European was seen to lie a decadent and corrupt society. How could one possibly pursue peaceful diplomacy with a nation which issued an edict 'stigmatising the English as dogs and sheep'? The tone of the texts reflected the affront felt by the English at the temerity of a nation who cast them as the 'barbarians'. A firm hand was felt necessary in dealings with China, as Innes explained in 1907:

> The conduct of the British was undoubtedly high handed, but it was held that if a less arbitrary attitude had been adopted toward such a power as China, the oriental mind would have supposed it due not to magnanimity or to justice, but to weakness....[9]

Firm diplomacy may have been in order, but the tone of this passage suggests that there were some of the same fears surfacing here which had informed British attitudes toward India. Rather than discussing the differential interests which might have come into play in negotiating spheres of influence abroad, the debate centres upon questions of difference in national character. The dangers of misreading the 'oriental' frame of mind had been well demonstrated in the errors of Clive and Hastings, and the need for force to defend British interests amply argued in the Indian Mutiny. The accepted 'duplicity' of the oriental was seen to make negotiations an untrustworthy medium for resolving disputes, particularly with a country so overtly hostile to the West.

When this view was coupled with the position that China must not be allowed to fetter the development of international trade, the approach of historians to events follows a predictable pattern. In the treatment of the first of the Opium Wars the textbooks provided little background to the conflict. There was a clear reluctance to associate the East India Company by name with the British defence of 'merchant' interests in the opium trade, showing the same unease that historians had expressed about associating the 'venal' and the 'higher' motives in British India. Additionally, having defended the right of the British to open China to commercial interests, it was demonstrably difficult to square this 'principle' with the acknowledgement that it was traffic in opium at issue. By the 1830s opium addiction was a serious problem in China, and attitudes toward the trading links with India (tea for opium) were hardening on the part of both court and followers. British history textbooks could hardly admit the key role played by the East India Company in the spread of drug addiction in China, even if they tacitly accepted widespread addiction as a price worth paying for the maintenance of the tea and silk trade.[10]

The more truculent of historians, such as Oman and Curtis, invited the student to add the Opium Wars in China to a list of 'the little wars in the East', a feature of Queen Victoria's long reign. Some, however, betrayed a sense of 'bad conscience' in the British camp, either by direct criticism or suggestive ambiguity. Bright devoted five pages to the first war, and did accept a number of errors on the part of the British, including those of British custom officials charged with overseeing the Chinese trade. He offered the view that opium was 'a questionable source of wealth for the British', and that reactions to the Chinese attempts to curtail it can 'scarcely be defended even by the plea of British interests'. Osmond Airy in 1893 told the student little of the origins of the conflict, but did state that 'we were completely in the wrong'. A number of writers throughout the period noted that the 'public conscience' of the British had been pricked over 'the attempt to force Indian opium on the Chinese'. There was a degree of sympathy for the Chinese in their decision to resist importation of the 'noxious drug'.[11]

Even among those historians who confined their observations to the 'absent-minded' school ('we found ourselves at war with China in 1840'), or an occasional ancillary remark ('While great events were happening in India we also fought a war with China'), there was little attempt to defend the opium traffic. Silence was perhaps thought better on such a controversial aspect of imperial ambitions. Those who broke the silence to condemn the trade were careful not to cast the English as total villains. China was universally held responsible for the inability to solve the crisis peaceably. The rights of commerce and private property, it seemed, needed to be upheld even when the cargo in question had such damaging human consequences. It is interesting to note the boundaries of the era's conscience. While the texts roundly condemned the enslavement of the African and waived any notion of property rights in human cargo, there was a reluctance to give up notions of commercial exchange and just compensation in the context of concern for the Chinese opium addict. The seizure of 20,000 chests of opium from ships in the harbour at Canton, according to both Bright and Hassall, placed the responsibility for a British response at the feet of the Chinese mandarins, who had inflicted treatment 'to which the representatives of a great power could scarcely submit'. Not only were the Chinese actions deemed illegal, but the 'insulting language and high handed conduct of their officials' was clearly inimical to reasonable dialogue between the parties concerned.[12]

These unresolved issues led to further conflict at the end of the 1850s, again emerging from a Chinese 'violation' of British trading rights. The capture of a British ship, the *Arrow*, was commonly seen as the precipitating incident. In this case there were few historians who agreed with Hassall that the Chinese were 'acting within their rights', either in seizing the ship or in refusing to apologise. More common was the response of Pringle, Warner and Marten, who referred to Chinese actions as 'an insult to the British flag', and offered this illegal and unilateral Chinese position as sufficient cause for the war which ensued. Here prestige was overtly at stake in the resort to armed response, and textbooks reminded the student that weakness could not be allowed at a time when mutiny threatened British India.[13]

Historians writing for the schoolchild seemed in clear agreement about the lesson to be learned from the two 'little wars'. Even Bright, who can usually be found to have reservations over British actions, could not avoid the following conclusion:

> If the moral question involved in the origin of the war is left out of sight, there is no doubt that its results were very advantageous.[14]

While none of the texts went into detail on the acquisition of treaty ports, or the cession of Hong Kong, all alerted students to the fact that war had produced the 'opening up of ports' to British trade.

The inference was that these developments were mutually beneficial, and none challenged Carter's note of the 'desirable increase of British influence in China'. The value of Hong Kong, noted as a critical factor in Britain's maintenance of a global trade presence, was celebrated unequivocally and served to diminish uncertainties about the means of its arrival in British hands.[15]

Textbooks which were published after the turn of the century might also include the 'Boxer Rebellion'. Again, little information was provided to the student which allowed him or her to comprehend the 'uprising' against foreigners in China, nor the links between internal conflicts and relations with Europe. The 'contempt and hatred of foreign influence' was again seen to be enough of an explanation for the prevention of peaceable relations between China and the West. The questions of European rivalry over China, and the interest of the United States, were avoided by most textbook writers, and those who, like Meiklejohn, suggested a 'scramble' for spoils in the area, nonetheless placed the blame for violence on the 'Boxers' – 'a sect of fanatics who rose in arms'. Exaggeration, compression and emotive language all contributed to an unsympathetic view of China during this period. Warner and Marten observed of the 'Boxers' little beyond their wish for 'all white men to be exterminated', similar phrasing to that employed in descriptions of Indian 'Thugs'. Buckley, writing for juniors, expressed a shared view of that 'determined and scheming woman', the Empress Dowager:

> She tried to drive Europeans out of China. Therefore she secretly encouraged a large body of rebels called 'Boxers', and a massacre of Europeans, chiefly missionaries, took place.[16]

The textbooks suggested that this 'irrational' purge of Westerners seemed to offer the European no alternative but to intervene and ensure protection of British lives and property.

Apart from brief references to the 'Opium Wars' and the Boxer Rebellion, historians did little more than suggest to the student that problems over trade had occurred in the past, Britain had achieved a foothold in Hong Kong, and that hostility toward foreign influence remained a reality. It was acknowledged by most that the 'China question' remained to be finally settled. There was an uncertainty expressed about developments in the East, based upon the unpredictable consequences of a 'rising' Japan and an 'awakening' China. The balance of power in global terms and the impact on British interests in India of these developments clearly produced some anxiety about the future. These uncertainties were countered, however, by the textbooks' unequivocal commitment to the use of British power for the maintenance of an 'open door' to China. Here, influence and profits might be maximised without the highly problematic division of spoils between competing imperial powers. Much depended as well on the future course of relations with Japan. History texts compared Japan favourably with its Eastern neighbour, not least because Westernisation, at least in the economic sense, was welcomed. Japanese influence was viewed as a useful counterbalance to the 'regressive' regimes in China and Russia, while at the same time causing some concern in its example to nationalist elements in India. That a 'new empire' might rise in the East to challenge the European was a distinct possibility (Japan would confirm this in a matter of decades). Historians suggested to the student that history would be made in the East, and Britain's self-interest would be closely involved with the course of events. Having already staked its claim in the nineteenth century, students were assured that Britain had done all it reasonably could to protect its interests in the area.[17]

Searching history textbooks written before the First World War shows interesting variations in the amount of space accorded to areas of imperial interest. In terms of pages and paragraphs alone, it is apparent that China came nowhere near the coverage of British India and was significantly less than that for Africa. The reasons for this have already been suggested, in attitudes toward the Chinese 'past' and the relatively minor consideration of China in a military, diplomatic or imperial context. That there was concern to inform the student of British economic interests in the area was clear, and maps of the treaty ports illustrated the significance of influence gained in the nineteenth century. Examination questions seldom called upon the student to display a knowledge of the 'opening' of China, a popular topic for India and Africa, and this may well be due to the less than heroic role played by opium in the acquisition of British influence. Lessons on the export of British institutions abroad were better served by British India, and for the military angle 'little wars' in Africa might suffice. These could be discussed without any troubling reference to drug trafficking or the long-standing hostility of a nation unwilling to accept the advance of European influence.[18]

History lessons did not offer much information on China, and rather confirmed its 'mystery'. There was a consistent view, however, across the period and among most historians, on certain aspects of China past and present. Characteristics of Chinese society were suggested even in the rationale for not providing more information – that is, the closed, static, and non-progressive nature of the country, its public and private institutions. This image of a people and society immobilised and unchanging suggested a rigidity and inflexibility damaging to China's own and the international community's self-interests. There was an assumption made in the history textbooks that non-alignment with the progressive outlook of modern states was in itself an unsustainable position and subject to challenge.[19]

China's hostility to foreigners was seen as emerging from its 'mistaken' adherence to insularity and the unfortunate impact of conservative leadership, and to have no relationship with its history of encounters with external agents. It was also clear that China did not meet the European definition of 'reasonable behaviour', either in its official diplomacy or in its resort to violence against outsiders and their property. Irrespective of 'mistakes' which might have been made over the opium trade, it was the arrogance of Chinese leaders which Britain, as a 'great power', could not ignore, and which inevitably led to clashes. China's reluctance to disrupt the internal order of its own society through the acceptance of the British doctrine of 'free trade' was a complex and perhaps difficult concept for young Britons to appreciate, having learned of the 'civilising' benefits of commercial exchange elsewhere.

The irony, of course, was that Britain could not accept China behaving as an imperial power. It was a grave concern that the Chinese refused, on occasion, to take the English as seriously as they would wish, and accord them the respect due to a 'great nation'. Refusal by the Chinese to accept British values was explained as the prejudice of the 'oriental mind', mired in its complexity and formalised into a ritual of self-protective policies. China's reluctance to enter the imperial orbit, either by persuasion or by force, left little option for the textbook historian. References were kept to a minimum, but within these few, telling, descriptions of the Chinese, the stereotypical image of China became fixed and familiar – a country rich and desirable for its wealth, strongly suspicious and hostile to outsiders, and needing a watchful eye as it emerged from its centuries of slumber.[20]

Notes

1 G. W. F. Hegel, quoted in R. S. Dawson, *The Chinese Chameleon*, London, 1967, p. 66.
2 Dawson, *The Chinese Chameleon*, chapter 4; V. G. Kiernan, *The Lords of Human Kind*, London, 1969, p. 159; A. H. Smith, *Chinese Characteristics*, London, 1906, p. 43; J. Ch'en, *China and the West*, London, 1979, p. 40; J. Haller, *Outcasts from Evolution*, New York, 1975, p. 138; E. Said, *Orientalism*, London, 1991, pp. 108–10.

3 See also F. Glendenning, 'School history textbooks and racial attitudes', *Journal of Educational Administration and History*, vol. 5, 1973, pp. 38–9.
4 T. Macauley, quoted in F. Glendenning, *The Evolution of History Teaching in British and French Schools in the 19th and 20th Century, with Special Reference to Attitudes to Race and Colonialism in History Textbooks*, unpublished PhD thesis, University of Keele, 1975, p. 162.
5 J. F. Bright, *A History of England for Public Schools*, London, 1887–1904, p. 1176, also pp. 189–91, 369, 223–4.
6 G. Warner and C. H. K. Marten, *Groundwork of British History*, London, 1912, p. 681.
7 *The Heroic Reader*, Book 2, London, 1897, p. 43; for 'hatred of foreigners' see Kiernan, *The Lords of Human Kind*, pp. 171–7; Ch'en, *China and the West*, pp. 58–63; Smith, *Chinese Characteristics*, pp. 260–5.
8 Bright, *A History of England for Public Schools*, pp. 71, 224; see also R. York-Powell and T. Tout, *History of England*, London, 1900, p. 957.
9 A. Innes, *History of England*, London, 1907, p. 482; see also Bright, *A History of England for Public Schools*, p. 74, 224; P. Barr, *Foreign Devils*, London, 1970, p. 121.
10 C. Oman, *History of England*, London, 1895, p. 693; J. C. Curtis, *Outlines of English History*, London, 1901, p. 65; Bright, *A History of England for Public Schools*, p. 71; M. Rolleston, *An English History Notebook*, London, 1902, p. 282; J. R. Green, *A Short History of the English People*, London, 1894, p. 1838; A. Hassall, *A Classbook of English History*, London, 1901, p. 546; G. Carter, *History of England*, London, 1899, p. 200; A. Buckley, *History of England for Beginners*, London, 1904, p. 352.
11 Oman, *History of England*, p. 693; Curtis, *Outlines of English History*, p. 65; Bright, *A History of England for Public Schools*, p. 72; O. Airy, *Textbook of English History*, London, 1893, p. 499; Hassall, *A Classbook of English History*, p. 546; Innes, *History of England*, p. 482; on Opium Wars see Kiernan, *The Lords of Human Kind*, pp. 158–60.
12 Bright, *A History of England for Public Schools*, p. 72; Hassall, *A Classbook of English History*, p. 546 ; see also Carter, *History of England*, p. 215; Innes, *History of England*, p. 482; York-Powell and Tout, *History of England*, p. 918; Oman, *History of England*, p. 222; Curtis, *Outlines of English History*, p. 67.
13 Hassall, *A Classbook of English History*, p. 557; R. Rait, *A School History of England*, Oxford, 1911, p. 91; R. S. Pringle, *Local Examination History*, London, 1907, p. 135; Warner and Marten, *Groundwork of British History*, p. 683; H. Ince and J. Gilbert, *Outlines of English History*, London, 1906, p. 127.
14 Bright, *A History of England for Public Schools*, p. 76.
15 Pringle, *Local Examination History*, p. 135; Carter, *History of England*, p. 215; Curtis, *Outlines of English History*, p. 66; Oman, *History of England*, p. 222; J. Meiklejohn and M. J. C. Meiklejohn, *A School History of England*, London, 1901, p. 455.
16 Buckley, *History of England for Beginners*, p. 354; see also Meiklejohn, *A School History of England*, p. 456; Warner and Marten, *Groundwork of British History*, p. 683; Rait, *A School History of England*, p. 190; on the Boxer Rebellion see Kiernan, *The Lords of Human Kind*, pp. 174–5; M. Edwardes, *The West in Asia, 1850–1914*, London, 1967, p. 195; J. M. MacKenzie, *Propaganda and Empire*, Manchester, 1984, p. 212.
17 For anxiety over the future of the East see Bright, *A History of England for Public Schools*, pp. 223–4; Hassall, *A Classbook of English History*, p. 587; Warner and Marten, *Groundwork of British History*, p. 683, Rait, *A School History of England*, p. 190.
18 London matriculation test papers in British history, 1888–1902, University of London; Higher school exam papers, 1904, University of London.
19 T. Livesey and B. Besonthorp, *History of England*, London, 1908, p. 165; Carter, *History of England*, p. 215; Hassall, *A Classbook of English History*, p. 182; Rait,

A School History of England, p. 190; Warner and Marten, *Groundwork of British History*, p. 683; M. Keatinge and N. Frazer, *A History of England for Schools*, London, 1911, p. 544.

20 Bright, *A History of England for Public Schools*, p. 71; Meiklejohn and Meiklejohn, *A School History of England*, p. 455; Innes, *History of England*, p. 482.

CHAPTER SIX

The yellow peril: China in children's periodicals

While China remained on the periphery of the historian's interest, publishers and editors of the juvenile periodicals recognised the attractions of the 'Celestial Kingdom' for their readers. The appeal of China lay partly in just the strangeness and mystery which had placed it outside the interest of the texts. Beyond the imaginative possibilities there remained the expectation of material rewards for those who managed to penetrate and overcome the legendary hostility to the 'foreign devils'. Anxiety about Britain's relations with this uncertain 'giant' also prompted imperial-minded publications to provide some answers on how to understand and potentially control its 'inscrutable' character.

Providing 'information' about the wider world was an important service in these journals, and concern over the 'awakening giant' and its future relations with Britain was reflected in the non-fiction sections of the middle-class publications. As China did not represent 'Empire' in the sense of extensive territorial control or white settlement colonies, the periodicals offered no evidence of a royal concern with the area. Neither did sections for potential emigrants offer China as a priority for the entrepreneur. The 'romance' of the resident trading community was not as compelling as the story of gold and diamonds in Africa. Contact between China and Britain, however, did form part of the 'Pictures from the Book of Empire', a series which ran in *Young England* in 1912–13, and included the defence of Lucknow and the Boer War among its entries. To these was added 'The Chinese war and the cession of Hong Kong':

> To those who believe that Great Britain has no right to Chinese soil, no business to be there, and would do well to withdraw ... the wars which we have waged with the Celestial Empire must count with the most inglorious in our history. To those, however, who study the situation in the second quarter of the nineteenth century, there is nothing surprising in the fact of that conservative empire and the progressive and commercial powers of Western Europe coming into open conflict.[1]

There was no direct criticism of the opium trade in the article, nor any suggestion of the legitimacy of a Chinese response. The 'quarrel', according to the writer, lay in China's refusal to deal with a foreign power on 'equal terms', and this 'far more than the wickedness of opium smoking'. The Emperor and his court, 'blind, ignorant, and obstinate', were held to account for misunderstanding the intentions of the British. Chinese outrage over the opium question was cast as an 'astute' manoeuvre calculated to provoke confrontation with potentially friendly British agents and drive them out of China.

[134]

These 'old stubborn attitudes' left the European with only two options – to 'withdraw altogether' or to 'compel respect at the sword's point'. The British case was further strengthened by the isolating of the enemy into a 'conservative and unenlightened' leadership, while potential allies in the Chinese business community remained willing to extend mutually beneficial contacts. With the 'Old China', however, 'nothing but a show of force' could change the 'haughty attitudes'. These attitudes were indeed swept aside in the 'great amity' which marked the signing of the Treaty of Nankin.[2]

In a series which had 'cleansed' the Boer War of controversy it is hardly surprising that the opium question should be neutralised into an issue manipulated by political interests. Material advantage became only a minor part of a conflict fought to ensure 'the rights and privileges of the Westerner'. The issue was not a loss of profit, but rather the loss of respect and potential influence. In 1913, from the imperial perspective, China's opium addicts held little concern either for the popular history or for the 'progressive' elements within China itself.[3]

This article also cast some light on attitudes toward the Chinese soldier, reflecting opinions which had been current in Britain since the Sino-Japanese War.

> Although there was some courage on the part of the Chinese soldiers there was little or no ability in the way they sought to repel the British advance.[4]

Chinese 'honour' was seen to play some part in a decision to 'fight to the death', but only the discipline of English officers, it was felt, could have effectively marshalled such desperate energy. The rules of 'oriental warfare' were clearly far from the European norm, and the exaggerated fears of the 'foreign barbarian' led Chinese troops to inexcusable excesses. These misconceptions contributed to one of the most 'deplorable' incidents of the war, the killing of Chinese women and children to prevent their capture. In this clash of military cultures, the Chinese were seen as culpable for their inability to recognise the restraint of European combatants, leaving the reader to ponder which army reflected a 'barbarian' character.[5]

While the military aspects of the encounter with China bolstered the view of British 'correctness', there were further articles which reflected contemporary concerns with the worrying intentions of a rising East. While there had been a reluctance in the popular papers to acknowledge the existence of either Indians or Africans living within Great Britain, the Chinese presence was an issue of concern. In 1892 *Chums* initiated the reader into the 'Terrors of the opium den', located not in Canton or Peking, but in the East End of London. A 'Chums Commissioner' was sent to investigate the work of the missions in the area, and accompanied a clergyman into the 'celestial haunts'. Hidden behind the 'front' of a barbershop were scenes of extraordinary degradation. Listlessly sprawled on rows of beds were the 'men who had taken their fill of poison and were reaping their rewards'. As an 'experiment', the *Chums* representative took a pipeful, while warning the reader that frightening hallucinations, illness and exhaustion were his only rewards. The 'romantic' image of opium as a stimulus to creative activity, popularised by De Quincey and others, clearly had no place in advice for the late-Victorian schoolchild.[6]

Together, *Chums* and the church worker passed a severe verdict on the Chinese in London. The 'peculiar smile' of the proprietor, Yan, was as deceptive as his barber's trade. Masquerading as legitimate services to the community, these dens of iniquity sent people to perdition and oblivion. Should any child's curiosity be aroused by the forbidden drug, the writer was quick to point out its noxious properties, and the state of the incoherent, lifeless, 'losers' within its grip. The owner, on the other hand, had all of his 'evil' wits about him, while he ruthlessly exploited the 'lower orders'.[7]

The terrors of the opium den were, however, only one aspect of the dangerously mobile Chinese. In 1910 the *Girl's Own Annual* felt it necessary to inform its readership of 'the Yellow Peril':

This enormous mass of humanity shows a marked tendency to spread out in all directions and overflow into the other countries of the world. It is this readiness of the Chinese to settle in the midst of other nations, and the evils which may follow in its train, which constitutes the 'Yellow Peril'.[8]

Opium dens were only the most obvious of the undesirable habits and customs which the aliens brought to Western societies. Apprehension centred upon the image of a 'nation within a nation' – 'secret societies which tend to keep them outside the control of the laws of the land in which they are sojourning'.[9] Danger also rested in their reproductive powers, for growing numbers could 'undersell and then replace white labour and industry'. Fears of the Chinese secretly 'boring from within' and undermining the strength of the West was shared by both Britain and America. By 1910 the US had already set about excluding further Chinese immigrants, and the *Girl's Own Annual* accepted that this was an 'urgent' matter for the British authorities. As befitted a paper of the Religious Tract Society, conversion was also seen as a positive step in neutralising the dangers.

Religion would provide an agency for control of oriental restlessness, and the writer urged the optimistic view that 'a Christian China would be no source of apprehension'.[10]

The image of Chinese people moving through the world seeking to establish footholds for private gain in 'advanced' societies appeared threatening, whether their energies were harnessed to illegal pursuits or legitimate competition with host workers. The papers made no concession to the usefulness of Chinese labour within the British Empire, nor mention of the problematic questions raised by the 'coolie' issue in South Africa. The use of 'foreigners' as migrant labour emerged only when, as with the Indians in South Africa, white administrators encountered problems of control.[11]

When the *Girl's Own Annual* travelled through areas of British settlement, 'From Aden to Sydney', its attitude toward the Chinese emigrants was telling. Girls would be disappointed if they expected these people to appear 'picturesque', for they quickly adopted a 'wretched travesty' of European attire. There was little pleasing to the eye in 'shops which are uniformly shabby' and have 'dirty windows'. The reader's attention was directed to the 'curious fact' of Chinese life. While all else in the China quarter appeared unexceptional and a second-rate imitation of European style, one characteristic stood out – 'for when anyone else appears only to be able to make a bare living, the Chinese can make a fortune'. The Chinese had somehow discovered the secret of effortless prosperity, and while 'apparently doing nothing', they amassed great fortunes. This was both mysterious and suspicious behaviour, for while overtly assuming Western ways, keeping their 'pigtails coiled up and hidden', their work patterns contradicted Western conceptions of visible industry. Unlike the picture of the closely regulated Indian community abroad or of the 'carefree', 'unreliable' African worker, the Chinese appeared to possess a talent and industry unfathomable by the Western observer. Again, as in the worries about the 'secret societies', the danger was that this overzealous foreigner, whose key to success was endemic and therefore 'alien', would challenge the foundations of the white economy.[12]

While young readers were alerted to the potentially expansive energies of the Chinese abroad, they were also offered an image of China reflected through the eyes of those who had worked in the country. The 'improving' annuals, in particular, directed at a mainly middle-class readership, featured tales of the humanitarians – nurses, teachers, and missionaries – who had served in the East. A special appeal was made in the *Girl's Own Paper* in 1910 by Lady Florence Cecil, who argued for 'The need for women workers in China'. Young

British women were encouraged to take up a 'special role' in emancipating their 'sisters' of the East, who had suffered from such 'cruel' traditions as foot binding and enforced marriage. Potential recruits were advised that the changing of 'barbaric' practices would not be easy, 'cooped up in a great Chinese city swarming with yellow men more or less inimical to their mission', but the women of China were pictured as responsive and eager to learn. Details of their plight featured in the annuals under such titles as 'A Chinese woman with crippled feet' and 'From a Chinese wedding', in which the bride was 'half-led, half-carried, half-dragged down the aisle'.[13]

Directing the energies of young British women toward the 'liberation' of their Chinese 'sisters' reflects the conservative domestic agenda of these papers. In the early 1900s they were endorsing a redirection of reformist zeal away from the imperfections in British society and toward the oppression of women abroad. Foot binding and enforced marriages seemed more important issues for the imperial minded than restrictions on the franchise at home. Rather than joining suffrage societies, imperial 'girls' were encouraged to forge 'bonds of love' with their counterparts abroad, an emphasis on service before political liberation.

While attitudes toward the status of women in China were uniformly critical, missionaries and teachers showed some ambivalence toward the Chinese they encountered in other aspects of their work. Those who were attempting to introduce Western religion and learning into China could not deny that this was a society which had contributed to the culture and knowledge of the world. Annuals made the young aware of Chinese inventions and praised both the status of education and the evolution of a system of civil law. Progressives and Christians, however, justified their intervention in China by stressing the evidence of a 'godless' and 'dormant' society, in decline from its previous splendours:

> The phlegmatic Chinaman ... cannot be expected to make way for the energy of the West. The age of Methusaleh touched the age of Edison and Marconi ... inactivity must give way to activity.[14]

For the readers, most of whom were or had recently been in school, a good illustration of this 'dormant' aspect of China lay in its education. The annuals contrasted the traditional learning with that offered in the mission schools. In Chinese schools, according to a *Chums* article of 1907, children did seem to appreciate the 'value of scholarship' and showed a healthy 'respect to their elders'. The relevance of the curriculum, however, was questioned:

They were taught how to form queer looking Chinese characters, and
learned long strings of maxims from the sage, Confucius.[15]

Missionary teachers, while admitting that the Chinese 'valued letters
and learning', argued that producing 'men of culture and deep reading
was not practical'. In the Christian schools the pupils were offered
Western 'skills', and the new atmosphere produced 'excellent' scholars
with a 'passion for education'. The young Chinese were pictured as
possessing strong 'imitative powers', and even in music they soon
produced 'full, round notes of which I had deemed a Chinese throat
incapable'.[16]

The image of the Chinese which emerged from the humanitarian's
interest in the country rested upon the belief that 'it is anxiously
looking for disinterested friends to guide it and sustain it'. The youth
of China, intelligent and diligent, appeared fertile ground for the
message of Christianity and its attendant social reforms. The 'old'
China was seen to be failing its citizens, both by inflicting misery
upon its women and by maintaining an irrelevant and outmoded
system of education for the young. Christianity was viewed as an
essential adjunct to the process of modernisation, encouraging a
progressive individual outlook and providing alternative models of
social behaviour. With the Chinese, however, a people more
'intelligent' and 'diligent' than other potential converts, greater
'knowledge and ability' were required of mission volunteers. The
'zeal' which might be enough to deal with 'simpler' races would not
suffice to dislodge the Chinese from their traditional practices.[17]

Success was particularly important in China, however, for although
all foreign missions were an important part of spreading the imperial
message, the Chinese in particular needed to be controlled. In the
annuals their conversion was linked more explicitly with countering
the threat of a people whose secret lives contained ambitions hostile
to British interests, at home and abroad. If China were to develop
as a friendly 'great power', it was both necessary and desirable that
its awakening include the acceptance of an indigenous Christian
community. The contrast between the 'disinterested service' of the
foreign missions and the activities of the emigrant Chinese community
could not be avoided. While a modern observer might note little
difference between the opium den and the 'opiate of the masses', for
the young reader the contrasting images of morality, public
spiritedness, and private gain provided a striking contrast between
the 'Yellow Peril' and the vanguard of enlightenment.

British inability or unwillingness to penetrate Chinese society
meant that there was relatively little information on the Chinese 'at

home'. What did appear, however, suggested a critical perspective on the conventions of society. In 'The heathen Chinee', which appeared in *Chums* in the 1890s, the author presented the formalities observed in a street encounter, characterising the interaction as proceeding in a series of ritualised exchanges and strictly prescribed vocabulary.[18] The formality appeared not only curious but rather comic, and certainly an odd manner in which to conduct a conversation. A Chinese inn, pictured in *Boys of the Empire*, illustrated the social life enjoyed in the country:

> Wretched places ... pigs wander in and out ... beetles, spiders, rats, vermin add to the general unpleasantness. The smells are indescribable.[19]

To an odd formality and the wretched surroundings of social intercourse might be added a 'cruelty' which was viewed as commonplace in Chinese society. At the everyday level it could be seen in a willingness to consume dogs and cats as staple fare or the degraded position of women, while at the level of official violence 'torture' was an accepted mode of punishment:

> The Chinese love of inflicting torture is shown in the case of the most common of their criminal punishments, the canque or yoke. It is eloquent of Chinese cruelty that the canque is one of the mildest forms of it.[20]

These selected examples of Chinese life suggested a society whose conventions and habits were far removed from the experience of British youth. Descriptions of 'barbaric' practices suggested that the Chinese, as was often ascribed to foreigners, placed a lower value on human and animal life than their counterparts in Europe. The 'twisted intelligence' which the West so often attributed to the 'oriental mind' was exercised in devising new forms of torture for the criminal element. If these references did increase youthful interest in the country and its peoples, it would be for further evidence of practices forbidden in a 'civilised' society, or for more examples of the 'strangeness' exhibited in every day life in China.

In the juvenile press one of the 'bridges' which could reduce the distance between British youth and the outsider was the world of sport. The Indian cricketer had helped to encourage the image of an exceptional alien learning the rules of the game and gaining a limited acceptance into British society. Missionaries in Africa wrote hopefully of their charges who acquired new attitudes through the discipline of games. China, however, was quite a different matter. The Chinese

[140]

people were not viewed as 'fine physical specimens', nor had they acquired the same affinity for British pastimes. *Young England* informed its readership in 1914 that the Chinese did not 'ever do anything brisk and energetic for pleasure'. A description of cricket as played in Shanghai seemed to confirm this, for local boys 'attached a string to the ball so it wouldn't go so far'. While an amusing image, it also signalled a lack of interest in 'healthy' pursuits, critically allied in the English mind with the development of character. That the Chinese in many senses did not 'play the game' clearly distanced them from British values and the young reader.[21]

The image of China which the non-fiction juvenile press offered to its readers reflected concerns which the British felt about the 'awakening giant' in the late-Victorian and Edwardian era. As a people outside the 'official' family of Empire, yet included within the orbit of imperial trade, the need was to understand and control, rather than assume responsibility for, a country with enormous potential and an uncertain future. There were a number of contradictory elements in the picture drawn in the non-fiction. On the one hand much criticism was directed toward elements in the Chinese character and society which represented a regressive, inward-looking, inflexible and static outlook. A lack of contact with the outside world had created an excessively self-referential society, shackled by form and ritual, and with a peasant population mired in poverty and pre-modern practices. The progressive, internationalist outlook of the imperial world encouraged the young to believe that these barriers should be lowered, and China opened to the influences of Western culture, trade and religion. The missionary view of the Chinese supported this view of a country awaiting the liberation of Christianity and Western education. The girls' papers invited recruits to work with those Chinese receptive to such a message, and stressed the intelligence and receptivity found among women and children in the country. The obstacles of entrenched prejudices and cruel practices were not denied, nor the very different customs of a society await-ing the awakening of a social conscience, but the human resources of this formerly great civilisation were seen as possessing great potential.

On the other hand, opening China's doors could pose real problems, and celebrating the possibilities of change for the Chinese 'at home' could turn to fear of their intentions once loosed upon the world. No other country was cast into an image like the 'Yellow Peril'. Ample evidence was provided in the annuals of the dangers for the West of Chinese in their midst, and the young would arguably have looked with fear and suspicion on Chinese encountered within the boundaries of their own country. Deception and secretiveness characterised the stereotypical opium peddler, ready to undermine the health and morals of the host society. No less threatening was the energetic, self-serving worker, whose 'closed' society gave little access to agencies of control, and whose success threatened the economic security of competing locals. These were people who needed to be watched carefully and monitored for their allegiances, and whose numbers called for a tighter immigration policy. Fear created an image of the Chinese abroad which was overtly racist and hostile, presenting a people of 'evil' disposition, unsavoury habits and immoral practices.

For the British there was no 'easy' or informal way of knowing Chinese society. Without the affinity of a sporting fraternity, a shared ethos of the ruling class, or the closeness bred of a shared history, China appeared to some degree 'unknowable'. This did not deter the authors of the annuals, however, from presenting to British youth generalisations about a Chinese character which contained few positive aspects. While the riches of China might encourage the need for a continued relation based on the exploitation of trade, few readers of the annuals would have felt encouraged to explore closer links with a people who appeared both hostile and dangerous.

In the world of fiction, where mystery, terror, and conflicts with evil were essential components of the adventure story, roles abounded for the Chinese. Fears and anxieties suggested in the textbooks and in the non-fiction found full expression in the writers' imaginative rendering of Chinese characters. Concurrently, threats posed by the old stereotypical agents of imperial China could be counterbalanced by imaginative projections of the 'new China', whose values might align positively with the British heroes. Chinese characters appeared in familiar formula stories, at public schools or with 'chums' abroad, and in invasion or detective serials, where they dominated the genre.

The mobility of the Chinese was a striking feature of the fiction, as it had been a central concern of contemporary observers. It was not surprising, then, that a young Chinese boy should find his way to Greyfriars, following in the steps of Hurree Singh and Sambo. 'The new boy at Greyfriars' arrived in 1908, an event 'unusual even by Greyfriars' standards'.

A young Chinese of about fourteen. His figure was well-formed, supple and graceful, but diminutive. He wore the loose garb of his native country, of a rich silken material, adorned with borders of strange characters. His face was oval, rather deep in colour, and not of the saffron hue some of the more imaginative Removeites had expected. His eyes had the curious obliqueness of the oriental ... it was the pigtail more than anything else that excited the interest of the Remove.[22]

As expected, it was Harry's concern for 'fair play' which brushed aside Bulstrode's taunts of 'Chin-chin Chinaman'. The decent lads' resistance to bullying, alongside Wun Lung's adaptability, assured the reader that good humour and tolerance would provide an atmosphere in which the young arrival might provide an interesting addition to school life. Hurree, in particular, as a fellow oriental, was deputised to help Wun Lung feel at home, with a game of chess.[23]

It soon became apparent that this rather meek and mild newcomer possessed surprising powers. Bulstrode was quickly floored with a display of jujitsu. Faced with quick wit and ready imagination, the 'Bold Explorers of the Remove' and the form master trembled in fear before a magnificent paper dragon. There was constant amazement at Wun Lung's ability to appear and disappear at will, removing himself handily from a scene of potential danger. Some talents, however, exasperated the chums, and lent great amusement to the stories. The ever-greedy schoolboys welcomed the offer of a Chinese cook in their midst, offering 'the common glub in my country'. As the Remove tucked in with their usual gusto, Wun quietly inquired, 'What you tinkee of dogee?', calmly finishing the stew as his friends 'gasped and groaned in anguish'.[24]

The limits upon his position in the school were made clear when Harry delegated his post as Form Captain to Wun Lung for a week in 1909. Quickly 'all hell broke loose' within Greyfriars. The idea of a 'Chinaman' assuming the 'serious' duties of the school was shown to be absurd. His inadequacies were particularly exposed in the school sporting fixtures, where he 'dressed for the part' as a mandarin, and put the school's athletic reputation in serious peril. It was with undisguised relief that Wun Lung greeted Harry on his return. 'Me had nuffee of being Captain! Me lesign.'[25]

It was not only the lack of sporting skills which alarmed Wun Lung's fellow schoolmates. There were several occasions in the stories when he seemed dangerously near to succumbing to the ways of the 'old China'. More than once the boys of the Remove showed their awareness of the dangers by interceding to save him. In 'Wun Lung's secret', the suspicions of Harry and Bob led them to follow their friend into the local village, where they found him in the company of a Chinese sailor. The boys immediately understood the origins of Wun's peculiar behaviour.

Bob: 'Opium!'
Harry: 'Yes. You know, it's a Chinese habit – they eat and smoke opium, same as some silly idiots in this country take morphia. It's a common thing out there – and there are opium dens in London, too, I've heard of them.'

Wun Lung – a mere lad, an opium fiend. It seemed too horrible to be true![26]

The British boys took matters in hand, condemning the vile habit, turning the culprit over to his ship's master, and escorting a 'penitent' Wun Lung back to the safety of Greyfriars.

The spectre of the 'other China' surfaced also in the guise of Wun Lung's uncle, who appeared at the gates of the school to rescue his nephew from the 'foreign devils'. Harry showed a remarkable knowledge of the issues informing the pressures on his 'chum'.

> He understood clearly enough the difference ... he had heard of the young China party, who wished to wake up their country on Japanese lines. He could understand the prejudices of the old mandarin, his horror of his nephew living, and receiving his education, in the midst of the 'foreign devils'.[27]

Harry and the Remove refused the uncle access to Wun Lung, and insisted that he be allowed to remain at the school. The young Chinese was pictured receiving the news with 'delighted thanks'.

The Chinese boy at school (there were no 'oriental' girls in the school stories until after the war) represented in fictional form the possibilities of youth to make connections where their elders had failed. As has been seen with Hurree and Sambo, the sense of 'fair play' represented by Harry and Bob allowed a tolerance of the peculiarities of the newcomer, whose gratitude cemented the alliance. There was in Wun Lung no evidence of the arrogance and contempt which the 'old China' held for the European. As long as he accepted the rules of the Remove, and had few pretensions, his clever tricks and practical jokes could be accommodated.

The problems emerged when Wun Lung connected with his fellow Chinese, who represented the undesirable face of China. The competition in the stories for the loyalty of Wun Lung mirrored the anxiety felt in Britain about the 'character' of the emergent China. That the British boys managed to help Wun Lung overcome the clutches of opium and escape the influence of his uncle provided a hopeful message for the future of British influence in the Chinese community. The boys of the Remove represented the 'best' of British boyhood, willing to assume a protective control over their new chum, with no mention of material reward. Unlike their 'reciprocal' friendship with Hurree, whose wealth eased the relations, there was no suggestion that the 'saving' of China had anything but disinterested motives. Once the danger of Wun Lung's alliance with the worst aspects of his heritage had been dispelled, the Chinese schoolboy could resume his position as the 'pet' of the Remove, a harmless and inventive companion.[28]

Foreigners outside the walls of the public school were more suspect. The Indian thief from the circus or the uncontrolled African performer had served as the target for righteous schoolboy heroes, and the Chinese would prove even more problematic. Again, the stories reflected the fears associated with a resident Chinese community, living in closed societies, and engaging in suspicious if not criminal activities. Wun Lung had been an exception to the rule, isolated from his compatriots, and admiring of the British way of life. A far more common image of the Chinese within Britain was the 'master criminal'.

The incidence of 'evil' conspirators, operating from the streets of Docklands, Camden Town or the Elephant and Castle, grew with the vogue of the detective story. Following in the steps of Sherlock Holmes, first introduced to the reading public in 1887, came Sexton Blake, Nelson Lee, Dixon Brett, Stanley Dare and Frank Ferret. Girl detectives such as Martia Wray, a 'female Sherlock Holmes', also found a place in the girls' magazines, although their cases tended to focus on domestic mysteries. From the pages of the story papers, *Pluck* and the *Magnet* in particular, the sleuths engaged each week with the pernicious underworld of crime. While the Chinese were favourite villains, they were by no means the only 'outsiders' with aberrant personalities, for Jews, Gypsies, Indians and even Frenchmen could take on the sinister roles.[29]

It was from China, however, that the 'master criminals' came, smarter, more cunning and unscrupulous than other adversaries. One description typifies the criminal persona:

> Li Lung was known to the world as a Chinese doctor, but secretly he was the owner of many of the worst gambling dens.

Under the guise of a helping profession, the doctor's real activities included 'murder, forgery, theft and gambling'. Possessed of a twisted scientific mind, he had perfected a 'master plan' to criminalise the West, a scheme to 'force innocent men to commit crimes by injecting them with germs obtained from criminals'. Pictured gloating in his laboratory, a 'crafty yellow face twisted by a thin lipped grin', he dreamed of limitless powers. Here incarnate was the danger of the 'enemy within', more fearsome than the ordinary criminal, whose life of crime was not just an individual quest for ill-gotten gains, but a plan for conquest of the world.[30]

[145]

In the face of such cunning adversaries, the detectives needed extraordinary powers, abilities which allowed them to succeed where the Foreign Office or the police had failed. Only 'subtle deductions and arguments' could unravel the clues which led to the secret societies and their masters, and the 'quick wits' to escape the clutches of a 'merciless' foe. Frank Ferret was a Cambridge graduate and a linguist, Nelson Lee a 'skilled tracker' from his years abroad, and Stanley Dare a 'master of disguise'. All 'knew' the characteristics of the Chinese intimately, recognising trouble from the imprint of a soft slipper or the sweet smell of drugs – 'the proof of Celestials'. Sexton Blake illustrated how they acquired first-hand knowledge of 'oriental habits':

> You see, before I went to see Mr Gladstone I took a small dose of a certain Eastern drug. We didn't know the effect of it and we wanted to find out. It appears that a measured dose of this drug lulls the moral sense. In other words, it makes the victim blind to common honesty and capable of any theft or unscrupulous piece of work.[31]

The detectives' physical and mental powers were stretched to their limits to outwit the criminal Chinese. Here British heroes met the imaginative extremes of a generalised fear of Chinese emigrants. Masters of secrecy and deceit, these aliens seemed able to adopt, chameleon like, the surface characteristics of 'civilised' individuals. The interrogator of one Chinese gang was an 'accomplished linguist', who spoke the 'correct English' of an educated man. It was, however, a cold and merciless intelligence, and the young detective knew that 'a human life more or less is nothing to them'. Impossibly clever tortures and sadistic death awaited the unsuccessful sleuth, while the destruction of a criminal without mercy was clearly justified. The stereotype of the Chinese villain has been an immensely popular feature in the world of juvenile literature, and it was here, in the journals of the pre-war era, that the outlines of the character became widely known. Emerging from long-held beliefs about the 'cruel intelligence' of the oriental mind, and compounded by the current fears of the 'yellow peril', these images were to breed fear and righteous indignation in generations of British youth.[32]

While the vigilance of the young detectives protected British society from internal enemies, others were anxiously watching the skies and shores for the threat of invasion. Published in 1906, William Le Quex's *The Invasion of 1910* was to sell one million copies and enjoy translation into 27 languages.[33] Perhaps nothing so much as the invasion fears illustrates the perceived vulnerability of Great Britain to external threats. The editor of the *Boy's Herald* in 1908 offered an explanation of this increasing hostility.

> It is no secret that the Britisher is hated abroad. We are not safe from insult or assault. Why? Because of our huge possessions and colonies, because of our enterprise and grit. Foreign nations are jealous of our progress. They fear that one day we will make a bid to be the conquerors of the world ... and make a concerted blow at every other nation.[34]

The physical and mental strength needed to meet this challenge could be acquired in a number of ways. 'Muscle and the boy', an article in the *Captain* in 1898, was just one of many articles which dealt with the question of physical preparedness, while reports on the Boy Scout movement and the Boys' Brigade encouraged the young to acquire discipline and martial skills. The dangers of weakness were both individual and social concerns, and a paramount issue was the defence of the British Isles.[35]

The 'unpredictability' of Chinese intentions, coupled with an acknowledged scientific and technical prowess, made their sudden appearance on British soil a common feature of invasion stories. 'Terror from the East', a long-running serial story in *Chums*, presented the Chinese in alliance with Japan, invading from Brighton's beaches, and taking advantage of Britain's preoccupation with mutiny in India:

> The yellow Peril that men had dreamt about had broken loose at last. Two nations, still obscured by the mists of barbarism, threw down the gauntlet.

Against this 'hissing crew of orientals, munching handfuls of rice as they fought' was hurled the best of British boyhood, coming forward from Scouts and Brigades – the factor 'to be reckoned with' by those who attempted to over-run Britain. While the 'cheers of conquering British boyhood' signalled the defeat of the invaders, the story displayed a notable anxiety about the combined human and naval power of the East, and portrayed the Chinese as ruthless and determined in their intention to contest the British for control of the world.[36]

Airborne vehicles also brought the spectre of unwelcome visitors, and in 'London in danger or the great Chinese invasion' Captain Ching clarified the ambitions of the interlopers.

> We will destroy the capitals of every power which has waged war against our Emperor. Ere another moon China will possess the whole world – that is certain.[37]

[147]

Landing on a hill which overlooked London, the crew of the aerial balloon fleet directed their attentions toward the prime target, the Bank of England, suggesting the ambitions for financial gain which the British had always feared from the Chinese presence. There was also the issue of revenge in the aftermath of the Boxer Rebellion. Captain Ching proclaimed himself a follower of the Empress Dowager, in her service to 'defy the world'. Contemporary concerns about the Chinese were evident throughout this *Marvel* story, both in the characterisation of the invaders and the warnings to British youth.[38]

The dangers posed by the Chinese as adversaries were expressed in the licence given to British defenders to 'show no mercy'. In the face of the invaders' determination to 'destroy the foreign devils', Reginald of the *Marvel* poisoned the entire crew with their own supply of 'noxious gas'. Much like the detectives, the annuals allowed that the intentions of the enemy lifted the ordinary rules of engagement, and extermination became a tolerable alternative to due process of law or the taking of prisoners. There was little evidence of the justification of a resort to violence which was felt necessary in dealing with either the Indian or the African.[39]

The portrayal of the Chinese threat to the security of Britain brought forth some of the most negative stereotypes of the annuals' fictional worlds. When a genuinely 'evil' character was called for, plotting world domination or germ warfare, the master criminal was often the 'oriental'. The origins of these images rested in the historical canon of their 'hatred' of the foreign barbarians and also the fear current in contemporary society about Chinese immigrants and the restless, mobile population of the 'Celestial Empire'. A sense that the Chinese harboured bitterness over European actions and were prepared to wreak revenge intensified the atmosphere of peril. When these feelings were fused with the characteristics of ambition, intelligence, ruthlessness and cruelty, the product was an image of the Chinese which provoked fear, concern, and a deep animosity. Young readers learned that unless isolated, outnumbered and pacified (like Wun Lung), the Chinese were dangerous. Security lay in vigilance and preparedness, for the individual and the nation, and knowing the enemy gave the essential skills for detection, whether in Camden Town, the night sky or on the beaches.

There was some relaxation in attitudes towards the Chinese when the setting for the encounter moved outside Britain. The bands of British boys who travelled the world in search of adventure did at times expand to include a young Chinese, and futuristic adventures in sky ships or submarines might need the skills of a neutral Chinaman. This was not, however, the case in British India, where the Chinese appeared working to 'undermine' British interests, and combined where possible with locals in 'oriental treachery'. When Europeans were in the majority, as in Australia, bonds of friendship might be struck between British heroes and a 'singular' Chinese. In 1910–11, the same years that it was running 'Terror from the East', *Chums* ran a serial story 'By southern campfires', set in the outback. Here the 'remarkable' powers of Wah Sing entered in partnership with two British boys, Eric and Bruce.[40] Binding the three together was a common goal – the recovery of £10,000 owed to Wah Sing by an Englishman working in the gold fields. The adventure was based on a journey to the isolated mining camp, and the encounters with a variety of hostile figures in the unwelcoming landscape. In action against the villains of the story, Wah Sing and the British youths worked together to protect their interests and their lives. The 'inscrutable Chinaman' possessed gifts which were instrumental in the success of the mission. Not only could he produce revolvers from the recesses of his sleeves, but he seemed to have access to information unavailable to the others:

> Men of his race, no matter what part of the world they happen to be in, always contrive to hear things, good or bad, strange or commonplace, before Europeans get any inkling of it.[41]

In other circumstances these qualities were deeply suspect, but once the boys had won Wah Sing's loyalty, such concerns disappeared. This transfer of affections emerged from the chums' determination to protect the Chinese boy from the prejudice and greed of other Europeans in the camp. It was clearly the intention of the story to place the fair-mindedness of the English as a major factor in their actions:

> As long as my partner acts in a straightforward and honest manner, I believe that he has as much right to work a claim in this country as, let us say, Germans or Russians or Jews.[42]

Tolerance toward Wah Sing set the British boys apart from the other Europeans in Australia, who did not work to the code of 'fair play' for all. In the lawless and 'uncivilised' environs of the mining camp, boundaries became fluid, and an interdependence of British and Chinese became possible. However, when the action moved to Sydney, where segregated patterns of housing and social intercourse were the norm, Wah Sing departed to live with his own. The author was also anxious to make of the Chinaman an exceptional figure, not 'your cook or washerman', for the disdain of Eric and Bruce for the residents of Chinatown was clearly stated. Interestingly their 'prize' for recognising the value of Wah Sing was a considerable share in the recovered money. It was not unexpected that, at the end of the story, the 'new friend' would 'naturally' return to his own country.[43]

Early science fiction stories, set again outside the boundaries of English life, also allowed more positive images of the Chinese in their characterisations. The crews of winged motor cars and sophisticated submarine vessels might contain Chinese within their international community. While invariably captained by an Englishman, who maintained a firm but fair discipline over the workers, these stories did provide positive commentary on the skills of China placed at the service of future-based heroes. Wah Tong in *Pluck* and Ching Lung in the *Magnet* provided examples of technologically astute aliens. This was in notable contrast to the consistent 'deskilling' of the Indian and the African, who seldom featured in any but the most menial of roles.[44]

In 1901 Wah Tung first made his appearance as the mechanic of the winged automobile, in a period when making a German inventor his overseer remained a feasible relationship. His resourcefulness was not limited to the smooth running of the craft:

He was adept, like most of his countrymen, in all manner of sly tricks and seemingly impossible slight of hand feats....[45]

Even in these stories the authors made a deliberate effort to alert the reader to the 'difference' between the exceptional Chinese and those of the London streets. In the *Magnet* stories, one aspect of the unfolding relationship between Ching Lung and Rupert was the growing realisation that neither fit the prejudices of the other. Their first encounter showed the 'baggage' of mutual suspicion:

Ching – Hallo, mistel, white foreign debbil!
Rupert – Hallo, yourself, you little yellow monkey. What a cute little urchin ... that lad would make a hundred pound a week at any decent music hall in London.

Class distinctions began to play their part in the story, and as Ching Lung began to demonstrate 'traces of princely bearing', he moved from cook to mechanic to leader of the expedition into China. Meanwhile his language altered as well, from 'Chinee' English to proper usage and a startling multilingualism. Without his 'wisdom', the company acknowledged that they might not have achieved their objectives.[46]

What was the reader to make of a people who in one issue represented evil incarnate, threatening invasion of Britain with twisted technology, and in the next gave invaluable assistance in aerial and underwater adventures? The essential differences were direction and control. If the balloons were drifting toward British shores with Captain Ching in charge, one must get ready to repel the 'yellow microbes'. If, on the other hand, new inventions were safely in the hands of the English, with Chinese energies directed toward shared goals, 'oriental' abilities could be appreciated. Isolation from the masses of China was also important, for the 'good' or 'exceptional' Chinese emerged within the confines of a controlled environment, where it was made clear that they were not the 'bad sort' of China-town or a representative of the 'old China'. In order for the independent Chinese to enjoy a positive image in the fiction set in the wider world, they had to be brought within the remit of the European order, colonised in fiction more completely than they would ever be in reality. This is what sets Wun Lung, Wah Sing, Ching Lung and Wah Tong apart from Captain Ching or the legions of master criminals. These stories betrayed a deep anxiety about the potential of a China unfriendly to European power, and a desire to reassure readers that they could match and ultimately contain China's 'inventive' powers.

Fiction set in China drew upon both the more pessimistic and the more hopeful images of the Chinese people. Here there were new kinds of characters, river pirates, smuggling gangs, Chinese princes and priests. Most stories set in China itself were of contemporary events and reflected current preoccupations, political and economic, reflecting both national priorities and the lack of a 'usable' past. Conflicts tended to centre on British economic interests in the region or European concern with defeating the old leadership and encouraging the forces of modernisation.

The difficulties of the British in establishing 'legitimate' trading interest within China provided the basis for many adventure stories. In some the heroes were direct representatives of Britain, and young employees of the Chinese Customs Service featured in serial stories which ran in *Chums* in 1907–8. Their opponents were the secret societies which sought to direct the riches of China into their own hands. In phrases reminiscent of the Thugs in India, societies such as 'The Dragon's Teeth' or 'The Society of the Glass Eye' pursued a reign of terror over the local population, including unscrupulous opium deals, highway robbery, and kidnapping of pro-Western Chinese. Young Britons, in confronting and defeating their powers, were portrayed as not only establishing the primacy of honest economic exchange, but also in freeing the peasant population of the 'scourge of oppression'. This associated, as it had in India and Africa, the extension of British economic power with the introduction of progressive reform, particularly in the arena of drug trafficking.[47]

Pirates also operated outside the law and showed little regard for the interests of European or fellow Chinese. Awareness of the threat to vital British interests was heightened by placing an encounter within sight of Hong Kong. Pirates attacked without warning and with what was seen as a total disregard for human life. Their image was perhaps the most negative of the Chinese 'at home', as their activities directly threatened the ethos of free trade, basic to a British view of the 'civilised' world. This was a 'gang which deserved the worst kind of death', according to a story in the *Captain* in 1898. The captains of British vessels wished to be merciful, but could not afford the luxury of 'civilised' behaviour toward those 'who desired with a wicked passion to see blood spilt before they died'. Their 'just' reward was extermination, often achieved by feeding them to the sharks which circled the ships. As Ogilvie prepared to toss one overboard, he paused to inform the reader:

Chinese pirates are creatures of course, but not fellow creatures; They're, oh hang it! I've no time for preaching! Savage wretches.[48]

These views of the criminal activities of societies within China and of pirates in the coastal waters reinforced the image of the Chinese as a people possessed of a spirit of enterprise, but one which ran directly counter to an open, honest, economic exchange, represented by the intentions of the British vessels. In China, as in Africa and India, British 'business' was contrasted with local activities which were extra-legal and deemed immoral, such as extortion, the slave trade, or drug dealing. This invested the British hero, the customs official, sea captain or trader, with a moral as well as economic imperative to eliminate the competition, seen as detrimental to the best interests of both China and Britain. The violence employed against these Chinese was quite extreme, matched only by the revenge against mutineers in India, and seldom encountered in conflict with African tribes.

The freedom of the European to engage in 'free trade' became elevated to a crusade against the 'evil demons' of the East. Apart from seeking to destroy the 'selfish' interests of China's illegal economy, young British heroes also became involved in the political struggles between the forces of the 'old' and 'new' China. This often involved 'befriending' a challenger to the power of the traditional ruling classes, and fighting with him to establish a 'new order' or assisting exile to the West. The figure of the Dowager Empress was an important symbol of the anti-Western tradition. These attitudes also found expression in the mandarins and priests of the traditional elites, anxious to protect their powers from the agents of modernisation. Adventures set in China reflected the contempt felt for this sector of Chinese society.

> They like to show their importance by keeping 'barbarian' visitors waiting. We shall have to observe the idiotic compliments and counter compliments that custom requires.[49]

Such arrogance toward British citizens was not easily accepted, despite an awareness that expediency might dictate an appearance of observing convention. Young British characters expressed their 'true feelings' by carving their names on a priest's 'favourite idol' before departing. This 'harmless act of vandalism' showed the resentment of British boys forced to 'kow tow' to inferior races. While the reader knew what the 'hero' really felt, generally common sense suggested that adopting 'appearances' and outwitting the opposition, rather than employment of physical force, was the preferred route to success. There was no 'imperial presence' to back up the individual if he became seriously imperilled or was hopelessly outnumbered, and all knew that capture meant a death by slow, unspeakable torture.[50]

Balancing the conservative and suspicious Chinese were those whose characterisation pointed toward the potential of better relations. His Imperial Majesty Kwang Su, 'the rightful ruler of China', assured Jack and Godwin as they arrived at court that he too was an enemy of the Empress, who was keeping him a virtual captive. An English governess in his employ reassures the lads that he was 'desirous, above all things, of peace with the Western powers'. Predictably, the 'new' Chinese ruler had adopted Western dress, perfect English and admiration for the English ways. In the story, with the boys' assistance, Kwang Su displaces the Dowager, and under his leadership, a new era of 'close alliances' between the British and Chinese is promised.[51]

Kwang Su was not the only pretender aided by the actions of British adventurers. When the search for a mysterious jewel turns into the discovery of Prince Liu, the English leader of the expedition concludes, 'I think we'll do China a good turn by helping to put him on the throne'. Before undertaking the task of assisting the young Prince, however, the Europeans establish an understanding with the Prince's supporters that his accession will serve Western interests. Liu's uncle reminds them that they may well find common ground:

My visits to English schools taught me that princes may make friends with English boys to their mutual advantage, if the friends are wisely chosen.[52]

In the fiction, whether friendly or hostile, Chinese figures represented aspects of the contemporary struggle to maintain and expand British influence. Those who acted with arrogance or outright hostility were the enemy, who must be displaced or defeated. Replacing their ascendancy, with British assistance, was the modern element in China, who adopted Western values and customs, spoke plain English and favoured European-style education. The 'new' leadership elicited the services of the adventurers against the old guard and together they worked toward a change in China's relations with the West, replacing suspicion and resistance with cooperation and friendship. Securing these ends was often the basis for adventure fiction set in China, encouraging readers to share with the heroes their appraisal of allies and adversaries, and thereby reaffirming the duality in the image of Chinese character.

Although they might not be overtly threatening to the advance of British fortunes, the 'masses' of China did not receive much respect in their natural environs. As adventurers passed through China they met with a society whose habits were strange and often 'immoral'. 'The fourth-rate town of Tung Hien', the setting for a *Pluck* serial in 1904–5, was populated only by gamblers and opium smokers. Violence and inhumanity were the norm. The foreigners were appalled by the eating habits of 'promiscuous and dirty feeders'.[53]

Descriptions of physical characteristics were also generally unfavourable. As a 'race' the Chinese were believed to possess little physical prowess, and were often described as weak and small-boned 'specimens'. The shape of the eyes was often noted, and whereas a beautiful and friendly princess was described as 'almond eyed', an attacking pirate looked at his prey through 'slits', gleaming like a cat or a crocodile. The more 'evil' a character was deemed to be, the more 'yellow' the skin, the longer the pigtail and the more drooping the moustache. Manchu or Tartar heritage could exaggerate the 'cruel' disposition of the facial expression, while contact with the West often 'opened' the features of the ally. In general the reaction to the physical appearance of the Chinese was not as positive, even with allies, as was the case with either the Indian or the African. The Indian prince might be described in terms of fine bearing or features, the African with an appreciation for 'savage' beauty, but the Chinese male was too slight and short to accord with standards of 'manliness'. Chinese 'maidens' were doll-like creatures, perhaps possessing beauty in a 'sparrow like' fashion, but essentially ornamental.[54]

For the British and indeed most Europeans China remained a 'difficult' reality throughout this period. While enjoying the profits from their hold on the treaty ports and Hong Kong, there was a great uncertainty about the future. Both fiction and non-fiction in the juvenile press expressed anxiety about the emergence of 'modern' China, including a potential alliance with Japan – a power block which could 'awake' and threaten the security and supremacy of the West. Many of the features and stories stressed the inroads made by Western ideas in mainland China or Britain's success in controlling Chinese influence abroad. In the broadest sense the 'message' of the periodicals supported these actions by discrediting the value and relevance of traditional China and endorsing the necessity of a new generation distanced from the patterns of the past.

China as 'menace' surfaced repeatedly in both the non-fiction and the fiction. Fears of the 'yellow peril' prompted strongly negative images of the behaviour of emigrants living within Britain and Australia, whose disregard for the wellbeing of the host society was evidenced in greed and corruption. Visits to 'opium dens' gave detailed information on the 'horrors' which accompanied the growth of a Chinese community. Even in areas where 'coolie' labour had been solicited, the social consequences were undesirable. Immigration restrictions were advocated if Britain was to be kept safe.[55] The fiction distilled these generalised social habits into individuals who became some of the best-known villains of the period, testing the powers of their British adversaries to the limit. Here a 'cunning intelligence' directed to the downfall of the old world order expressed the final revenge planned against the white devils of the West. In addition, there were fears of 'invasion' by an army of the 'East', 'yellow microbes' poised to penetrate British defences.

Scientific ideas and imagery did feature in the characterisation of China in an interesting way. Social Darwinism, of course, was used to buttress the distinction between progressive and non-progressive peoples, and had a great influence on the image of Africa. But there was also the recognition that in this new century the mastery of technology and the skills of invention would give an advantage in the competitive world. The African's encounter with the cinema and electricity produced much humour, suggesting an inability to deal with modern phenomena. India's doctors were viewed as second-rate professionals, clearly inferior to those trained in Britain. The Chinese relationship with scientific knowledge and discovery was rather different. They were seen to have declined from an early genius into a degenerate state, which left them with the intelligence to conquer science but with a concern about how they might use this power. For example, their use of drugs, like opium, was seen as life threatening rather than a social good. Evil doctors and scientists used their skills to destroy rather than contribute to useful knowledge. As physical specimens the Chinese were viewed as not much of a threat in combat, but when armed with germ warfare or toxic gases the balance of power could shift. The fear of an 'enemy within', the Chinese immigrant, was symbolised by the image of hostile microbes invading the body, small, numerous and endlessly reproducing. Children of Britain were, meanwhile, being encouraged to appreciate the wonders of science, and to try their hands at a few simple experiments. The image of a people who could master the complexities of scientific knowledge, but lacked a moral or social conscience in its application, was a particularly frightening and powerful one. In the anxious years before the First World War, these fears took on a heightened relevance.[56]

Given that very little was learned of the Chinese from textbooks, the image of China which the youth of Britain did receive in the period came mainly from the pages of their popular journals. While there were positive images of better relations with the 'new China' – Wun Lung, Wah Sing or Kwang Su – which showed the possibilities of reciprocal interests and personal friendships, these were in a minority. Apart from the fact that the Chinese served so well as fictional adversaries, there was also less reason, and less of a realistic basis, for picturing the Chinese as either faithful or loyal to Britain's imperial ethos. While it was always a delicate balance between using the 'evil' Chinese to sell the excitement of the story, and reassuring the reader the British really had the situation under control, a victory over such an astute opponent carried more positive messages about the strength of British character and fewer concerns about the abuse of power than stories of conflict in India or Africa.

The resistance of the Chinese to British influence also made it more difficult for authors to dramatise or 'humanise' personal relations. There was no parallel to the 'adoption' of the English into African tribes, or stories of brother turning against his own to save an English life. The rigid constraints of a complex and hierarchical Chinese society, with customs and manners incomprehensible to the European, and without the long association of imperial government, made it difficult for the British to 'know' the Chinese, and this made their observations particularly dismissive of cultural differences. Ignorance about the Chinese and the lack of a history of 'significant' contacts denied British youth the same complacent superiority over a people of acknowledged intelligence and a great, if dormant, civilisation.

While the Chinese character might have in reality remained less controlled, and less 'knowable', than either the Indian or the African, this did not deter the annuals from creating an image of the country which reflected national concerns and abiding stereotypes. Where gunboat diplomacy had failed, it was hoped the Christian missions might win, and the young were encouraged to see the Chinese as a particularly challenging field in which to sow a new morality and civilising spirit. Here the 'evils' of the old China might be challenged through the 'softer' targets of oppressed women and receptive children. This was acknowledged, however, to be a long and difficult task. In the fiction of adventure and detection, young Britons achieved a command over the Chinese which in reality they were unsure of obtaining. The idea of young British boys playing a crucial role in the dynastic struggles of China may have seemed fantastic, but it suggested the kind of influence which was desired. British characters in charge of flying machines and submarines, with the Chinese in supporting roles, was an ideal arrangement for harnessing the talents of the East. Fiction touched the deepest anxieties about the ability to meet the challenge of sustaining fruitful relations with the East, and played its role in reassuring the reader that the 'old China' could be successfully transformed. The villains would remain, but they would never win, and increasingly the conversion of China, by religion, commerce, and the force of British character, would become a reality.[57]

Notes

1 'The Chinese War and the cession of Hong Kong', *Young England*, vol. XXXIV, 1912–13, p. 304.
2 *Ibid.*, pp. 304–7.
3 *Ibid.*, p. 306.
4 *Ibid.*, p. 306; R. S. Dawson, *The Chinese Chameleon*, London, 1967, p. 160; V. G. Kiernan, *The Lords of Human Kind*, London, 1969, p. 171.
5 'The Chinese War and the cession of Hong Kong', p. 306.
6 'The terrors of the opium den', *Chums*, vol. 1, no. 11, 23 November, 1892, p. 166; for romantic image see E. Said, *Orientalism*, London, 1991 edn, p. 192; Dawson *The Chinese Chameleon*, pp. 70–3; J. Ch'en, *China and the West*, London, 1979, p. 45.
7 'The terrors of the opium den', p. 166.
8 C. Tarring, 'What is the yellow peril?', *Girl's Own Annual*, vol. XXI, 1909–10, p. 359; for 'yellow peril' see Kiernan, *The Lords of Human Kind*, pp. 177–9.
9 *The Chinese Chameleon*, pp. 359, 360.
10 *Ibid.*, p. 359.
11 'From Aden to Sydney', *Girl's Own Annual*, vol. X, 1891, pp. 724–6; D. O. Judd, *Balfour and the British Empire*, London, 1968, pp. 199–203; see also Hugh Clifford quoted in Chai Hon Chen, *The Development of British Malaya, 1896–1909*, Oxford, 1964, pp. 105–6.
12 'From Aden to Sydney', p. 726; 'A quaint scene at the Cape', *Chums*, vol. VIII, no. 366, 13 September, 1899, p. 54; J. W. Heslop, 'The hut by the river', *Chums*, vol. XV, 1906–7, p. 245.

13 'The mid China mission', *Children's World*, vol. III, February, 1893, pp. 18–20; 'What is the yellow peril?', p. 360; Lady F. Cecil, 'The need for women workers in China', *Girl's Own Annual*, vol. XXI, 1910, pp. 209–12; 'A Chinese woman with crippled feet' and 'A Chinese wedding', *Children's World*, vol. III, June, 1893, pp. 169–70, 183; for missionary image see Dawson, *The Chinese Chameleon*, chapter 5; A. H. Smith, *Chinese Characteristics*, London, 1906, pp. 329–30.

14 'From Pekin to the Great Wall', *Boy's Own Annual*, vol. XXXII, 1909–10, p. 778; 'Chinese civilisation', *Chums*, vol. I, 1892–93, p. 351; for 'degenerate' civilisation see Said, *Orientalism*, pp. 231–4.

15 'At school in China', *Chums*, vol. XVI, no. 779, 1907, p. 9.

16 'The need for women workers in China', p. 209; for imitative powers see Ch'en, *The Development of British Malaya, 1896–1909*, pp. 45–56; Kiernan, *The Lords of Human Kind*, pp. 167–8.

17 'The need for women workers in China', p. 209; Mrs Bryson, 'Shanghai, the model settlement', *Young England*, vol. XXI, 1899, pp. 452–4; A. H. R., 'A woman's day in Shanghai', *Girl's Empire*, vol. III, 1903–4, pp. 170–2; 'The chinaman's wheelbarrow', *Young England*, vol. XXXIV, 1912–13, p. 192.

18 'The heathen Chinee', *Chums*, vol. I, 1892–93, p. 616.

19 'A Chinese inn', *Boys of the Empire*, vol. I, no. 4, 17 November, 1900, p. 66; for Chinese social habits see Smith, *Chinese Characteristics*, chapter XV; Ch'en, *The Development of British Malaya, 1896–1909*, p. 44; R. Knox, *The Races of Man*, London, 1862, p. 226.

20 'When in the Canque', *Chums*, vol. VIII, no. 414, 15 August, 1900, p. 821; 'The need for women workers in China', p. 209; for cruelty see Smith, *Chinese Characteristics*, p. 213–15.

21 'Cricket in strange places', *Young England*, vol. XXXV, 1913–14, p. 452; for sport in imperial image see J. A. Mangan, ed., *The Cultural Bond*, London, 1992, pp. 1–10.

22 F. Richards, 'The new boy at Greyfriars', *Magnet*, vol. I, no. 38, 17 October, 1908, p. 14; F. Richards, 'Aliens at Greyfriars', *Magnet*, vol. I, no. 6, 26 October, 1910, p. 141; see also E. S. Turner, *Boys will be Boys*, London, 1948, pp. 199–220.

23 Richards, 'The new boy at Greyfriars', p. 14; F. Richards, 'The cheerful Chinee', *Magnet*, vol. II, no. 47, 1 January, 1909, p. 3; F. Richards, *Autobiography*, London, 1952, p. 38.

24 F. Richards, 'The Greyfriars Chinee', *Magnet*, vol. I, no. 39, 24 October, 1908, p. 2; Richards, 'The cheerful Chinee', pp. 5, 11, 14.

25 F. Richards, 'The Chinee captain', *Magnet*, vol. I, no. 55, 27 January, 1909, pp. 2–3.

26 F. Richards, 'Wun Lung's secret', *Magnet*, vol. VII, no. 276, 24 May, 1913, p. 21.

27 Richards, 'The Greyfriars Chinee', p. 10.

28 Richards, 'The new boy at Greyfriars', pp. 2, 14; Richards, 'Wun Lung's secret', p. 22; Richards, 'The Greyfriars Chinee', p. 10.

29 Turner, *Boys will be Boys*, p. 149; in 1900 the Aldine Library contained 250 detective titles, and many of the annual detectives, such as Nelson Lee, appeared in library series of their own; for a picture of women detectives see 'Martia Wray, the female Sherlock Holmes', *Pluck*, vol. X, no. 235, 1899; for a view of other groups portrayed as villains see 'The thief of the black ruby', *Pluck*, vol. II, no. 52, 1895, pp. 1–3 (Indian); 'Vengeance', *Pluck*, vol. V, no. 114, 1897, pp. 1–2 (Gypsy); 'The three fold mystery', *Pluck*, vol. IV, no. 105, 1896, pp. 1–2 (Jew); 'The anarchist mystery', *Pluck*, vol. XIV, no. 342, 1901, pp. 12–14 (French).

30 H. Rich, 'A tale of three cities', *Pluck*, vol. XVIII, no. 2, 1904–5, p. 29; for master criminal see Turner, *Boys will be Boys*, pp. 152–3.

31 'BB, A tale of a London secret society', *Pluck*, vol. VI, no. 160, 1898, p. 1; see also Turner, *Boys will be Boys*, p. 154; 'Frank Ferret's first case', *Pluck*, vol. XIV, no. 346, 1901, pp. 4–5; 'Stanley Dare, boy detective', *Magnet*, vol. V, no. 138, 1910, p. 26; 'Captain Twilight', *Pluck*, vol. VIII, no. 186, 1898, pp. 1–2.

32 'Frank Ferret's first case', p. 7; 'BB, A tale of a London secret society', p. 13.

33 W. LeQuex, *The Invasion of 1910*, London, 1906, pp. x–v; for invasion fears see Turner, *Boys will be Boys*, chapter XI; I. F. Clarke, 'The battle of Dorking', *Victorian Studies*, vol. 8, no. 4, June, 1965, pp. 309–27; also 'For England', *Chums*, vol. XVI, no. 801, 1908, p. 430.
34 *Boy's Herald*, vol. VIII, 1908; for the psychology of 'hatred' in the colonised see O. Mannoni, *Prospero and Caliban*, London, 1956, pp. 74–83.
35 *Chums* was the official journal of the Boy Scouts, see frontispiece, vol. XIX, 1910–11; R. Baden-Powell, 'The Boy Scout', *Boys of the Empire*, was a regular column throughout 1900; E. Sandow, 'Muscle and the boy', *Captain*, vol. I, 1898, p. 54; 'Physical culture for girls', *Girl's Own Annual*, vol. XXI, 1909–10.
36 'Terror from the East', *Chums*, vol. XIX, nos 940–60, September 1910 – February 1911, p. 13; *ibid.*, pp. 328, 383; see also 'How to become an Imperial Scout', *Chums*, vol. XIX, no. 948, 1910, p. 178; 'The editor chats', *Chums*, vol. XIX, no. 949, 1910, p. 187.
37 'London in danger or the Great Chinese Invasion', *Marvel*, vol. XV, no. 365, 1900–1, pp. 1–12.
38 *Ibid.*, p. 4.
39 *Ibid.*, p. 12; for military encounters see Kiernan, *The Lords of Human Kind*, pp. 174–6.
40 India – 'The Treaty of Tibet', *Chums*, vol. XIX, no. 942, 28 September, 1910, p. 72; see also 'Lost in the jungle', *Boy's Comic Journal*, vol. XXXI, no. 781, 26 February, 1898, p. 204; J. Liley, 'By southern campfires', *Chums*, vol. XIX, nos 947–959, 2 November 1910 – 25 January 1911.
41 'By southern campfires', no. 959, pp. 180, no. 948, p. 166.
42 *Ibid.*, no. 958, p. 336.
43 *Ibid.*, no. 950, pp. 209, 210, no. 959, p. 374; for a desire to 'return' Chinese see C. Holmes, *John Bull's Island*, London, 1988, pp. 77–80; for Chinese in Australia see Sir C. Dilke, *Problems of Greater Britain*, London, 1890, pp. 356–7.
44 'Southward Ho', *Pluck*, vol. XV, no. 371, 1901–2, pp. 2–7; S. Drew, 'Beyond the eternal ice', *Magnet*, vol. VI, no. 192, p. 25; see also Turner, *Boys will be Boys*, chapter XII.
45 'Southward Ho', p. 6.
46 S. Drew, 'Wolves of the deep', *Magnet*, vol. VI, no. 169, 1911, p. 24; see also S. Drew 'Lion against bear', *Magnet*, vol. VI, no. 179, 1911, p. 23; for music hall image of Chinese see J. MacKenzie, *Propaganda and Empire*, Manchester, 1984, chapter 2.
47 'The opium smugglers', *Chums*, vol. XVI, no. 807, 1908, p. 565; C. Payne, 'The glass eye', *Chums*, vol. XVI, no. 810, 1908, p. 802; 'The dragon's teeth', *Chums*, vol. XVI, no. 799, 1908, p. 824.
48 'Such a coward', *Boys of the Empire*, vol. 1, no. 6, 1 December, 1900, p. 104; see also 'The quest of the black pearl', *Chums*, vol. XIX, no. 975, 17 May, 1911, p. 656; W. Gray, 'The pirate Chung Li Sen', *Captain*, vol. I, 1898, pp. 212–15.
49 'The mysterious jewel', *Young England*, vol. XXXV, 1913–14, p. 126; 'London in danger', pp. 9, 12; for Chinese customs see Ch'en, *China and the West*, p. 44; Smith, *Chinese Characteristics*, chapter 4.
50 'The mysterious jewel', p. 311; for brash imperial boy see P. Dunae, 'Boys' literature and the idea of Empire, 1870–1914', *Victorian Studies*, vol. 24, no. 1, autumn, 1980, pp. 105–22; L. James, 'Tom Brown's imperialist sons', *Victorian Studies*, vol. 18, September, 1973, pp. 89–99.
51 'London in danger', pp. 7–12; for modern China see 'Dry bones stirring in China', *Spectator*, 24 September, 1898, pp. 395–6; Ch'en, *China and the West*, pp. 70–1; Kiernan, *The Lords of Human Kind*, pp. 165–66
52 'The mysterious jewel', p. 309, 499; for Chinese and Western education see Ch'en, *China and the West*, pp. 63–72, 159–73.
53 S. Hooke, 'The wraith of Buddha's tower', *Pluck*, vol. XII, no. 2, 1904–5, p. 23.
54 Hooke, 'The wraith of Buddha's tower', p. 24; 'The mandarin's quest', *Pluck*, vol. III, no. 69, 1905, p. 19; 'A Chinaman's revenge', *Chums*, vol. I, no. 33, 1 April,

1893, p. 314; 'Such a coward', p. 104; 'The black pearl of Peihoo', *Boy's Own Annual*, vol. XXXVI, 1913–14, p. 410; for Chinese physical characteristics see Ch'en, *China and the West*, p. 43–4; P. Murrell, *The Imperial Idea in Children's Literature, 1840–1902*, unpublished PhD thesis, University of Swansea, 1975, pp. 134–7.

55 On immigration restrictions see Holmes, *John Bull's Island*, pp. 53–4, 77–80.
56 For interest in science see Turner, *Boys will be Boys*, chapter X.
57 For image of Japan, see Kiernan, *The Lords of Human Kind*, pp. 181–93; 'Editor speaks', *Chums*, vol. XIX, no. 946, 1910.

CHAPTER SEVEN

The inter-war years

There has been a tendency among historians to view the great wars as watersheds in the narrative of history. It is perhaps useful then to consider whether the inter-war years brought significant change in the images forged before the First World War, or whether the patterns of representation set in an earlier period remained substantially intact.

In the period when Britain was assimilating the lessons of the First World War, part of the process did involve a questioning of the role of history in society. Certainly voices were raised which pointed to a possible correlation between overtly nationalistic history and international misunderstandings. Among them was Bertrand Russell, who wrote in 1922, and again in 1937, on the dangers of miseducating the young:

> Throughout the western world boys and girls are taught false history, false politics, false economics. Children learn in school the faults of other nations, but not the faults of their own.[1]

Leonard and Virginia Woolf published a book in 1929 by a young member of the Teachers Labour League, Mark Starr. *Lies and Hate in Education* was a forceful attack on the race and class bias of the history textbooks used in British schools. It also emphasised the relationship between history texts and the cheap adventure fiction which 'children read with avidity outside the school'. Starr deplored the regularity with which the 'old patriotic histories' were reissued in the post-war era. To reinforce his argument he quoted Ramsay MacDonald's address to the World Conference of History Associations in 1925:

> The history that is taught by every nation today is deplorable. It is far more national propaganda than an exposition of truth.[2]

There were also moves initiated by the League of Nations to study the effects of textbooks on international understanding, and under its auspices a series of texts was issued which professed the aim of fostering a spirit of toleration through education. There was clearly a concern among certain segments of society that a new approach to history was an essential part of rebuilding the post-war world.[3]

Historians took up the debate over a 'desirable' curriculum with enthusiasm. Discussion centred on issues such as the move away from insularity, and a proper inclusion of world history within the syllabus. Criticism of a history which had overemphasised politics at the expense of social or economic history also surfaced. A critical aspect of the debate was the place of imperial history in the classroom. J. F. Findlay, in his influential book *History and its Place in Education*, wrote in 1923:

> To leave our children as ignorant as their fathers were of the state of Europe and Asia, lulled in the pride of the past and a conceited security of our exalted power, is to invite disaster.[4]

The Board of Education did respond to the new atmosphere and showed itself willing, with reservations. While H. A. L. Fisher did assert in a 1923 circular that 'some general notion of world history' should be offered to the young, he insisted that the history of 'their native country will naturally claim the prerogative share of attention'. Rather optimistically the pamphlet also claimed a notable improvement in the quality of textbook writing, while still insisting that a question on imperial and one on military or naval affairs appear in every examination paper in later periods of British history.[5]

The Hadow report in 1927 also emphasised world history as the setting for national history, but showed concern that 'good training in history is impossible where the work is confined to the textbook'. Again, in 1927 a *Handbook for Teachers in Elementary Schools* endorsed a fuller history of the overseas dominions as an 'integral part of the story of the British peoples'. Perhaps more instructive is the admission that 'there is seldom time for the systematic teaching of foreign or world history'. A report on books used in public elementary schools in 1928 recommended regular review of their contents to ensure the inclusion of modern research. It virtually acknowledged that the shortcomings of the books still in use reflected the continued dominance of the 'old type' of history text, particularly in their treatment of the dominions.[6] By 1937 the Board of Education was still suggesting to teachers, in a rather resigned tone:

> A respect for other civilisations than that of Western Europe will best grow out of a knowledge, however small, of their history. Even to hear that the Chinese were a cultured people when our ancestors were savages may exercise a lasting effect on the outlook of the child.[7]

Despite laudable sentiments in the public arena and informed debate among the historical and educational establishment, there were forces at work which resisted the implementation of significant change. This is particularly true in the treatment of imperial history, and the images it presented of non-Europeans. One important factor was the long shelf life of history textbooks published before the war,

[163]

notably those which had secured the approval of examining boards and sold well. Influential texts such as S. R. Gardiner's *A Student's History of England* and Warner and Marten's senior school history were successively reprinted and used well into the 1930s. Some pre-First World War texts were still found in schools in the 1960s.[8]

Histories written after the war did devote more space to modern history and in some cases offered a more comprehensive treatment of Britain's dominions. There is little evidence, however, that significant change had occurred in the treatment of the Indian, the African or the Chinese. Although attitudes toward India as Empire had undergone revision after the war, acknowledging its contribution to the war effort and the emerging nationalist movements, there continued traditional views of important events in the history of British India and of groups/individuals from the history of India. The division which had been made in the earlier texts between 'good' and 'bad' rulers saw little revision. Nana Sahib and Siraj ud Daula continued to be portrayed as 'oriental tyrants', with little attempt to offer explanation for their hostile actions. The 'massacre' at Cawnpore and the loss of life in the 'Black Hole' remained as events illustrating the cruelty and duplicity of those who would overthrow British power. Clive and Hastings retained their positions as great empire builders. Textbooks still praised the 'amazing work in setting things straight' on the subcontinent. In general there was significant praise for the servants of Empire, stressing their skill, dedication, and self-sacrifice in the Indian service.[9]

In both junior and senior texts the attitude toward the British in India was overwhelmingly positive. In George Southgate's *The British Empire*, successively reprinted from 1936, great stress is laid upon the justice of British administration in India, in particular 'the very great benefits' brought to the Indian peoples after the Mutiny. Roads, railroads, famine relief, public health, education and administrative reforms were achieved despite the 'oriental fatalism' of the people. While accepting the need for the introduction of free institutions in India, he views the Indian National Congress as somewhat irresponsible. In an unconsciously ironic observation he notes that 'history was falsified and every British measure misrepresented in the worst possible way'. His textbook suggests that the pace of change must be controlled by the British, whose job it is, despite the 'hostile races, castes, language and illiteracy' to apply 'the restraining hand of a superior power'. Rayner and Airey in *A Concise History of Britain*, written in 1938, also emphasised that the British government 'tries to meet the discontent by the largest practicable grant of self-government'.[10]

Between the wars the textbooks were eager to stress the benefits of British rule for India, past and present, and mounted quite a strong defence against considering that the potential end of British rule in India signified failure. The treatment of the Mutiny, which now provided greater detail on complex causes yet continued to stress misunderstandings on the part of the sepoy and clemency by the British, reflects the pre-war tendency to blame the Indian for the outbreak of violence. A. P. Newton wrote in 1929, of the period from 1870 to 1900, that it was the 'unbroken prosperity' which helped to obliterate the memories of the Mutiny and 'gives lie to the belief that British imperialism connotes selfishness and tyranny'. Texts of the inter-war period suggest that the problems which remain are due to the character of the Indian peoples, their fatalism, illiteracy, backwardness, conservatism and natural improvidence. As Newton observed, 'only those guided by passion or prejudice deny the healing influence of British rule'.[11]

These texts also continued to acknowledge the contributions of the loyal Sikhs on the battlefield, and supported the ambitions of responsible Indian leaders, expounding a traditional stereotypical view of Indian relations with the structures of power. There was little sympathy for the crucial problems of the subcontinent, and little real understanding of the genesis of nationalist sentiments. While anticipating the time when India would take its place among the dominions of 'Greater Britain', little information was offered to the student which would alter the ethnocentric assumptions of the pre-war textbooks. Indians in the mass continued incapable of progress without a firm British presence, and history suggested an Indian character at once treacherous, cruel and generally 'uncivilised'. The 'imperial image' of India's people remained virtually intact.[12]

China and Africa fared no better in the years before the Second World War. Not until very recently have history textbooks moved beyond attitudes formed toward the Chinese in the nineteenth century. Information continued to be centred on encounters in the Opium Wars, the *Arrow* incident, and the Boxer Rebellion. There was no significant revision of the causation of these events, and attention continued to focus on the hostility shown towards 'foreign devils'. The 'arrogance' of Chinese officials still figured strongly in the course of events, without offering to the student any explanation of possible Chinese grievances against the West. Events in China in the 1920s and 1930s had done little to increase sympathy for or understanding of the country, and revolution seemed to distance China more than ever from the Western tradition. Both these factors and the rise of Japan suggested the need for Britain to continue with a strong naval

[165]

presence in the Pacific. Opium remained the 'problem' of the Chinese peoples, while a lack of respect for the British continued to illustrate a flawed character, the Boxers rebelled without clear cause, and internal struggles destabilised the course of progress. Only Hong Kong remained proof of the possibilities of a modern world view on the part of the Chinese, and of success in compelling the reluctant giant to concede to Western values.[13]

Some texts, whether in the light of Australian labour problems or in reference to British anti-immigration legislation, kept alive the idea of the 'yellow peril'. China was believed to be 'teeming' with surplus population, and a watchful eye was suggested as necessary if white Australia was to be protected from 'coolie' labour. Attitudes toward the Chinese were mixed, but judgements were most favourable when they stayed at home, cooperated with Western trading and strategic needs, and provided a buffer against Japanese expansionist tendencies.[14]

As late as the mid-seventies, David Killingray was still finding that 'for the majority of schools Africa's past is still either ignored, denigrated, or distorted'. This was essentially the approach of textbooks in the inter-war years. Africa's past continued to figure only in relation to the British exploration, settlement, and/or economic penetration of the continent. Tribes might be described in sweeping generalisations of their main characteristics, the Bantus as 'virile', Zulus, Basutos, Ashanti and Matabele as 'warlike', Hottentots as 'primitive', Bushmen as 'uncivilised', and so on. The Zulus remained a 'race apart' in the African context, admired for martial skills, strong leadership, and physical stature.[15]

The treatment of South Africa and the Boer War in particular illustrates how little progress had been made in presenting a more balanced view of the 'natives'. A major concern in the area was the fact that, as Southgate put it, 'the native population substantially exceeds the white'. Junior texts as well noted that the 'coloured peoples of Africa are numerous and strong, they increase very fast'. Much emphasis was placed upon the 'racial character' of the problems which emerged in the area. Hostilities between the Boer and the British were presented as exacerbated by the 'native' question; indeed, some historians questioned whether there would have been such mis-understandings without 'natives playing one race off against another'. Southgate further illustrates the complexity of the race question in the case of 'Asiatics' imported to replace local labour. The overwhelming impression of the inter-war commentaries on South Africa and the African in general was a clear sense of dealing with inferior peoples, who created troubles between Europeans, but whose 'burden' had to be accepted in order to enjoy the demonstrable economic gains of occupying a rich continent.[16]

A resistance to change in the history textbooks' characterisation of peoples encountered in imperial expansion has been quite striking. The historian Peter Fryer, writing in 1989, observed that 'the essential racism of the official version of our history is seen above all in its glorification of the British Empire and its arrogant attitude to those who were the empire's subjects'. As late as 1985, in the Swann report, *Education for All*, the author advised that racism in the curriculum be addressed. The History Working Group for the National Curriculum in 1990 advocated the application of historical skills learned in the classroom to 'combating racial and other forms of prejudice and stereotypical thinking'. While there is clearly greater awareness of the role which history can play in correcting the consequences of its abuse, particularly in advocating critical thought, it is equally certain that negative imagery and distortions have been difficult to eradicate.[17]

In the world of popular magazines, important developments did follow the First World War. Ever conscious of the audience, the publishing houses responded to the social changes which affected their young readers. By 1918 the Education Act had raised the school-leaving age to 14, ensuring that the vast majority of the population remained at school for at least nine years. This factor was important in extending the period of childhood, and establishing more widely the idea of leisure time for boys and girls. Ever more titles appeared for the juvenile market, responding to the influence of the cinema, greater spending power, and the diminishing encroachment of 'work' on children's time.

Two trends in particular seem important to consider as relevant to this study. One is the decrease in the 'improving' type of paper, and the other is the increase in commercial fiction for schoolgirls. The entry of D. C. Thompson of Dundee into the popular market was a major innovation, challenging and eventually surpassing the popularity of the Harmsworth monopoly on popular titles. While the *Magnet* and the *Gem* began to fall behind in the circulation race, Thompson's 'Big Five', *Adventure* (1921) *Rover* (1922), *Wizard* (1922), *Skipper* (1930), and *Hotspur* (1933) captured the twopenny market. Harmsworth's Amalgamated Press responded with the launch of 28 papers in the 1920s and 1930s, particularly concentrating their efforts on schoolgirls. Among the older weeklies, only the *Boy's Own Paper* held its own throughout the period. Studies of children's reading habits in the inter-war years confirm the consumption of at least two or three storypapers a week by school-age children.[18]

Just as more children were staying on at school, so the numbers able and willing to buy and exchange popular papers was on the increase. The possibilities for the young to enter into the world of mass-produced fiction was eased by both the increasing literacy of the era and the papers' own emphasis on appealing to the 'modern' reader. Kirsten Drotner, in her excellent study of magazines for the English youth market, has noted how the publications of these years gradually discarded realism for the exuberant formula of rapid action, blurring the distinction between fact and fiction, rapidly changing the casts of characters, and introducing a new 'type' of girl and boy. Yet as the magazine market expanded, it continued to depend on a cast of 'alien' characters in its stories and features. While much of the 'improving' material began to disappear, reflecting the move toward a youth-centred culture, Indian, African and Chinese characters still played an important role in stories and features. In both boys' and girls' magazines the school story remained a popular feature, with 'dusky' chums continuing to provide narrative interest. Young Britain still roved the world in search of adventure, meeting friends and adversaries on their home ground. Annuals continued the practice of retelling the stories of famous defences and residency sieges, a time-tested source of thrills and danger. Foreigners remained a source of curiosity, whether as the newest troop of international Scouts, interesting statistics, or quaint customs. Girl aviatrix, while a new character type, found themselves on familiar ground, flying into China, for example, to rescue women and children stranded in isolated villages.[19]

In older titles, like the *Boy's Own Paper* and *Young England*, imperial tales of India still appeared. Hunting continued to operate as a paradigm of dominance. Each generation of readers learned anew both that 'the flag is immortal' and that Indian agitators 'wished to sit in the seat of power'. Danger to the Empire rested in the actions of mutinous crowds 'all bent on murder and loot'. British fears about German ambitions for world power surfaced in conspiracies to defeat the Empire in Asia. In one story it was a German arms dealer named Marx who encouraged 'an India in arms and mad with bloodlust'. The Indian 'masses' were portrayed as susceptible still to the manipulation of unscrupulous agitators.[20]

'Information' about India and its peoples was still provided in the non-fiction of the more traditional papers. 'Notes from Overseas', a long-standing feature of the *Boy's Own Paper*, explained the duties of a forest officer in India, discussed the Scouting movement, and introduced boys to the type of games favoured on the subcontinent. In 1927 this section featured the 'Tortoise race', suitable for a climate where the heat demanded limited physical exertion, and therefore demanding 'self-control and mental strength' instead. Indian cricketers continued to appear as exemplary ambassadors for their country, and the recounting of a famous cricket match between an English and a Sikh side offered the observation that Sikh batsmen 'show the same grit and good faith that your race show when they give their best for England'. Overall, the presentation of India differed little from the pattern of the pre-war papers, an amalgam of reassurance and distortion in the non-fiction, giving way to the stuff of adventure in the serial stories.[21]

In the popular papers founded before the war, such as the *Marvel* and the *Magnet*, familiar formulas continued through the inter-war years. Hurree Jamset Ram Singh survived in the *Magnet* until 1940 with concessions neither to time nor social change. School stories were also a prominent feature of the newer boys' and girls' magazines which came on to the market in the 1920s and 1930s. Bessie Bunter returned home from Cliff House School for Christmas in 1934 to find Gunda Lal, a Hindu fortune teller, invited to 'enliven' the festivities. The Red Circle School in the *Hotspur* featured a 'colonial house' for boys from the dominions. This story from 1937 illustrated that the Indian schoolboy was still viewed as a useful device for those who wrote for the modern papers. While the pre-war papers confined their newcomers to the princely class, the *Hotspur*, reflecting a more 'egalitarian' atmosphere in the fictional inter-war schools, introduced a story which featured the conflict between Ranji Das and Ahmed Singh, Hindu untouchable and Sikh, who refused despite all efforts of the English chums to become friends. The resources of the schoolboys were stretched to their limits in an attempt to overcome this hostility in time to play them together in a crucial football match. The solution found was to dupe them both by covering every inch of their skin with white sticking plaster. In this disguise Ranji unwittingly saved Ahmed's life, proving that 'different castes or not, they could not go on being enemies'. Both went on to score goals and ensure victory in the school cup.[22]

This is an interesting story for the late 1930s. British boys show themselves as fair minded and concerned with mediating irrational prejudice in the Indian. The use of white sticking plaster suggests that whiteness brings with it a willingness to ignore what are presented as ridiculous caste and religious prohibitions. The sporting ethos is seen as instrumental in overcoming individual antagonisms. It is another example, familiar in the imagery of India, of the British superiority over attitudes and behaviour which was held to have worked against unity and progress on the subcontinent. India, it seemed, still had much to learn from the values of British boyhood. On the eve of war in Europe the story also presented an image of Britain's peacemaking role, eager to disarm, rather than join, the troublemakers.

While the distinguishing 'difference' of India was often described in terms of custom, observance, or behaviour, racial distinctions also featured strongly. In the story above, one of the key aspects of neutralising the conflict was the elimination of colour in the two Indian boys. Other stories reversed the experience by showing British boys in India disguising themselves to escape detection. Stories such as the 'Irrepressible snake charmers' in the *Wizard* (1925) made clear to the reader the English reaction to falling into a bath of skin stain:

> Tim: 'Crumbs, I'm a Hindu'.
> Jim: 'Crumbs, they're black. I've gone bad'.
> Tim: 'My brother with a black face? Never let it be said'.
> Jim: 'It's better to have a black skin than none at all'.[23]

While de-emphasising the overt imperial messages of the pre-war publications, the magazines of the inter-war years continued to propagate images of the Indian forged in the colonial context. The Indian as adversary, duplicitous, cruel, and cunning, still crept toward the Residency. Indian schoolboys still spoke 'flowery' English, and still needed the spirit of 'fair play' to overcome their own irrational prejudices. Pindharis and Thugs continued to challenge the rule of law, while upper-class Indians upheld British custom and intervention. Snake charmers and fakirs remained a curious mystery. And the 'blackness' of India was used to represent an unchallengeable superiority in the Anglo-Saxon world.[24]

Africa was a favoured setting for adventure in the years between the world wars, and African characters of long standing retained their popularity. Pete was still in the *Marvel* after the war, and successfully transferred to film in 1919. The loyal, fun-loving, comic was repeated in other figures like 'Nelson the Nig' in the *Wizard* and Topsy in the *Schoolgirls' Own*. This continued the image of the African as good tempered, impulsive, sentimental, and a firm friend of white companions.[25]

Racial characteristics figured large in both the presentation and the action. Topsy, 'black as the proverbial pitch', enters the story in 'striking contrast' to her 'mistress' Peggy Blake, daughter of an English businessman in South Africa. In many stories the stock figure of the 'candid coloured girl' and the capable or daredevil white girl joined forces. While the 'coloured' character rested on familiar stereotypes, the resourceful girl heroine was a new and very popular convention of the 1930s. Girl 'castaways' now encountered 'natives' in their adventures, with a 'Girl Friday' as a faithful servant. The 'Old Kaffir', family retainer and source of local wisdom to young master or mistress was another stock character, again familiar from pre-war adventures in Africa. These confident British boys and girls showed that they 'knew' Africa by speaking local languages and defending their servants from the racism of other, less enlightened Europeans. Pluck and daring had their place as well, in the face of 'savage tribes', and reinforced the image of resourceful and competent characters in the young expatriate community.[26]

Despite the introduction of modern elements in the stories – the cinema, aeroplanes, an emphasis on trade to the exclusion of sport and missionary work – the updated British characters encountered predictable African stereotypes. A story from 1933 set on the Guinea coast included a black airman, a 'coal coloured Colossus', called Tupper. Although he presents himself as a doctor, as the story unfolds he reveals himself as a dealer in diamonds, ivory and gold. The author reminds the readers that despite appearances Tupper was no more than a 'modern day witch doctor'. Indeed, witch doctors of the traditional variety continued to hold a fascination for the story writers, guaranteed to introduce an air of mystery and magical violence into the course of events. They continued to be portrayed as holding superstitious 'natives' in their grip, extorting money and tribute in return for the promise of protection from evil spirits.[27]

Pictures continued to be drawn of friendly and unfriendly, more and less advanced, tribal societies, with tribal 'hierarchy' little changed from the pre-war years. The Zulu and the Bantu were generally well received, serving the interests of the white characters. Their physical characteristics were described in more flattering terms – 'tall and well-formed' specimens of manhood. Pygmies rested at the other end of the scale, described as 'repulsive, cruel and unintelligent'. A story of Jimmy and QP, 'radio pals' on a spree in Central Africa, showed the stories making the standards of judgement explicit to the reader:

Jimmy: 'Are they fond of sport?'
QP: 'Are they loyal to the British?'
Consul: 'Yes, the Hausas are one of the finest races in Africa.'[28]

While the interests of the British characters showed them as 'up to date', the action owed much to accepted formulas. Young adventurers continued to discover lost white men and women in the jungle, some kings or 'she queens' of local tribes. When Bessie Bunter and her gang landed in Central Africa, Mabs, blonde and pretty, casts a 'spell' over the Zulus by realising the legend of the white queen. M'Lizi, the legitimate African queen, has to be painted white in order to spirit Mabs away from the 'grovelling' natives. In the *Schoolgirl* of 1935, Claire, a young British actress on location in Africa, discovers a 'female Tarzan', Kanda, 'whose sensitive and loveable nature had survived even the roughness of a native upbringing'. While it is clear that young girl heroines had outgrown their earlier domestic constraints in these stories, and assumed an 'active' imperialism, their relations with 'natives' tend to confirm, rather than challenge, existing stereotypes.[29]

The *Boy's Own Paper* combined its fiction set in Africa with narratives of natural wonders and short informative pieces. Episodes from the nineteenth-century 'little wars' remained popular, as did trips on the African railways, and slices of life from tribal societies. Economic development continued to bring benefits to Africa – railroads, farms and mines were viewed as 'blessings' to the local workers. The picture of the African seemed untouched by the passage of time. While British boys and girls were products of a 'new age', the African retained a position and a persona seemingly untouched by the progress of 'civilisation',[30] a view which supported the maintenance of British influence in the region.

Chinese characters continued to feature in the periodicals in a variety of situations, set both in China and the wider world. The children's press did suggest that great changes were taking place within China and there were hints of revolutionary ideas, people's parties and internal power struggles. The English were presented as the friends of 'legitimate' and progressive merchant interests in the country, and generally portrayed as defenders of a peasantry caught in the cross currents. Enlightened Chinese were pictured allying with the British to defeat the intentions of 'secret societies' or 'tongs' who worked against the public interest and commercial development. One such story, set in the city of Shanghai, featured the joint efforts of a British and a Chinese detective to unmask the evil of Dr Kwang. In fiction, the two faces of China, one progressive, educated, English-speaking, the other stereotyped 'Chinks', robbers, pirates, and hostile political leaders, had altered little from the pre-war stories. Chinese torture remained a threat lurking in the background. While many modern Chinese characters dressed in the Western style, there was still the 'pig tail' to identify those who adhered to the old customs and represented a threat to British interests.[31]

On the high seas and outside China, Chinese characters appeared in predictable roles as washermen, cooks, opium smugglers and jewel thieves. International conspirators were often of Eastern origin, playing upon the popularity of Fu Manchu and the continued appeal of detective stories. Stories set in Malaya and Australia expanded the opportunities for Chinese characters to appear, as did the new journals appealing to girl readers.[32]

While pre-war papers had shown that the position of Chinese girls was a disadvantageous one in their home society, the sympathy of British schoolgirls for the 'oriental' girl now took fictional form in the inter-war stories. The *Schoolgirl* in 1929 featured a number of stories with young Chinese characters. In 'Cinderella of the circus', a Chinese lady acrobat becomes close friends with an English girl, Mimi. While noting her 'quaint' manner of speaking, the English girls also value her loyalty and pretty manners. Selina, the bad girl, calls Lo San 'an ignorant foreigner', but Mimi knows better, and calls her 'a wonderful little friend'. The same year, in 'The mystery of the miniature pagoda', a Chinese family suddenly appears in a Devon town, and while the story informs the reader 'that funny things happen when the Chinese are about', the young daughter becomes firm friends with Dot. Dot describes her new chum as 'beautiful in her eastern way', with 'refined features' and 'lovely inscrutable eyes'. The ending of the story reveals that the young Chinese girl is royalty in her own country. While there is little good to say about Chinese men in the girls' papers – Castaway Jess and other roaming girls freely refer to 'John Chinaman' and 'Chinks' – there was a clear tendency in the papers to approve of the refined Chinese woman, demure, pretty and generally anxious to foster relations with English girls. This pattern echoes the ability of women in the pre-war stories to forge alliances with upper-class 'Eastern' princesses, but does little to challenge the received image of 'decorative' Chinese women.[33]

The juvenile market was immensely prolific in the inter-war years, and the large cast of 'alien' characters was an important part of their continued appeal to the audience. It appeared a free and easy world compared with the pre-war publications. Fewer heroes and heroines were fettered with the 'white man's burden' or the imperative of consolidating the interest of Empire. The foreigner, however, still enjoyed an existence predicated upon old stereotypes recycled in new settings. While Empire was declining, racism was not, and the authors and editors seemed little interested in redrawing the Indian, the African or the Chinese character. While there were examples of new 'types' of character, like Chinese girl chums, they drew upon available images from an earlier age of delicate princesses. Indeed, with the decline of Empire and young characters less constrained by the manners of the Victorian or Edwardian era, confident boys and girls became strident in their language and actions, and this often resulted in a more overt racism in the narrative. Arguably, stereotypes set in an earlier era were reinforced as effortless superiority became integral to the English characters, and a casual, yet often harsh and superficial, judgement of 'alien' characteristics became the norm.

When the representations of the children's popular press are allied with a world of textbook history where change came slowly, if at all, one can see the forces for sustaining the images created before the war. Neither the First World War nor the imminent second one would dislodge significantly the entrenched racial attitudes which informed the presentation of African, Indian and Chinese in history textbooks and juvenile publications. For over forty years the images remained deeply ingrained in the public and private consciousness of editor, writer and reader, generally impervious to changing times. Children continued to take with them into adulthood the memory of their reading in formative years, and to find these images reinforced by cinema, newspapers and public policy. Change would come only slowly, as the old villains were replaced by new, and as the multicultural society exercised some caution in the propagation of the more overt racial stereotypes. For the large part of this century, however, the message to the youth of Britain was unequivocal. It was acceptable, entertaining, even necessary, to hold these images of the outsider. Myths generated to sustain the Empire continued to play a large part in the acculturation of British boys and girls. The discourse of dominance would prove resistant to the external realities of colonial independence and imperial decline.

Notes

1 B. Russell, *Education and the Social Order*, London, 1922, p. 137; this echoes the views of J. A. Hobson that society seeks in children's education 'to poison its early understanding of history by false ideals and pseudo-heroes', *Imperialism*, London, 1902, pp. 229–30.
2 M. Starr, *Lies and Hate in Education*, London, 1929, p. 160.
3 H. E. Cooper, *British Education, Public and Private, and the British Empire 1880–1930*, unpublished PhD thesis, University of Edinburgh, 1979, pp. 270–5; see also P. M. Kennedy, 'The decline of nationalistic history in the West', in W. Z. Laquer and G. L. Mosse, eds, *Historians in Politics*, London, 1974, pp. 141–4; G. McDiarmod and D. Pratt, *Teaching Prejudice*, Toronto, 1971, chapter 1.
4 J. Findlay, *History and its Place in Education*, London, 1923, p. 178.
5 H. A. L. Fisher, *Report on the Teaching of History*, London, 1923, p. iii.
6 *Consultative Committee Report on the Education of the Adolescent*, London, 1927, p. 203; *Handbook for Teachers in Elementary Schools*, London, 1927, pp. 123–5;

Report of the Consultative Committee on Books in Elementary Schools, London, 1928, p. 114.

7 Board of Education, *Handbook of Suggestions for Teachers*, London, 1937, p. 416.

8 S. Bates, 'School libraries shelve the fall of Empire', *The Guardian*, 19 December, 1990, p. 1; F. Glendenning, 'School history textbooks and racial attitudes, 1804–1911', *Journal of Educational Administration and History*, vol. 5, no. 22, 1973, p. 35; B. J. Elliott, *The Development of History Teaching in England, 1918–39*, unpublished PhD thesis, University of Sheffield, 1976, pp. 183–200; E. F. Lawrence, *Forms of Bias in History Writing for Schools*, unpublished MA thesis, University of Sussex, 1967, p. 19; J. MacKenzie, *Propaganda and Empire*, Manchester, 1984, p. 190.

9 F. Glendenning, *The Evolution of History Teaching in British and French Schools in the 19th and 20th Century, with Special Reference to Attitudes to Race and Colonialism in History Textbooks*, unpublished PhD thesis, University of Keele, 1975, pp.268–70; L. Hanson, *New World History Series*, London, 1920, pp. 129–41; *Handbooks of English History*, London, 1927, pp. 63–71; A. P. Newton, *The British Empire since 1783*, London, 1929, pp. 3–20; R. Rayner and W. T. G. Airey, *A Concise History of Britain*, London, 1938, pp. 403–4; R. B. Mowatt and T. Kelly, *Mayflower Histories*, vol. 3, London, 1940, pp. 216; G. Warner and C. H. K. Marten, *Groundwork of British History*, London, 1932, p. 691.

10 G. Southgate, *The British Empire*, London, 1936, pp. 175–234; Rayner and Airey, *A Concise History of Britain*, p. 630.

11 Newton, *The British Empire since 1783*, pp. 116–20; Rayner, *A Concise History of Britain*, p. 569; for Newton see R. Aldrich, 'Imperialism in the study and teaching of history', in J. Mangan, ed., *Benefits Bestowed*, Manchester, 1988, pp. 28–31.

12 Mowat, *Mayflower Histories*, vol. 3, London, 1940, pp. 156–61; Elliott, *The Development of History Teaching in England, 1918–39*, p. 200; Lawrence, *Forms of Bias in History Writing for Schools*, p. 36; MacKenzie, *Propaganda and Empire*, pp. 191–3.

13 Hanson, *New World History Series*, p. 163; Newton, *The British Empire since 1783*, p. 105; Warner and Marten, *Groundwork of British History, 1603–1932*, p. 683; E. H. Dance, *History the Betrayer*, London, 1960, p. 25.

14 Southgate, *The British Empire*, pp. 123–4; Rayner and Airey, *A Concise History of Britain*, p. 736.

15 D. Killingray, 'Africa in the classroom', *Teaching History*, no. 17, February, 1977, p. 7; Glendenning, *The Evolution of History Teaching in British and French Schools in the 19th and 20th Century*, p. 355; Mowatt and Kelly, *Mayflower History*, p. 171.

16 Southgate, *The British Empire*, pp. 161–72; see also Mowatt and Kelly, *Mayflower Histories*, vol. 3, p. 882; Warner and Marten, *Groundwork of British History, 1603–1932*, p. 704; Hanson, *New World History Series*, p. 658.

17 P. Fryer, *Black People in the British Empire*, London, 1989, p. xiii; *Education for All*, Swann report, London, 1985; *Final Report History Working Group for the National Curriculum*, London, April, 1990, p. 184.

18 K. Boyd, 'Knowing your place', in J. Tosh and M. Roper, eds, *Manful Assertions*, London, 1991, p. 148; see also P. W. Musgrave, *From Brown to Bunter*, London, 1985, pp. 226–30; MacKenzie, *Propaganda and Empire*, pp. 218–20; E. S. Turner, *Boys will be Boys*, London, 1948, pp. 221–3.

19 K. Drotner, *English Children and their Magazines 1751–1945*, New Haven, 1988, chapter 13; P. Cadogan and M. Craig, *You're a Brick Angela*, London, 1976, pp. 134–5; Musgrave, *From Brown to Bunter*, p. 225; 'Mistress of the air', *Warnes' Pleasure Book for Girls*, London, 1938, pp. 20–34.

20 G. Rochester, 'The flying beetle', *Boy's Own Annual*, vol. 49, 1926–27, pp. 2–8; W. J. May, 'The fight for the Residency', *Young England*, vol. 52, 1940, pp. 251–3; W. J. May, 'The raid that was foiled', *Young England*, vol. 52, 1940, pp. 160–4; 'Hunting – a leopard's mistake' and 'Jungle thunder', *Boy's Own Annual*, vol. 54, 1931–32, pp. 447, 342; 'A startling intrusion', *Young England*, vol. 52, 1940, pp. 133–4.

21 'Notes from Overseas', *Boy's Own Paper*, vol. 49, no. 1, p. 55, vol. 49, no. 2, p. 94–95, vol. 49, no. 2, p. 539; 'Walking on stones', *Young England*, vol. 52, 1940, p. 83; on cricket, see 'The last century bat', *Boys' Own Annual*, vol. 49, 1926–27, pp. 542, 475.

22 'The magic of the Hindu', *Schoolgirl*, vol. 11, no. 282, 22 December, 1934, pp. 5–6; 'Red turban against green turban', *Hotspur*, no. 218, 30 October 1937 – 5 November 1937.

23 'Irrepressible snake charmers', *Wizard*, no. 123, 24 January, 1925, pp. 87–94.

24 Rochester, 'The flying beetle', p. 8; 'Kalgar does his bossing', *Wizard*, no. 128, 28 February, 1925, p. 230–2; 'Kid from the jungle', *Wizard*, no. 129, 7 March, 1925, p. 256; J. Goodfellow, 'A knowledge of the game', *Warnes' Pleasure Book for Boys*, 1933; Captain G. A. Hope, 'The thanks of the government of India', *Oxford Annual for Boys*, 1930, p. 73; Major F. A. Robertson, 'Zam Zummah', *Oxford Annual for Boys*, 1930, pp. 141–4; M. S. Tustin, 'The white queen's secret', *Boy's Own Annual*, vol. 54, 1931–32, pp. 107–11.

25 'Out East with Thunderbolt', *Wizard*, no. 124, 31 January, 1925, pp. 118–25; 'Thunderbolt, Frank, and Nelson', *Wizard*, no. 133, 4 April, 1925, pp. 234–9; 'The ivory seekers', *Schoolgirls' Own*, vol. 2, no. 31, 3 September, 1921.

26 E. Rogers, 'Castaway Jess', *Schoolgirls' Own*, vol. 1, no. 1, 5 February, 1921, pp. 15–18; 'The ivory seekers', pp. 17–18; 'Mistress of the air', *Warnes' Pleasure Book for Girls*, 1938, pp. 20–34; Cadogan and Craig, *You're a Brick Angela*, p. 259; 'The girl who made good', *Warnes' Pleasure Book for Girls*, 1938, pp. 3–4; 'The orphan of the jungle', *Schoolgirl*, vol. 11, no. 285, 12 January, 1935, pp. 24–8; 'Babs and Co in the Secret City', *Schoolgirl*, vol. 11, no. 266, 1 September, 1934, pp. 2–4; C. B. Rutley, 'The wonders of mischief', *Boy's Own Annual*, vol. 54, 1931–32, pp. 295–300.

27 'Medicine man's medicine', *Warnes' Pleasure Book for Boys*, 1933; 'Study by name', *Warnes' Pleasure Book for Boys*, 1933; 'The rampart of sneezes'. *Wizard*, no. 658, 13 July, 1935, pp. 31–3; M. C. Gilson, 'Taboo', *Boy's Own Annual*, vol. 54, 1931–32, pp. 33, 513, 557; see also D. Butts, 'Imperialists of the air', in J. Richards, ed., *Imperialism and Juvenile Literature*, Manchester, 1989, pp. 136–41; for cinema see J. Richards, 'Boys' Own Empire: feature films and imperialism', in J. MacKenzie, *Imperialism and Popular Culture*, Manchester, 1986.

28 'A wireless story', *Wizard*, no. 139, 16 May, 1925, pp. 190–2; see also 'The shadow of the Assegai', *Hotspur*, no. 200, 26 June, 1937, pp. 352–4; 'Leopard tamer', *Champion*, 1939, pp. 184–90; 'A rescue in the bush', *Oxford Annual for Boys*, 1930, pp. 94–6.

29 'Mabs, queen of the jungle', *Schoolgirl*, vol. 11, no. 265, 25 August, 1934, pp. 7–9; 'The orphan of the jungle', *Schoolgirl*, vol. 11, no. 285, 12 January, 1935, pp. 24–8; 'The white queen's gold', *Boy's Own Annual*, vol. 49, 1926–27, pp. 737–41; Cadogan and Craig, *You're a Brick Angela*, pp. 230–5.

30 'The fearful eye', *Boys' Own Annual*, vol. 49, 1926–27, pp. 25–6; see also 'An arden of Thane', 'The captured bugle', and the 'Northern Rhodesian native' in the same volume; 'The making of a great Scout', 'From Mombasa to Kisume: a journey on the Ugandan railway', *Young England*, vol. 52, 1940, pp. 42–3.

31 'Coolies hostage', *Oxford Annual for Boys*, 1930, pp. 152–6; 'The trail of the hatchet man', *Wizard*, no. 633, 19 January, 1935, pp. 59–61; 'The venture of Red Star Roberts', *Wizard*, no. 655, 22 June, 1935, pp. 316–18; H. Jones, 'A sword of Nippon', *Boy's Own Annual*, vol. 54, 1931–32, pp. 1–19; 'A night of terror', *Boy's Own Annual*, vol. 54, 1931–32, pp. 372–3.

32 'Green scorpion', *Oxford Annual for Boys*, 1930, p. 230; 'The game is greater', *Warnes' Pleasure Book for Boys*, 1933; 'The story of a head', *Boy's Own Annual*, vol. 49, 1926–27, p. 222; 'My chum Tsalong', *Boy's Own Annual*, vol. 49, 1926–27, p. 375; 'Ask Jimmy', *Wizard*, no. 150, 1 August, 1925, pp. 115–20; 'Pete and the silver mine', *Marvel*, no. 799, 17 May, 1919, p. 2; for Fu Manchu and imitators see P. Howarth, *Play up and Play the Game*, London, 1973, p. 134; see also Turner, *Boys will be Boys*, pp. 152–3.

33 'Castaway Jess', *Schoolgirl's Own*, vol. 1, no. 3, 19 February, 1921, pp. 15–16; 'Cinderella of the circus', *Schoolgirl*, vol. 1, no. 2, 11 August, 1929, pp. 35–8; 'The mystery of the miniature pagoda', *Schoolgirl*, vol. 1, no. 14, 2 November, 1929, pp. 381–6; J. S. Bratton, 'British imperialism and the reproduction of femininity in girls' fiction, 1900–1930', in J. Richards, ed., *Imperialism and Juvenile Literature*, Manchester, 1989, pp. 195–215, shows girls taking up imperial views after 1914.

CONCLUSION

The idea of race has always been to some degree a construct of social necessity. This study has shown that Britain, at the zenith of Empire and in its aftermath, believing it to be necessary and expedient, deployed racial imagery to build 'character' at home and maintain the Empire abroad. What followed was both a positive definition of Anglo-Saxon characteristics and the creation of stereotypical representations of Indian, African and Chinese peoples. One of the most significant aspects of this process was its ability to take over, and to some degree subvert, channels of communication to the young, using history and the popular press to secure new generations in the ethos of 'Greater Britain'.

Ideas of racial difference and hierarchy were certainly alive in Britain before the end of the nineteenth century. However, even if one adds in the powerful influence of social Darwinism, it is unlikely that ideas of racial determination and significant hierarchies would have found their way into the consciousness of the general public without the driving force of the imperial ethos. The need of Empire to expand and to justify its subordination of other peoples gave a dynamic to the characterisation of the 'outsider' which was not at work before the imperial 'scrambles' of the 1880s. For example, while there is no doubt that the representation of India began to harden after the Mutiny of 1857, renewed fears of Indian nationalism and a general insecurity about the safety of the Empire in the early twentieth century certainly made the judgements of 'troublemakers' even harsher.[1]

It was in the thirty years before the First World War that the British public became the targets of widely disseminated propaganda, the contents of which had previously been reserved for the elite discourse of those directly involved in the administration of Empire. There were a number of reasons for spreading the message, and extending 'ownership' of the imperial ideal. The Empire was felt by its defenders to underpin Britain's claim to respect and power in the world, and there were fears of becoming a second-rate nation. On a more practical level, the Empire was clearly profitable, if not to all Britons, then at least to those who were most vocal in its defence. The armed forces also had a vested interest in promoting patriotic sentiments, and ensuring that this translated into preparedness for imperial and European defence. Those who feared a loss of social purpose and unity within domestic society also found that the imperial rhetoric served the purpose of quieting class and gender discontent. On the individual level, it was hoped that 'imperial youth' would also embrace the 'muscular Christianity' formerly reserved for the public schools, as this would be a route to combating 'degeneracy' and the 'savage' instincts of the urban poor. While this study has only touched upon the class and gender messages carried within racial representations, it is certain that the popularity and longevity of the 'colonial subject' within the classroom and popular literature rested upon the multiple lessons it carried for the schoolchild.[2]

In an important sense, what one views in the construction of racial images, and in the portrayal of the Indian, the African and the Chinese peoples, is a process of colonisation in the text, and the 'mastery' which this offered the young. One of the characteristics of these racial constructs in the history textbooks and popular publications was their flexibility and responsiveness to the needs of nationality and Empire. The reality of the British Empire was that it encompassed a great variety of peoples and places. This fact made available an extraordinary amount of 'raw material' for the historian seeking an heroic past, and for the adventure writers who placed their fiction in the far corners of the globe. Because 'subject peoples' were under the control of the writer, they could be summoned to support more than one aspect of the imperial ethos. The representation of India might primarily validate the structures of government and administration which had developed under the Raj. Africa repeatedly showed itself receptive and grateful for the humanitarian efforts of antislavery and missionary initiatives, while positively benefiting from the growth of British economic investment. China represented the challenge of a people on the periphery of Empire, who nonetheless needed to be 'understood' for their ambitions and hostility toward the West. Each group entered the texts on the condition that they supported different but complementary aspects of imperial ambition, while operating within the prevailing notions of racial hierarchy. In the texts which children encountered at school and at home, the colonial subject was essentially dehumanised and recast as a rationale for the maintenance of European dominance.[3]

Was this indoctrination of the young? It is difficult to know how many young people were sold on the idea of maintaining the British Empire by enjoying the supremacy which it offered over 'inferior peoples'. These ideas could not stop the disintegration of the Empire in the twentieth century. It is certainly arguable that history lost its claim to discovery and debate in the textbook treatment of the imperial world. Received 'truths', which included the assertion of Anglo-Saxon supremacy, were the order of the day. The popular press recognised a winning formula when they saw it, and claimed to be both entertaining and improving its readership in the process. The circulation figures of the juvenile market seem to prove the first assertion, but cannot persuade us of the second. If the young were being ill-served by a denial of balanced history and the distortions of race in their leisure reading, it is unlikely that they recognised it. The materials, in particular the adventure fiction, but also the heroics of a shared past, invited the child to join the forces of good over evil, of power over weakness, and of progress over 'darkness'. The stereotypes might be crude, but they spoke to deeply felt needs in the individual, and were particularly attractive when associated with fair play toward a 'dusky chum' or joining in the fun offered by the antics of a 'funny foreigner'.[4]

The images of race, however, continued into the inter-war years, and increasingly became dissociated from the maintenance of a dwindling Empire. What remained, however, was the association of national and individual identity with racial superiority, and this was passed to generations of children as an active legacy of the imperial era. Heroes and villains continued to be identified by racial difference, as imperial constructs began to assume a life independent from the realities of a contracting Empire. In the post-colonial world, efforts have been made to remove the distortions from materials which children encounter in their formative years. This study belongs partly to that already considerable body of literature which seeks to 'deconstruct' the colonial discourse and disempower the images created by collusive forms of knowledge. One of the challenges of the post-colonial perspective is to find a form of language which can carry understanding and respect, without the old patterns of dominance. To this end, studying the images of the 'other' in an earlier age helps us to understand how, in a particular time and place, a false historicism and racial mythologies permeated the 'education' of the young and entered the consciousness of generations to follow.[5]

Notes

1 On 'energising myths' see M. Green, *Dreams of Adventure, Deeds of Empire*, London, 1980, p. xi.

2 P. Brantlinger, *Rule of Darkness*, Ithaca, 1988, pp. 8–13; V. Ware, *Beyond the Pale*, New York, p. xv; G. Orwell, 'Boys' weeklies', in *Selected Essays*, London, 1957, pp. 196–8.

3 On the 'colonisation' of subject peoples in the textbooks, see R. Young, *White Mythologies*, London, 1990, pp. 2–20; for the post-colonial perspective see G. Spivak 'Can the subaltern speak?', in C. Nelson and L. Grossberg, eds, *Marxism and the Interpretation of Culture*, London, 1988, pp. 233–71.

4 See P. Dunae, 'New Grub Street for boys', in I. Richards, ed., *Imperialism and Juvenile Literature*, Manchester, 1989, pp. 12–33; also P. Fryer, *Black People in the British Empire*, London, 1989, pp. 73–7.

5 Two particularly important works in relation to the post-colonial perspective are E. Said, *Orientalism*, London, 1991 edn, and M. Foucault, *The Order of Things*, London, 1970; see also F. Barber, *The Politics of Theory*, Colchester, 1983.

BIBLIOGRAPHY

I. Official reports and regulations

New Code of Regulations, Education Department, 1890, LV.423.
Code of Regulations for Public Elementary Schools, Board of Education, 1904, Cd 2074, LXXVI.
Suggestions for the Consideration of Teachers and Others Concerned in the Work of Public Elementary Schools, Circular 883, Board of Education, Comd 2638, HMSO, 1905 (reissued 1914).
The Teaching of History, Board of Education Circular 599, HMSO, 1908.
Fisher, H. A. L., *Report on the Teaching of History*, Board of Education, HMSO, 1923.
Consultative Committee Report on the Education of the Adolescent (Hadow report), HMSO, 1927.
Handbook for Teachers in Elementary Schools, Board of Education, HMSO, 1927.
Report of the Consultative Committee on Books in Elementary Schools, HMSO, 1928.
Handbood of Suggestions for Teachers, Board of Education, HMSO, 1937.
Education for All (Swann report), HMSO, 1985.
Final Report of the History Working Group for the National Curriculum, HMSO, April 1990.

II. Textbooks

* Texts recommended by examination boards.
S = senior texts, J = junior texts.

Airy, O., *Textbook of English History*, Longman, 1893. S
Avon Historical Readers, Pitman, 1895. J
Bosworth, G., *A History of the British Empire*, Macmillan, 1905. S
——, *Cambridge Historical Readers*, Cambridge University Press, 1911. J
Bright, J. F., *A History of England for Public Schools*, Longman, 1887–1901. S*
Buckley, A., *History of England for Beginners*, Macmillan, 1904. J
Callcott, Lady, *Little Arthur's History of England*, J. Murray, 1913. J
Carter, G., *History of England*, Relfe, 1899. S*
Chambers' New Scheme History Readers, Chambers, 1901–1905. J
Curtis, J. C., *Outlines of English History*, Curtis, 1901. S*
Dakers, A. W., *Jack Historical Readers*, Jack, 1905. J
Davis, M. O., *The Story of England*, Clarendon Press, 1912. J*
Donald, H. W., *Handbook of Pictorial History*, Charles and Dible, 1914. J

Fearenside, C. S., *Matriculation Modern History*, Clive, 1902. *S**
——, *A School History of England*, Clive, 1904. *S**
Fletcher, C. R. L., *An Introductory History of England*, Murray, 1909. *S*
——, and Kipling, R. A., *School History of England*, Clarendon Press, 1911. *S**
Gardiner, S. R., *A Student's History of England*, Longman, 1892. *S**
Graphic History of the British Empire, Nelson, 1890. *J*
Green, J. R., *A Short History of the English People*, Macmillan, 1894. *J*
Hankin, J. T., *The Story of the Empire*, Murray, 1912. *S*
Hanson, L., *New World History Series*, Collins, 1920. *J*
Hassall, A., *The Making of the British Empire*, Blackie, 1896, 1910. *S*
——, *A Classbook of English History*, Rivingtons, 1901. *S*
Hawke, E., *The British Empire and its History*, Murray, 1911. *S*
Hayens, H., *The Making of the Homeland*, Collins, 1909. *J*
Henty, G. A., *The Sovereign Reader*, Blackie and Son, 1901. *J*
Herbertson, J. A., and Howarth, O. J., *Oxford Survey of the British Empire*,
    Clarendon Press, 1914. *S*
Heroic Reader, Jarrold, 1897. *J*
Highroads of History, Thomas Nelson, 1915. *J*
Ince, H., and Gilbert, J., *Outlines of English History*, Gilbert, 1906. *S**
Innes, A., *History of England*, Cambridge University Press, 1907. *S**
Keatinge, M., and Frazer, N. L., *A History of England for Schools*, Black,
    1911. *S*
Livesey, T., *Granville History Readers*, Burn & Oates, 1902. *J*
——, and Besonthorp, B., *Macmillan's History Readers*, Macmillan, 1891–
    95. *J*
——, and ——, *History of England*, Longman, 1908. *S*
Longman's British Empire Readers, Longman, 1905. *J*
Longman's Historical Readers, Longman, 1895. *J*
McCartey, J., *England Before and After the Reform Bill*, London, 1899. *S*
Meath, Lord, *Our Empire Past and Present*, Cassell, 1901. *S*
Meiklejohn, J., *A School History of England*, Holden, 1901. *S**
——, and Meiklejohn, M. J. C., *New World Histories*, Collins, 1920. *J*
Mowat, R. B., *A Short History of the British Empire*, Rivingtons, 1933.
——, *Mayflower Histories*, Chambers, 1940. *J*
Newton, A. P., *The British Empire since 1783*, Methuen, 1929. *S*
Oman, C., *History of England*, Edward Arnold, 1895. *S**
——, and Oman, M., *A Junior History of England*, Edward Arnold, 1904. *J*
Patriotic Historical Readers, Collins, 1898. *J*
Pringle, R. S., *Local Examination History*, Heywood, 1907. *S**
Rait, R., *A School History of England*, Clarendon Press, 1911. *S**
Raleigh History Reader, Blackie, 1898. *J*
Rayner, R., and Airey, W. T. G., *A Concise History of Britain*, Longman,
    1938. *S**
Rolleston, M., *An English History Notebook*, Davis and Houghton, 1902. *S*
——, *A School History of England*, Clarendon Press, 1911. *S*
Southgate, G., *The British Empire*, J. M. Dent and Sons, 1936. *S**
Spalding, E., *Piers Plowman Histories*, Geo Philip, 1913–22. *J&S*

[183]

Tait, C. W., *Synopsis of History*, Macmillan, 1898. *S**

Temple, A., *The Making of the Empire*, A. Melrose, 1895. *S*

Tout, T. F., *Short Analysis of English History*, Macmillan, 1891. *J*

——, *History of Britain*, Macmillan, 1902–6. *S*

Tower History Readers, Pitman, 1907. *J*

Walker, R., and Carter, G., *Local Examination History of England*, Relfe, 1905. *S*

Warner, G., and Marten, C. H. K., *Groundwork of British History*, Blackie, 1912, 1932. *S**

Warwick History Readers, Blackie, 1895–96. *J*

Yonge, C., *Westminster Reading Books*, National Society Dispensary, 1890–92. *J*

York-Powell, R., and Tout, T., *History of England*, Longman, 1900. *S**

III. Juvenile periodicals

Blackie's Girls' Annual, Blackie (annually), 1923.

Boy's Comic Journal, E. Brett (weekly), 1897–1901.

Boys of the Empire, A. Melrose (weekly), 1900–3.

Boys' Friend, Harmsworth (weekly), 1907–9.

Boy's Own Annual, ed. G. Hutchinson, Religious Tract Society (weekly until 1906, then monthly to 1967), 1880–1915, 1926–27.

Captain, G. Newnes (monthly), 1899–1906.

Champion, Amalgamated Press (weekly), 1939.

Children's World, Church Missionary House (monthly), 1893.

Chums, Cassells (weekly), 1890–1913, 1931.

Gem, Amalgamated Press (weekly), 1907–10.

Girl's Empire, Melrose (monthly), 1902–5.

Girl's Friend, Harmsworth (weekly), 1906–8.

Girl's Own Annual, Religious Tract Society (weekly, monthly in 1909), 1890–1914.

Girl's Realm Annual, Hutchinson (monthly), 1898–1900.

Girl's School Magazine, Glen & Hall (monthly), 1892–95.

Greyfriars Boys' Herald, Amalgamated Press (monthly), 1915–16.

Harmsworth Magazine, Harmsworth (monthly), 1900–2.

Herbert Strang's Annual, Henry, Frowde, Hodder & Stoughton (monthly), 1909.

Hotspur, D. C. Thompson (weekly), 1937.

Magnet, Amalgamated Press (weekly), 1908–14.

Marvel, Amalgamated Press (weekly), 1900–22.

Oxford Annual for Boys, Oxford University Press (annually), 1930.

Pluck, Harmsworth (weekly), 1895–1906.

Public School Magazine, A. & C. Black (monthly), 1898–1900.

Schoolgirl, Amalgamated Press (weekly), 1929–35.

Schoolgirls' Own, Amalgamated Press (weekly), 1921–22.

Warnes' Pleasure Book for Boys, Warne & Co. (annually), 1933.

Warnes' Pleasure Book for Girls, Warne & Co. (annually), 1938.

Wizard, D. C. Thompson (weekly), 1925–35.
Young Days, Sunday School Association (monthly), 1905–10.
Young England, Youth Missionary Society (monthly), 1895–1914, 1940.

IV. Secondary works

Adkins, F., 'Significant history for the upper standards', *History,* vol. 1, no. 1, 1912, pp. 20–33.
Afro-Caribbean Educational Resources Project, *Racism and the Black Child,* London, 1982.
Aldrich, R., 'Imperialism in the study and teaching of history', in J. Mangan, ed., *Benefits Bestowed: Education and British Imperialism,* Manchester, 1988.
Allen, J. W., *The Place of History in Education,* Edinburgh, 1909.
Allport, G., *The Nature of Prejudice,* New York, 1958.
Anglo, M., *Penny Dreadfuls and Other Victorian Horrors,* London, 1977.
Anonymous, 'Dry bones stirring in China', *The Spectator,* September, 1898.
——, 'The fighting power of the negroes', *The Spectator,* November, 1898.
——, 'Penny fiction', *Quarterly Review,* vol. CLXII, 1890, pp. 150–71.
Anstey, F., *Baboo Jabberjee BA,* London, 1897.
Arnold, G., *Hold Fast for England,* London, 1980.
Ashley-Montagu, R., *Man's Most Dangerous Myth,* New York, 1952.
Avery, G., *Childhood's Pattern,* London, 1975.
Baden-Powell, R., *Indian Memories,* London, 1915.
Ballhatchet, K., *Race, Sex and Class under the Raj,* London, 1980.
Banton, M., *White and Coloured,* London, 1959.
Barbour, I., *Myths, Models and Paradigms,* London, 1974.
Barker, A. J., *The African Link: British Attitudes to the Negro in the Era of the Slave Trade, 1550–1807,* London, 1978.
Barnard, J., *Nationality, its Nature and Problems,* London, 1929.
Barr, P., *Foreign Devils,* London, 1970.
——, *The Memsahibs,* London, 1976.
Barzun, J., *Race, a Study in Superstition,* London, 1938.
Baudet, H., *Paradise on Earth,* New Haven, 1965.
Bearce, G., *British Attitudes Towards India, 1784–1858,* Oxford, 1961.
Beckett J., and Cherry, D., eds, *The Edwardian Era,* London, 1987.
Benedict, R., *Race and Racism,* London, 1959.
Bhabha, H., 'Difference, discrimination, and the discourse of colonialism', in F. Barker, ed., *The Politics of Theory,* Colchester, 1983.
Bibbey, G., *The Testimony of the Spade,* London, 1962.
Biddiss, M., *Images of Race,* Leicester, 1979.
——, ed., *Gobineau: Selected Political Writings,* London, 1970.
Billington, R., *The Historians' Contribution to Anglo-American Misunderstandings,* New York, 1966.
Birkett, D., *Spinsters Abroad,* London, 1986.
Bland, L., *Banishing the Beast: English Feminism and Sexual Morality 1885–1914,* London, 1995.

Bloch, M., *The Historian's Craft*, Manchester, 1954.

Boime, A., *The Art of Exclusion*, London, 1990.

Bolt, C., *Victorian Attitudes to Race*, London, 1971.

——, 'Race and the Victorians', in C. Eldridge, ed., *British Imperialism in the 19th Century*, London, 1985.

Booth, C., *Life and Labour of the People of London*, London, 1902.

Boskin, J., *Sambo: The Rise and Demise of an American Jester*, Oxford, 1986.

Bowle, J., *The Imperial Achievement*, London, 1974.

Brantlinger, P., *Rule of Darkness: British Literature and Imperialism, 1830–1914*, Ithaca, 1988.

Bratton, J. S., *The Impact of Victorian Children's Fiction*, London, 1981.

——, et al., *Acts of Supremacy: The British Empire and the Stage, 1790–1930*, Manchester, 1991.

Bristow, J., *Empire Boys*, London, 1991.

Bryce, J., *The Relations of the Advanced and Backward Nations of Mankind*, London, 1902.

Burrows, J., *A Liberal Descent*, Cambridge, 1981.

Bury, J., *The Idea of Progress*, London, 1955.

Cadogan, M., and Craig, P., *You're a Brick Angela*, London, 1976.

Cairns, H. A., *Prelude to Imperialism*, London, 1965.

Carlyle, T., *Critical and Miscellaneous Essays*, London, 1905.

Chamberlain, M. E., *Britain and India*, Newton Abbot, 1974.

Chancellor, V., *History for their Masters*, Bath, 1970.

Charles Edwardes, T., and Richardson, B., *They Saw it Happen*, Oxford, 1974.

Chen, C. H., *The Development of British Malaya, 1896–1909*, Oxford, 1964.

Ch'en, J., *China and the West*, London, 1979.

Chesneaux, J., et al., *China from the Opium Wars to the 1911 Revolution*, London, 1977.

Chirol, V., *Indian Unrest*, London, 1910.

Clarke, I. F., 'The battle of Dorking', *Victorian Studies*, vol. 8, no. 4, June, 1965, pp. 309–27.

Collingwood, R., *The Idea of History*, London, 1946.

Comas, J., *Racial Myths*, Paris, 1958.

Coombes, A., *Reinventing Africa*, New Haven, 1994.

Cox, J., *Take a Cold Tub, Sir*, Guildford, 1982.

Cramb, J., *The Origins and Destiny of Imperial Britain*, London, 1900.

Cunningham, H., 'The language of patriotism', *History Workshop*, no. 12, autumn, 1981, pp. 8–33.

Cunningham, H., *The Children of the Poor*, Oxford, 1991.

Curtin, P., *The Image of Africa*, London, 1965.

Curtis, L. P., *Apes and Angels*, Newton Abbot, 1971.

Dabydeen, D., ed., *The Black Presence in English Literature*, Manchester, 1985.

Dance, E. H., *History the Betrayer*, London, 1960.

Davin, A., 'Imperialism and motherhood', *History Workshop Journal*, vol. 5, 1978, pp. 9–65.

Davison, B., *The African Past*, London, 1964.

Dawson, R., *The Chinese Chameleon*, London, 1967.

Del Fattore, J., *What Johnny Shouldn't Read*, London, 1992.

Dent, H., *A Century of Growth in English Education*, London, 1970.

Dilke, Sir C., *Problems of Greater Britain*, London, 1890.

——, *On Education*, London, 1870.

Dixon, R., *Catching Them Young*, London, 1977.

Doyle, B., *Who's Who of Boys' Writers and Illustrators*, London, 1964.

Drotner, K., *English Children and their Magazines, 1751–1945*, New Haven, 1988.

Dunae, P., 'Penny dreadfuls', *Victoria Studies*, vol. 22, no. 2, winter, 1979, pp. 133–50.

——, 'Boys' literature and the idea of Empire, 1870–1914', *Victorian Studies*, vol. 24, no. 1, autumn, 1980, pp. 105–22.

Edwardes, M., *The West in Asia, 1850–1914*, London, 1967.

——, *Red Year*, London, 1973.

Egerton, H. E., *A Short History of British Colonial Policy*, London, 1897.

Egoff, S., *Children's Periodicals of the 19th Century*, London, 1951.

Ellis, A., *A History of Children's Reading and Literature*, Oxford, 1968.

Faber, R., *The Vision and the Need*, London, 1966.

Fage, J. D., *An Introduction to the History of West Africa*, Cambridge, 1962.

Fairchild, H., *The Noble Savage*, New York, 1961.

Fang, Wu Ting, 'China', a paper delivered at the Universal Races Congress, University of London, 1911.

Farwell, B., *Queen Victoria's Little Wars*, London, 1973.

Ferro, M., *The Uses and Abuses of History*, London, 1984.

Field, J., *Toward a Programme of Imperial Life*, Westport, 1982.

File, N., and Power, C., *Black Settlers in Britain*, London, 1981.

Findlay, J., *History and its Place in Education*, London, 1923.

Forrester, W., *Great Grandma's Weekly: the GOP 1880–1901*, London, 1980.

Foucault, M., *The Order of Things*, London, 1970.

French, D., 'Spy fever in Britain 1900–15', *Historical Journal*, no. 21, 1978, pp. 355–70.

Froude, J. A., *Oceana: or England and her Colonies*, London, 1886.

Fryer, P., *Staying Power*, London, 1984.

——, *Black People in the British Empire*, London, 1989.

Gardiner, J., ed., *The History Debate*, London, 1990.

Geyl, P., *The Use and Abuse of History*, New Haven, 1955.

Gillis, J., *Youth and History*, London, 1981.

Glendenning, F., 'Racial stereotypes in school textbooks', *Race Today*, vol. 3, no. 2, 1971 February, pp. 52–4.

——, 'School history textbooks and racial attitudes, 1804–1911', *Journal of Educational Administration and History*, vol. 5, 1973, pp. 33–44.

Gooch, G. P., *History and Historians in the 19th Century*, London, 1952.

Gordon, D., *The Moment of Power*, Englewood Cliffs, 1970.

Gough, B., ed., *In Search of the Visible Past*, London, 1975.

Green, M., *Dreams of Adventure, Deeds of Empire*, London, 1980.

Greenberger, A. J., *The British Image of India*, Oxford, 1969.

Gregg, H., 'The Indian mutiny in fiction', *Blackwood's Magazine*, vol. CLXL, no. 976, February, 1897, pp. 218–31.

Grey, H., *The Public Schools and the Empire*, London, 1913.

Gundara, J., Jones, C., and Kimberly, K., *Racism, Diversity and Education*, London, 1986.

Guy, J., *The Destruction of the Zulu Kingdom*, London, 1979.

Haggard, H. R., *She: A History of Adventure*, London, 1887.

Haining, P., *The Penny Dreadful*, London, 1975.

Haldane, R., *Education and Empire*, London, 1902.

Haller, J., *Outcasts from Evolution*, New York, 1975.

Hannam, C. L., 'Prejudice and the teaching of history', in M. Ballard, ed., *New Movements in the Study and Teaching of History*, London, 1971.

Harris, M., *The Rise of Anthropological Theory*, London, 1968.

Hatch, S., 'Coloured people in school textbooks', *Race*, vol. 4, no. 1, November, 1962, pp. 63–71.

Hearnshaw, F., 'The place of history in education', *History*, vol. i, no. 1, 1912, pp. 34–40.

Hertz, F., *Nationality in History and Politics*, London, 1944.

Hobsbawn, E., and Ranger, T., eds, *The Invention of Tradition*, Cambridge, 1983.

Hobson, J. A., *Imperialism*, London, 1902.

Hodglin, T., 'The teaching of history in schools', *Historical Asociation Leaflet*, no. 10, 1908.

Hoggart, R., *The Uses of Literacy*, London, 1957.

Holmes, C., *John Bull's Island*, London, 1988.

Honey, J. R., *Tom Brown's Universe*, London, 1977.

Houghton, W., *The Victorian Frame of Mind*, Oxford, 1957.

Howarth, P., *Play Up and Play the Game*, London, 1973.

Howat, G., 'The 19th c history textbook', *British Journal of Educational Studies*, no. 13, May, 1965.

Hsu, I., *The Rise of Modern China*, Oxford, 1983.

Humphries, S., *Hooligans or Rebels*, Oxford, 1981.

Hunter, W. W., *The India of the Queen*, London, 1908.

Huxley, J., and Haddon, A., *We Europeans*, London, 1935.

Hynes, S., *The Edwardian Turn of Mind*, Princeton, 1968.

Isaacs, H. R., *Images of Asia*, New York, 1972.

James, L., 'Tom Brown's imperialist sons', *Victorian Studies*, vol. 18, September, 1973, pp. 89–99.

Jeal, T., *Baden-Powell*, London, 1989.

Jenkinson, A., *What Boys and Girls Read*, London, 1940.

Johns, B. G., 'The literature of the streets', *Edinburgh Review*, January, 1887, pp. 40–65.

Johnson, B., *Letters from John Chinaman*, London, 1901.

Johnston, Sir H., *On the Urgent Need for Reform in our National and Class Education*, Conway Memorial Lecture, London, 1911.

——, *The Backward Peoples and Our Relations with Them*, London, 1920.

Judd, D. O., *Balfour and the British Empire*, London, 1968.

Keane, A. H., *The World's Peoples: A Popular Account of their Bodily and Mental Characters, Beliefs, Traditions, Political and Social Institutions*, London, 1908.

Keatinge, M. W., *Studies in the Teaching of History*, London, 1910.

Kennedy, P. M., 'The decline of nationalist history in the West', in W. Z. Laquer and G. L. Mosse, eds, *Historians in Politics*, London, 1974, pp. 329–52.

Kenyon, J., *The History Men*, London, 1983.

Kidd, B., *Social Evolution*, London, 1894.

——, *The Control of the Tropics*, London, 1898.

Kiernan, V. G., *The Lords of Human Kind*, London, 1969.

Killam, G. D., *Africa in English Fiction*, Ibadan, 1968.

Killingray, D., 'Africa in the classroom', *Teaching History*, no. 17, February, 1977, pp. 7–12.

Kipling, R., *Something of Myself*, London, 1937.

Klein, G., *Reading into Racism*, London, 1985.

Knox, R., *The Races of Man*, London, 1862.

Koebner, R., and Schmidt, H., *Imperialism: the Story and Significance of a Political Word, 1840–1960*, Cambridge, 1964.

Kuper, L., ed., *Race, Science and Society*, London, 1975.

Kuya, D., 'Biggles is a fascist beast', *Sunday Times*, 12 June, 1977.

——, 'Racism in children's books in Britain', in R. Preiswerk, ed., *The Slant of the Pen*, Geneva, 1980, pp. 26–45.

Lambert, J. C., *The Romance of Missionary Heroism*, London, 1907.

Laquer, W. Z., and Mosse, G. L., eds, *Historians in Politics*, London, 1974.

Lawrence, F., 'Textbooks', in W. Lamont, ed., *The Realities of Teaching History*, London, 1972.

Leitis, M., 'Race and culture', in *The Race Question in Modern Science*, UNESCO, London, 1975.

LeQuex, W., *The Invasion of 1910*, London, 1906.

Levine, L., *Black Culture and Black Consciousness*, New York, 1977.

Lewis, R., and Foy, Y., *The British in Africa*, London, 1971.

Little, K., *Negroes in Britain*, London, 1947.

Lofts, W., and Adley, D., *The Men Behind Boys' Fiction*, London, 1970.

Lorimer, D., *Colour, Class and the Victorians*, Leicester, 1978.

——, *Race, Race Relations and Resistance*, London, 1993.

Low-Beer, A., 'Books and the teaching of history in schools', *History*, no. 59, October, 1974, pp. 392–404.

Lowndes, G., *The Silent Social Revolution*, London, 1937.

Lucas, Sir C., 'On the teaching of imperial history', *History, new series*, vol. 1, no. 1, 1916, pp. 5–12.

Lyall, Sir A., *Asiatic Studies*, London, 1882.

Mack, E. C., *Public Schools and British Opinion Since 1860*, New York, 1941.

Mackenzie, D., 'Eugenics in Britain', *Social Studies of Science*, no. 6, 1976, pp. 499–532.

MacKenzie, J., *Propoganda and Empire: The Manipulation of British Public Opinion 1880–1960*, Manchester, 1984.

——, ed., *Imperialism and Popular Culture*, Manchester, 1986.

——, *The Empire of Nature*, Manchester, 1988.

——, *Orientalism: History, Theory and Art*, Manchester, 1995.

Mackinder, H. J., 'Man power as a measure of national and imperial strength', *National Review*, vol. XLV, March–August, 1905, pp. 136–43.

Macnamara, N. C., *The Origins and Character of the British People*, London, 1900.

Maitland, F. W., *Essays on the Teaching of History*, London, 1901.

Mangan, J. A., 'The concept of duty and the prospect of adventure', *Journal of Educational Administration and History*, vol. 12, no. 1, 1980, pp. 31–9.

——, *Athleticism in the Victorian and Edwardian Public School*, London, 1981.

——, ed., *Pleasure, Profit, Proselytism*, London, 1988.

——, ed., *Benefits Bestowed*, Manchester, 1988.

——, *The Cultural Bond: Sport, Empire and Society*, London, 1992.

——, ed., *The Imperial Curriculum*, London, 1993.

——, and Walvin, J., eds, *Manliness and Morality*, Manchester, 1987.

Mannoni, O., *Prospero and Caliban*, London, 1956.

Mannsaker, F., 'East and West: Anglo-Indian racial attitudes as reflected in popular fiction', *Victorian Studies*, vol. 24, no. 1, autumn, 1980, p. 33–52.

Marsh, P., *The Conscience of the Victorian State*, Syracuse, 1979.

Marten, C. H. K., 'Some general reflections on the teaching of history', *History*, vol. 2, no. 2, 1913, pp. 86–98.

——, *On the Teaching of History and other Addresses*, Oxford, 1938.

Mason, P., *Prospero's Magic: Some Thoughts on Class and Race*, London, 1962.

——, *Patterns of Dominance*, London, 1970.

Masterman, C., *The Heart of the Empire*, London, 1901.

McDiarmod, G., and Pratt, D., *Teaching Prejudice*, Toronto, 1971.

McDonald, R., *The Awakening of India*, London, 1910.

Meacham, S., *A Life Apart: The English Working Classes, 1890–1914*, London, 1977.

Meath, Lord, *Essays on Duty and Discipline*, London, 1911.

Milner, D., *Children and Race: Ten Years On*, London, 1983.

Montagu, M. F., *The Concept of Race*, London, 1964.

Morris, D., *The Washing of the Spears*, London, 1973.

Mowat, C., 'A study of bias in British and American history textbooks', *British Association for American Studies Bulletin*, vol. X, June, 1965, pp. 31–9.

BIBLIOGRAPHY

Mphahlele, E., *The African Image*, London, 1962.

Mudford, P., *Birds of a Different Plumage*, London, 1974.

Musgrave, P. W., *From Brown to Bunter*, London, 1985.

Nelson, C., and Grossberg, L., eds, *Marxism and the Interpretation of Culture*, London, 1988.

Neuberg, V., *Popular Literature*, London, 1977.

Nottidge, C., *Origin and Character of the British People*, London, 1900.

Oliver, R., and Atmore, A., *Africa Since 1800*, Cambridge, 1981.

Oman, Sir C., *On the Writing of History*, London, 1939.

Orwell, G., *Selected Essays*, London, 1957.

Pemberton, M., *Sixty Years Ago and After*, London, 1936.

Piaget, J., 'The development in children of the idea of homeland', *Journal of Social Psychology*, no. 58, pp. 91–108, 1951.

Pickering, M., 'White skins: black masks: nigger minstrelsy in Victorian Britain', in J. S. Bratton, ed., *Music Hall: Performance and Style*, Milton Keynes, 1986.

Pieterse, J. N., *White on Black: Images of Africa and Blacks in Western Popular Culture*, London, 1995.

Pitt, G., *A History of England with the Wars Left Out*, London, 1893.

Plumb, J. H., *The Death of the Past*, London, 1969.

Poliakov, L., *The Aryan Myth*, London, 1974.

Porter, B., *Critics of Empire*, London, 1968.

Postgate, R., and Vallance, A., *Those Foreigners*, London, 1937.

Preiswerk, R., *The Slant of the Pen*, Geneva, 1980.

Price, R. N., *The Imperial War and the British Working Class*, London, 1972.

Quayle, E., *The Collectors' Book of Boys' Stories*, London, 1973.

Quigley, I., *The Heirs of Tom Brown*, London, 1982.

Read, D., *Documents from Edwardian England*, London, 1973.

Reed, J. R., *The Old School Tie: the Public School in British Literature*, New York, 1964.

Reynolds, K., *Girls Only: Gender and Popular Children's Fiction in Britain, 1880–1910*, London, 1990.

Richards, F., *Autobiography*, London, 1952.

Richards, J., ed., *Imperialism and Juvenile Literature*, Manchester, 1989.

Roach, J., 'History teaching and examining in secondary schools, 1850–1900', *History of Education*, vol. 5, no. 2, 1976, pp. 127–40.

Robbins, K., 'History, the historical association, and the national past', *History*, October, 1981, pp. 413–25.

Roberts, R., *The Classic Slum*, Manchester, 1971.

Robinson, R., and Gallagher, J., *Africa and the Victorians*, London, 1981 edn.

Rollington, R., *The Old Boys' Book*, Leicester, 1913.

Rose, J., *The Case of Peter Pan*, London, 1984.

Rose, K., *Superior Person*, London, 1969.

Rotberg, R., *Africa and the Explorers*, Cambridge, 1970.

Russell, B., *Education and the Social Order*, London, 1932.

Said, E., *Orientalism*, London, 1991 edn.
——, *Culture and Imperialism*, London, 1993.
Salmon, E., 'What girls read', *Nineteenth Century*, vol. 20, October, 1886, pp. 515–29.
Salmon, G., 'What boys read', *Fortnightly Review*, vol. 39, January–June, 1886, pp. 248–59.
Sandison, A., *The Wheel of Empire*, London, 1967.
Schumpeter, J., *Imperialism and Social Classes*, Oxford, 1951 edn.
Scott, J., *The Menace of Nationalism in Education*, London, 1926.
Searle, G. R., *Eugenics and Politics in Britain, 1900–14*, Leyden, 1976.
Seeley, J. R., *Our Colonial Expansion*, London, 1887.
——, *The Expansion of England*, London, 1883.
Selous, F. C., *Sunshine and Storm in Rhodesia*, London, 1896.
Semmel, B., *Imperialism and Social Reform*, London, 1960.
Sencourt, R., *India in English Literature*, New York, 1923.
Shannon, R., *The Crisis of Imperialism*, London, 1974.
Silver, H., 'Aspects of neglect: the strange case of Victorian popular education', *Oxford Review of Education*, vol. 3, no. 1, 1977, pp. 57–69.
Simon, B., *Education and the Labour Movement*, London, 1964.
——, and Bradley, I. *The Victorian Public School*, Dublin, 1975.
Smith, A. H., *Chinese Characteristics*, London, 1906.
Smith, S., *Towards World Understanding: Bias in History Textbooks and Teaching*, London, 1962.
Soloway, R., 'Counting the degenerates: the statistics of race degeneration in Edwardian England', *Journal of Contemporary History*, vol. 17, 1982, pp. 137–64.
Spear, P., *Oxford History of Modern India, 1740–1947*, Oxford, 1965.
Spencer, H., *Essays on Education*, London, 1911.
Spiller, G., ed., *Papers on Inter Racial Problems*, London, 1911.
Springhall, J., *Youth, Empire and Society*, London, 1977.
——, *Coming of Age: Adolescence in Britain, 1860–1960*, London, 1986.
Starr, M., *Lies and Hate in Education*, London, 1929.
Steiner, Z., *Britain and the Origins of the First World War*, London, 1977.
Strachey, J., *The End of Empire*, London, 1959.
Street, B., *The Savage in Literature*, London, 1975.
Sturt, M., *Education of the People*, London, 1967.
Symonds, R., *Oxford and Empire*, London, 1986.
Temu, A., and Swai, B., *Historians and Africanist History*, London, 1981.
Thornton, A., *The Imperial Idea and its Enemies*, London, 1959.
——, *For the File on Empire*, London, 1968.
Thwaite, M. F., *From Primer to Pleasure*, London, 1963.
Tidrick, K., *Empire and the English Character*, London, 1990.
Toll, R., *Blacking Up*, London, 1974.
Tonkin, E., *et al.*, eds, *History and Ethnicity*, London, 1987.
Tosh, J., *The Pursuit of History*, London, 1984.
——, and Roper, M., eds, *Manful Assertions*, London, 1991.
Tout, T. F., *The Teaching of History in Schools*, London, 1907.

Trease, G., *Tales out of School*, London, 1964.
Tressell, R., *The Ragged Trousered Philanthropist*, London, 1983, 3rd edn.
Trollope, J., *Brittania's Daughters*, London, 1983.
Turner, E. S., *Boys will be Boys*, London, 1948.
UNESCO, *Looking at the World Through Textbooks*, Paris, 1946.
Unwick, E. J., *Studies of Boy Life in our Cities*, London, 1904.
Visram, R., *Ayahs, Lascars and Princes*, London, 1986.
Walvin, J., *Black and White: the Negro in English Society 1555–1945*, London, 1973.
——, *A Child's World*, London, 1982.
Ware, V., *Beyond the Pale: White Women, Racism and History*, New York, 1992.
Warner, P., *The Best of British Pluck: a History of the Boys' Own Paper*, London, 1976.
Warwick, P., *Black People and the South African War, 1899–1902*, Cambridge, 1983.
Webb, W. H., 'History, patriotism, and the child', *History*, vol. 2, no. 1, 1913, pp. 53–4.
Weeks, J., *Sex, Politics and Society*, London, 1981.
Welldon, J. C., *Youth and Duty: Sermons to Harrow Schoolboys*, London, 1903.
Wells, H. G., *An Englishman Looks at the World*, London, 1914.
——, *The Salvaging of Civilisation*, London, 1921.
Wertham, F., *The Seduction of the Innocent*, London, 1955.
White, A., *Efficiency and Empire*, London, 1901.
Whitehouse, J. H., *Problems of Boy Life*, London, 1912.
Williams, F., *Dangerous Estate*, London, 1959.
Williams, R., *The Long Revolution*, London, 1961.
Williamson, G., 'On learning and on teaching history in schools and on the results obtained by such teaching', *Transactions of the Royal Historical Society*, vol. 5, 1891.
Witte, C., *Tambo and Bones*, Westport, 1971.
Wolpert, S., *A New History of India*, Oxford, 1989.
Wormell, D., *Sir John Seeley and the Uses of History*, Cambridge, 1980.
Young, R., *White Mythologies: Writing History and the West*, London, 1990.
Younghusband, F., 'Interracial relations', *Sociological Review*, vol. 3, 1910, pp. 151–3.
Zimet, S., *Print and Prejudice*, London, 1976.

V. Contemporary periodical sources

Journal of Education, vol. XII (1890), vol. XXI (1900), vol. XXXII (1910), vol. LII (1920).

VI. Examination papers and examiners' reports

London matriculation test papers in English History, 1888–1902, Cambridge, 1902.

University of London senior-school and higher-school examination papers, London, 1904.

Oxford and Cambridge local examination papers in English history, 1881–90, London, 1891.

Oxford higher local examination papers, Oxford, 1902–14.

Oxford local examiners' reports, Oxford, 1895–1914.

VII. Unpublished theses

Castle, K., *American Minstrelsy 1879–90*, unpublished MA thesis, University College, London, 1978.

Cooper, H. E., *British Education, Public and Private, and the British Empire, 1880–1930*, PhD, University of Edinburgh, 1979.

Duckworth, J. W., *The Evolution of the History Syllabus in English Schools, with Special Reference to the Influence of Public Schools, 1900–25*, MPhil, University of London, 1972.

Elliott, B. J., *The Development of History Teaching in England, 1918–39*, PhD, University of Sheffield, 1976.

Glendenning, F., *The Evolution of History Teaching in British and French Schools in the 19th and 20th Century with Special Reference to Attitudes to Race and Colonialism in History Textbooks*, PhD, University of Keele, 1975.

Hadkins, L., *An Analysis of Prejudice in Textbooks on Irish History*, MPhil, University of London, 1976.

Lawrence, F., *Forms of Bias in History Writing for Schools*, MA, University of Sussex, 1967.

Murrell, P., *The Imperial Idea in Children's Literature, 1840–1902*, PhD, University of Swansea, 1975.

Pilsbury, W., *A Consideration of Some of the Textbooks on Modern History Used in Secondary Schools since 1860*, MA, University of Reading, 1944.

Springhall, J., *Youth and Empire: A Study of the Propagation of Imperialism to the Young in Edwardian England*, PhD, University of Sussex, 1968.

Steele, J., *A Study of the Formative Years in the Development of the History Curriculum in English Schools, 1833–1901*, PhD, University of Sheffield, 1974.

Wilkins, D., *A Consideration of History Textbooks Published Between 1750 and 1839 in Relation to the Teaching of History in English Schools*, MEdn, University of Nottingham, 1969.

INDEX